SCREENING GENERATION X

To my mother and father, Gerk Hong and Eng Guan Lee.
And in memory of Goldsworthy.

Screening Generation X

The Politics and Popular Memory of Youth in Contemporary Cinema

CHRISTINA LEE
Curtin University of Technology, Western Australia

ASHGATE

Published by
Ashgate Publishing Limited
Wey Court East
Union Road
Farnham
Surrey, GU9 7PT
England

Ashgate Publishing Company
Suite 420
101 Cherry Street
Burlington
VT 05401-4405
USA

www.ashgate.com

British Library Cataloguing in Publication Data
Lee, Christina.
   Screening Generation X : the politics and popular memory of
   youth in contemporary cinema.
   1. Youth in motion pictures. 2. Generation X.
   I. Title
   791.4'365235-dc22

Library of Congress Cataloging-in-Publication Data
Lee, Christina, 1976-
   Screening Generation X : the politics and popular memory of youth in contemporary
cinema / by Christina Lee.
      p. cm.
   Includes bibliographical references and index.
   ISBN 978-0-7546-4973-1 (hardback) -- ISBN 978-0-7546-9073-3 (ebook)
   1. Motion pictures and youth. 2. Generation X. I. Title.

PN1995.9.Y6L44 2009
791.43'65235--dc22

2009026738

ISBN 9780754649731 (hbk)
ISBN 9780754690733 (ebk)

Mixed Sources
Product group from well-managed
forests and other controlled sources
www.fsc.org Cert no. SA-COC-1565
© 1996 Forest Stewardship Council

Printed and bound in Great Britain by
MPG Books Group, UK

Contents

Acknowledgments   *vii*
List of Illustrations   *ix*

Introduction   1

1   The Subcultural Style of Generation X   11

2   Rebels with a Cause: Popular Youth Cinema, Unpopular Politics   27

3   Taking Out the Trash: The Politics of Remembering (and
     Forgetting) Molly Ringwald   43

4   Girl Power: The Politics of Pop   59

5   Violent Femmes: Angry Girls in Youth Cinema   77

6   Club Casualties: Go-Go(ing) Girls of Rave   95

7   Boys to Men and Back Again: The Historian and the
     Time Traveler   111

8   Another Sunrise, Another Sunset: Beyond Generation X   133

Conclusion: Thanks for the Good Times, Where to Now?   151

Bibliography   *155*
Filmography   *171*
Index   *175*

Acknowledgments

As this book began as a PhD dissertation, its journey from conception to completion has been a long, but rewarding, one. Many thanks go to John Tulloch, Anne Cranny-Francis, Howard McNaughton, and Timothy Shary for having encouraged the publication of this book back when it was still a thesis, and to Tara Brabazon who was instrumental in the formative stages of this project.

I am extremely grateful to Neil Jordan and Pam Bertram at Ashgate Publishing for getting me over the finish line, and to Rebecca Pate at The Picture Desk for her assistance in the acquisition of the images. Many thanks to Patrick Cole and Pete Waterhouse for their expertise during the copy-editing and proofing stages. The Humanities Publication Grant from Curtin University of Technology provided financial assistance to complete the manuscript. Thank you to my colleagues at the Department of Communication and Cultural Studies for their advice and friendship throughout the whole process. Special mention goes to Ron Blaber, Ann McGuire, David Buchbinder, Margaret Macintyre, and Jon Stratton.

I am indebted to Adam Trainer and Miyume Tanji who read early drafts of the manuscript and generously offered invaluable suggestions. Heartfelt thanks go to Kathryn Locke, Pamela Kerpius, Martin Laszkiewicz, Kara-Jane Lombard, Caroline Hamilton, Denise Woods, Russell Bishop, and to my sister and brother, Josephine and Jason, for their support and sympathetic ears.

A special shout-out to Alzena D'Costa for her friendship, her bottomless well of optimism, and for being my second pair of eyes. The journey would not have been the same without a kindred spirit to share the laughter and angst with. To Christian Rigby, thank you for the encouragement, hugs, and countless discussions on all things 1980s. Deepest gratitude to my parents, Gerk Hong and Eng Guan, who have always supported my endeavors and love of movies. I could not have asked for a better education in film than at Goldsworthy's open-air cinema. Forever thank you.

List of Illustrations

List of Illustrations

1.1 Generation Xploitation of collage culture: Hitmen, Vincent Vega (John Travolta) and Jules Winnfield (Samuel L. Jackson), in *Pulp Fiction* (1994)   23

2.1 License for thrills: Sloane (Mia Sara), Cameron (Alan Ruck), and Ferris (Matthew Broderick) on a mission for serious fun in *Ferris Bueller's Day Off* (1986)   35

2.2 Rebel with a cause: Pirate DJ, Happy Harry Hardon (Christian Slater), in *Pump Up the Volume* (1990)   39

3.1 High school confessions: Bender (Judd Nelson), Andy (Emilio Estevez), Allison (Ally Sheedy), Claire (Molly Ringwald), and Brian (Anthony Michael Hall) in *The Breakfast Club* (1985)   47

4.1 Space invaders: The proud, loud, and popular feminism of the Spice Girls in *Spice World: The Spice Girls Movie* (1997)   71

5.1 The bitchy, bold, and beautiful: Veronica Sawyer (Winona Ryder) and "the Heathers" (Kim Walker, Lisanne Falk, and Shannen Doherty) in *Heathers* (1989)   83

5.2 Violent femme: Vanessa Lutz (Reese Witherspoon) on her way to Grandma's trailer park in *Freeway* (1996)   91

6.1 Going nowhere fast: Claire (Katie Holmes) and Ronna (Sarah Polley) in *Go* (1999)   104

7.1 Masters of the temporal universe: Doc Brown (Christopher Lloyd) and Marty McFly (Michael J. Fox) in *Back to the Future* (1985)   122

7.2 Dystopian vision of the 1980s: Donnie (Jake Gyllenhaal), Gretchen (Jena Malone), and Frank the Rabbit (James Duval) in *Donnie Darko* (2001)   128

8.1   Art imitating life: Julie Delpy and Ethan Hawke as nameless
        characters in *Waking Life* (2001)   140

8.2   Nostalgic interplay: The nine-year reunion between Celine
        (Julie Delpy) and Jesse (Ethan Hawke) in *Before Sunset* (2004)   146

Introduction

I think it's safe to say that this party is about to become a historical fact.
(Duncan in *Some Kind of Wonderful* [dir. Howard Deutch, 1987])

My high school education began long before I was sent to boarding school in the city at thirteen years of age. Like so many others, it started at the open-air cinema in my preteen years. And, as it was the 1980s, the plethora of teen films flowing out of Hollywood was unavoidable in the curriculum. As a result, my youth was as informed by *The Karate Kid* (dir. John G. Avildsen, 1984) and *Footloose* (dir. Herbert Ross, 1984) as it was traipses to the local creek. I became enamored with John Hughes' *The Breakfast Club* (1985) when it was first released, and whatever I lacked in personal experience of Saturday detention was compensated with piqued curiosity. At the time, I had the strange sensation that I was witnessing something important unfolding on the silver screen, but uncertain of why. It was not until several years later when I saw the film again, this time as a high schooler, that I *got* what Hughes had been trying to say. The profundity of the revelation—the identification with the pressures of youth—was a deeply affective experience.

Screening Generation X: The Politics and Popular Memory of Youth in Contemporary Cinema addresses a cultural fascination with the genre of youth cinema, with particular focus upon post-1980s films. While not all films presented in this book are strictly classified as portraying Generation X, they do represent the historical context (the 1980s and 1990s) in which this cohort came of age. Instead of attempting to write the definitive history of Generation X in cinema—for instance, the works of Kevin Smith are glaringly absent for reasons pertaining to the scope and constraints of the current project, rather than any perceived lack of their importance—the book is a more modest venture. It provides a series of snapshots of cinematic icons and experiences to create a collage-like portrait. At times, the films offer ambiguous and problematic impressions of youth, underscoring the complexities of a group that has more often than not been simplified as caricatures—the tired trope of the slacker being a case in point—and misunderstood in the media. My opening anecdote signals the three core aspects of this book, that is, the pleasures, politics, and popular memory of youth cinema. More than just a study of cinema, *Screening Generation X* adopts a Cultural Studies perspective to analyze representations of Generation X in relation to their contexts of production. It is a commentary on the intergenerational divide between Generation X and their predecessors, the sociopolitical milieu of post-Second World War America (and, to a lesser extent, Britain), and the continued struggle of youth to find a voice and identity in increasingly unstable times.

By exploring the iconography and ideologies that pervade the landscape of post-1980s youth cinema, I argue that there is a political and pedagogical function to the genre. Prom politics and mallrat musings have a cultural currency that speaks in the literacies of its audience. Considering the few outlets available to youth to exercise agency and instigate change, popular culture takes on even greater onus and significance. Seldom just mindless entertainment, youth cinema performs important cultural work. A pivotal tenet of the book borrows from the subcultural theory aphorism that a society's structural inequalities and major movements are manifested most noticeably in its youth. As these changes ripple through a community, it is the marginalized who are subjected to the strongest pull of the undertow. Angela McRobbie posits that youth subcultures are important as they play back a version of social reality, functioning as "strong social texts, signs of response that indicate an active registering of broad social changes over which such groupings otherwise have no control" (1994: 160). Henry Giroux echoes this sentiment, arguing that representations of youth in popular culture work as signposts that register society's own crises of community, vision, and meaning (2002: 170). McRobbie's and Giroux's assertions underscore the motivations behind this book. I am interested in examining filmic texts in relation to the context in which they were produced.

The pedagogic function of popular cinema has often been undermined, stressing instead its role as a cultural panacea—the "mythic fantasy and lure of entertainment" for the masses, and mere diversion from the everyday (Giroux 2002: 3). Take, for instance, Robin Wood's flippant remark about high school movies, "The first question is, I suppose, Why? Why bother, when everyone knows these films are trash?" (2002: 2). Viewers do not, however, abandon their sense of self and society even within the darkened theater. Giroux states,

> Deeply imbricated within material and symbolic relations of power, movies produce and incorporate ideologies that represent the outcome of struggles marked by the historical realities of power and the deep anxieties of the times; they also deploy power through the important role they play connecting the production of pleasure and meaning with the mechanisms and practices of powerful teaching machines. (Giroux 2002: 3)

In youth cinema, especially films targeted at an adolescent set, these "material and symbolic relations of power" reach hyperbolic proportions. The obligatory "anthropology shot" as Roz Kaveney terms it, that is, panning and cutting to stock shots of the various high school cliques to indicate their social division— the alternative crowd, the sorority sisters and fraternity brothers crowd, the nerd crowd, the ethnic crowd—is a perfect example of such hierarchies at play (2006: 56). Inequalities are articulated through narrative and characterization. Through vilification, validation, and negotiation, we implicitly learn the limits of acceptable behavior and the consequences of deviancy. Who is dominant in the narratives, and who occupies the edges? In this book, I focus upon inequalities of generation, gender, and class. While race, ethnicity, and sexuality have become important issues raised in youth cinema, such as in *Boyz N the Hood* (dir. John Singleton, 1991), *Boys Don't Cry* (dir. Kimberly Peirce, 1999), and *Get Real* (dir. Simon Shore, 1999), they are not broached here.

While youth cinema as a window to society cannot be overstated, neither should the intensely personal experience of watching a film be underestimated. Its dynamic relation with the audience separates it from the way we interact with other technologies, such as radio and television. Watched in darkness and without the continual interruption of commercial advertising, cinema offers a uniquely intimate experience. The suture between the audience and the unfolding narrative is tight. Only when we are disturbed by other patrons talking loudly during the screening, or when we glimpse an usher patrolling the aisles with a flashlight, are we reminded that we have temporarily surrendered our senses and willingly suspended our own reality to occupy another time and space. To borrow from the cliché, the characters and the plot become "larger than life." Projected onto the immense, white canvas of the Cineplex, emotions and events become magnified and loaded with gravity—the intricate contours of a face, the subtly of a sigh, and the prosaic quality of daily rituals take on greater relevance. In his discussion of "talking pictures," John Hartley argues that even the most private images and the "detritus of everyday life" become politically charged (1992: 33–4). We do not passively absorb a film, but actively engage with the text to produce meaning.

The revival of the teen film in the 1980s, after a relatively quiet period in the late 1960s and 1970s, would see youth on the popular culture stage once more. And by the 1990s, the genre had become a mainstay in multiplexes. While the motion picture industry continued to create movies of the usual formulaic fare, such as *Mystery Date* (dir. Jonathan Wacks, 1991), *Encino Man* (dir. Les Mayfield, 1992), *Jawbreaker* (dir. Darren Stein, 1999), and a slew of slasher/horror copycat films that saw another generation of teenagers being gutted and hacked to pieces, the decade also witnessed a burgeoning number of films with a self-referential and sardonic edge, such as *Clueless* (dir. Amy Heckerling, 1995), *Scream* (dir. Wes Craven, 1996), *Pleasantville* (dir. Gary Ross, 1998), and *Ghost World* (dir. Terry Zwigoff, 2001). The teen invasion at the movies was one facet of a teenage takeover in popular culture. For instance, television programs, such as *Beverly Hills, 90210* (1990–2000), the critically acclaimed but short-lived series *My So-Called Life* (1994–1995), *Buffy the Vampire Slayer* (1997–2003), *Dawson's Creek* (1998–2003), and *Freaks and Geeks* (1999–2000), would spur the lucrative exercise of luring the teenage and young adult crowd back to television. This trend was also echoed in the pulp literature of fanzines, entertainment magazines, and high-profile fashion and style editorials that recognized the dollar value of this niche market. Many high couture magazines now produce a subsidiary, teen-downed version of their publications. For instance, *Teen Vogue* is an offshoot of *Vogue* that focuses exclusively on fashion, beauty trends, and issues applicable to teenagers, and features young celebrities and personalities. In a 1997 edition of *Entertainment Weekly*, Chris Nashawaty proclaimed, "a youth-quake is blowing the lid off Hollywood" (1997: 24–5). He wrote,

According to the Census Bureau, there are 37 million 10- to 19-year-olds right now, and that number will soar to 42 million in the next decade. (Call it *Baby Boomers: The Sequel.*) And with this population explosion comes a hungry horde of consumers itching to spend what amounts to $82 billion per year in disposable income. (Nashawaty 1997: 31)

In July 2003, *Vanity Fair* dedicated the issue to "kid culture" (Wolcott 2003: 70–87, 132–3). The front cover was an attractive double-spread of nine of the industry's most recognized and influential female celebrities under the age of 20 wearing designer couture—Amanda Bynes, Ashley Olsen, Mary-Kate Olsen, Mandy Moore, Hilary Duff, Alexis Bledel, Evan Rachel Wood, Raven, and Lindsay Lohan. Although the feature included several boy wonders, the emphasis was upon the powerful princesses of pop culture. It cited that the then 16-year-old Olsen twins presided over the Dualstar Entertainment Group, which is responsible for marketing the billion-dollar empire of the pair's franchise line. The duo's net worth was an estimated $150 million in 2003 (Wolcott 2003: 72). Clearly, youths were no longer just the target market; they had become the producers of popular culture. The formidable clout of youths in, and supporting, the entertainment industry would, by the next decade, be the rule rather than the exception. Fast-forward five years, and *Vanity Fair* would again be paying homage to the teen and twentysomething titans of the film, television, and music industry (Wolcott 2008: 92–105). While Hollywood's next wave had graduated to twittering on their Blackberries and professing their approval of the United States' first African-American president, it was nevertheless a continuation of the youth-quake that Nashawaty had described over a decade earlier. The issue boasted "27 kids who will own the next ten years." Yet again it would be four fabulous females on the front page—Kristen Stewart of *Twilight* (dir. Catherine Hardwicke, 2008) fame, Blake Lively from *Gossip Girl* (2007–), Emma Roberts who was the super-sleuth in the film *Nancy Drew* (dir. Andrew Fleming, 2007), and Amanda Seyfried, whose breakthrough role was in *Mean Girls* (dir. Mark S. Waters, 2004) before she danced and sang her way through *Mamma Mia!* (dir. Phyllida Lloyd, 2008). Although the entertainment industry continues to pander to the pin-up male idols of teendom, the star treatment has unequivocally been centered on female personalities. Similarly, *Screening Generation X* places considerable attention on female icons. However, it should be stressed that it is not this author's intention to attempt an exhaustive study of female representation in youth cinema. Shifts in gender roles are indicative of wider movements in society.

Any study of youth requires a return to the past, whether it is an exercise in historic mapping or reminiscence of seminal events in our own lives. We cannot escape this regression. On occasions when out socially with friends, we will catch ourselves making some sort of commentary on "kids these days." During our banter, it will dawn upon me that we are really talking about ourselves. The focus upon the teenager with the baggy jeans and the crotch that falls to his knees is merely an anchor point for our articulation of difference, identity, and place in history. There is a knowing community, even though our teenage years are long gone, sharing images, iconography, and ideas that are as fresh and lucid as when they were first experienced decades ago. The past persists in the present, with rifts and rivulets of social change marking cultural texts and memory sites.

The pull of the past saw a trend in films of the 1990s revisiting the 1980s. They ranged from narratives about young adults rekindling their adolescent years, to films that poached unashamedly from the iconography and distinctive plotlines of well-known films of the decade, such as *Romy and Michele's High School Reunion* (dir. David Mirkin, 1997), *Grosse Pointe Blank* (dir. George Armitage, 1997), *The Wedding Singer* (dir. Frank Coraci, 1998), and *Not Another Teen Movie* (dir. Joel Gallen, 2001). Lesley Speed argues that these films appeal to nostalgic and revivalist tendencies, with revivalist texts entailing,

> audiences, texts, and culture industries (including music and screen industries) participating in a shared recognition and manipulation of signs with reference to a particular historical period … Revivalist texts tend to highlight the selective and often contrived aspect of narrativizing history by placing an emphasis on material objects associated with the past. (Speed 2000: 24, 25)

An example of this would be *Napoleon Dynamite* (dir. Jared Hess, 2004). While it is set sometime in the mid-1990s, the film borrows heavily and consciously from the 1980s. For instance, Napoleon (Jon Heder) wears t-shirts with iron-on transfers, sports a large afro, plays tetherball, and busts out a dance routine to the tune of "Canned Heat" that is a strange mixture of Michael Jackson and *Fame/Footloose*-inspired moves. Deb's (Tina Majorino) fashion at the school dance is a homage to the excessive stylings of the decade—the side-ponytail and a hideous pink frock complete with puffed sleeves. There is an emphasis on antiquated technologies of the analog era—the VCR, cassettes, the Walkman, and landline telephones. At one point, Napoleon's elder brother, Kip (Aaron Ruell), and Uncle Rico (Jon Gries) even talk about acquiring a time machine that will transport Rico back to 1982 (the crowning glory of his youth). Nicolaas Mink convincingly argues that *Napoleon Dynamite*'s throwback to the 1980s exposes deep-seated anxieties and fears between mainstream America and the rural West by portraying the latter as caught in a time warp, whilst also creating a "white cultural world" that bridges the divide between the two (2008: 156).

In acknowledging the active recognition and manipulation of signs in the revivalist texts, Speed implies that nostalgia does not perform the same function. This is reminiscent of early understandings of nostalgia which saw it as a sickness—a melancholy for what is gone and irretrievable. Bryan Turner proposes that nostalgia, as a cultural discourse, is a response to moral uncertainty, the collapse of values, the loss of individual freedom with the death of God, the loss of personal authenticity, simplicity, and emotional spontaneity, and the departure from an age of "homeliness" (1987: 150–1). This assumes that the past is like a cadaver that nostalgia has clothed and preened, until even the stench of formaldehyde smells like sweet perfume. However, the nostalgic evocations in current youth cinema, resulting from historical displacement, are streaked with skepticism that is as critical of the past as it is of the present. It runs counter to David Lowenthal's proposition that "nostalgia is memory with the pain removed" (1985: 8). In the case of films about Generation X youth, the uses of memory arising from this generation's movement into post-youth are far from sugarcoated and misty-eyed.[1] I argue that reflective nostalgia (which shall be discussed in further detail in Chapter 3) is able to activate critique, rather than just function as a masking device to smooth over historical imperfections and to indulge in sentimental investments. Earlier films about youth, such as *American Graffiti* (dir. George Lucas, 1973), *Quadrophenia* (dir. Franc Roddam, 1979), and *Stand By Me* (dir. Rob Reiner, 1986), also register the hedonism and opportunities of a past youth, but all come with a coda that is only possible through hindsight, whether it is the filmmaker's historical vantage point years after an event, or a character's authorial narration. For instance, Jimmy (Phil Daniels) sends his scooter careening off a precipice at the end of *Quadrophenia* to forecast symbolically the demise of the Mods and Rockers era. In *Stand By Me*, Gordie (Richard Dreyfuss), 26 years after a boyhood adventure with friends to find a dead body, overlays his memory of events with the following commentary, "We'd only been gone two days, but somehow the town seemed different, smaller." Serving as a cultural time travel machine, *Screening Generation X* retrieves artifacts from the past to gauge the present—it remembers the past without resorting to unchecked celebration— where the party of today becomes, as one character suggests in the epigraph, the historical fact of tomorrow.

Before proceeding further, it is important to qualify what I mean by "youth cinema." As many writers have argued before, the genre is itself amorphous and its boundaries porous. While many would unequivocally classify *Say Anything...* (dir.

---

1   An example of this is Nancy Savoca's film *Dogfight* (1991). A young marine, Eddie Birdlace (River Phoenix), returns to San Francisco in 1966 after serving three years in Vietnam. The majority of the film is an extended flashback to one night in November 1963 which Eddie spent with dowdy Rose Fenny (Lili Taylor). The humorous nature of the narrative is set up from the exposition when we learn that he has only asked out the waitress to win a "dogfight"—a competition in which the marine who brings the most unattractive date to a party wins a wager. Rose severely reprimands Eddie when she finds out, prompting his change of heart and sincere efforts thereafter to earn her forgiveness. The proceedings of the evening are at times hilarious (they fake having to attend Eddie's grandfather's funeral so that they can buy Eddie a dinner jacket after store hours, and they cuss like sailors in a fancy restaurant) and tender (the first awkward kiss at a penny arcade). *Dogfight*, however, is far from a fluffy, date movie. The film ends with Eddie's homecoming, physically and emotionally scarred after having witnessed his friends die in Vietnam, to Rose who is now in charge of the family-owned café. As they embrace, the camera's tight close-up on their faces conveys a deep sadness and innocence lost as they reflect on the past. River Phoenix's own death after a tragic drug overdose in 1993 further became a point for nostalgic reflections on youth and mortality for a generation who had grown up watching the actor's films.

Cameron Crowe, 1989) as belonging to the genre, the same cannot be so easily said for *River's Edge* (dir. Tim Hunter, 1987). In the former, Lloyd Dobler (John Cusack) asks out the class valedictorian, Diane Court (Ione Skye), after graduation. They fall in love but, as to be expected, numerous obstacles threaten to tear them apart. However, love prevails and the young couple jump on a plane bound for England with their whole future ahead of them. In *River's Edge*—loosely based on true events of a teenage homicide in Milpitas, California in 1981—Samson "John" Tollet (Daniel Roebuck) boasts to his gang that he has murdered his girlfriend, then takes them to the site of her decomposing body. The various responses are a mixture of revulsion, reverence, and nonchalance. The film concludes with the dissolution of the group (Matt, played by Keanu Reeves, is racked with guilt and informs the authorities) and Samson's death. The film paints a morbid picture of dead-end youth, immorality, desperation, and exploitation. The naiveté and optimism of *Say Anything...* locates the film firmly within the genre of youth cinema, whereas the solemn tone and depravity of its characters renders *River's Edge* a digression, even though both films are essentially coming-of-age narratives. Similarly, the controversy surrounding *Kids* (dir. Larry Clark, 1995) indicates the elastic borders of the genre. While the film was initially given an NC-17 rating by the Motion Picture Association of America (and later released without a rating), and promotional material came with a warning that it was for mature audiences only, director Larry Clark maintains that it was a teenage movie as it grappled with teenage issues (such as underage sex, drugs, and peer pressure), was written by a teenager (Harmony Korine), and starred teenage actors. Clark states,

> Well, I always wanted to make the teenage movie that I felt America never made … I knew my film had to be from the inside, so I called this kid writer I knew through skateboarding, and he came over and I told him what I wanted, and he said, 'I've been waiting all my life to write this,' and he knocked out the screenplay in three weeks. I think when you see the movie *Kids* that most of us—not all of us, but most of us—will say, 'Yea, that's the way we were, that's the way kids are.' (Clark n.d.)

In conceding that even the "teenager" is a relative term in youth cinema, Adrian Martin provides one of the most succinct descriptions of the genre, "At the one end is craziness, characterised by free-for-all fun, sex, drugs and rock 'n' roll … But at the other end, and equally importantly is innocence, uncomplicated conflict with another human being, the unformed, impossible dream of a better world tomorrow" (1994: 67).[2] This oscillation between extremities in representations of youth signals a *rites de passage*. This latter concept has been applied in the past by anthropologists to explain the myths and rituals surrounding the transition from childhood to adulthood in various cultures, but still has important application.

---

2   While Adrian Martin specifically calls his subject "teen movies," I have expanded the parameters to "youth cinema."

Screening Generation X departs from the approaches taken by previous writers, such as David Considine (*The Cinema of Adolescence*, 1985), Timothy Shary (*Generation Multiplex*, 2002), and Jon Lewis (*The Road to Romance and Ruin*, 1992), which provide studies of subgenres within the broader genre of youth cinema. While such a method has merits in terms of giving coherence and order to an otherwise amorphous body of films, I have opted for the style taken by Peter Hanson in *The Cinema of Generation X: A Critical Study* (2002). Even though Hanson's project is not exempt from classifying the movies under discussion—there is the obligatory slacker section—his interest resides in the cultural influences that informed the filmmakers of Generation X cinema as a collective and as individual artists. Instead of cataloging generic themes and narratives, Hanson's book is a study of the sociocultural climate that gave rise to this genre of films. The chapters do not act as sacrosanct and divisive boundaries between topics, theories, and ideas, but as spaces for transgression, integration, and juxtaposition of subjects and style. For instance, in Chapter 3, entitled "Culture Vultures," the arthouse drama *sex, lies, and videotape* (dir. Steven Soderbergh, 1989) finds company with the violent *Reservoir Dogs* (dir. Quentin Tarantino, 1992), and the farcical exploits of *Jay and Silent Bob Strike Back* (dir. Kevin Smith, 2001). *The Cinema of Generation X* emphasizes the synergy between text, producer, and readership through social critique. This paradigm has been adopted in *Screening Generation X*.

Chapters 1 and 2 lay the conceptual foundation for the major arguments presented in the book. In Chapter 1, I argue that youth is a constructed, elastic category whose boundaries are stretched and pulled in relation to the ideologies that dominate its sociohistorical context. As Lawrence Grossberg states, "Youth *is* a historical construct" (1994: 27). Employing subcultural theory, the chapter looks to the rituals and practices of youth as symbolic acts of resistance that respond to historical conditions, thereby paving the way for a discussion of the politics of popular youth culture and the subcultural style of Generation X. As I am interested in cinema as a medium for social commentary, it is necessary to establish the significance of the 1980s to the emergence of Generation X as not only a populace/ target market, but also a style and mentality. This cannot be done without recourse to the importance of popular culture to identity formation.

Chapter 2 starts to explore the representational politics of youth cinema, validating the study of a genre that has often been debased for its mass appeal and supposed crassness. Through the representation of the rebel who transgresses social boundaries and occupies liminal spaces (an analogy that can be applied to youth itself), we can see the unpopular politics of the disempowered at play and the pedagogic function of cinema. Continuing on from the previous chapter, Chapter 2 stresses the process of meaning-making that occurs between the film and its audience, and the importance of acknowledging cultural context in any form of cultural critique. As John Fiske proposes, the meanings of texts are only triggered in their circulation in social and intertextual relations, and how they are articulated and used (1989: 3). I focus upon the 1980s with reference to the 1950s. Both decades were landmarks for their conservative values and materialism, and the tidal wave of youths in popular cinema and, by extension, popular culture. This chapter introduces the first of our cinematic icons—Harry Hardon, the rebel with a cause from *Pump Up the Volume* (dir. Allan Moyle, 1990)—in relation to the juvenile delinquent films of the 1950s.

In Chapter 3, I look at Molly Ringwald as actor and icon of a decade. It is no understatement to claim that she was *the* archetypal teenager of the 1980s—a time that was marked by economic and political restructuring, and the booming industry of youth cinema. Spearheading the teen invasion in, and at, the movies, and in collaboration with writer-director John Hughes, Ringwald's popularity and box-office clout was meteoric. Her descent into obscurity soon after and our response to her aging reveals how the present impinges upon the past to freeze time and history, raising a host of assumptions and myths of the 1980s. Recollections of the Ringwald–Hughes collaborations speak volumes of personal and collective investment in popular memories of the decade, as well as the experience of youth. The chapter further argues that cinema functions as a valuable source of documentation that captures and validates transitory moments of emotional intensity.

Chapter 4 investigates the relationship between pop and politics, and idolatry and identification that underscores many aspects of popular youth culture. I focus specifically on the global phenomenon of the Spice Girls with reference to the Riot Grrrl Movement of the 1990s. Popular culture has become the coliseum for the showmanship and struggle for young people, with celebrity status working as a platform for vocal demonstration, such as the advocating of a feminist agenda. The Spice Girls present a particularly interesting example of how polysemic reading strategies by fans are important to formation of identity and agency. As with many popular artists in the 1950s, the success of the Spice Girls' music would lay the foundations for their foray into cinema. While a discussion of the Spice Girls may seem an odd inclusion to the book, they exemplify the power of the mediated image (not only in cinema, but also television and magazine culture), the accelerating speed of popular culture redundancy in the postmodern age, and a feminism with a distinctively Generation X sensibility.

Chapter 5 focuses upon the "bitch" in youth cinema, that is, the violent femme who is a permanent fixture in the genre. The bitch is comparable to the femme fatale of *film noir*. The 1980s and 1990s in particular saw images of the angry girl come to prominence in film, and these were not always pretty but, at times, disturbingly raw and brutal. As violence has often been synonymous with males, adding the aggressive female into this equation becomes deeply problematic. It uncovers cultural anxieties of a transgressive, excessive femininity. This chapter proposes that the threat posed by the bitch, unlike her femme fatale forerunner, has the potential to act as the agent of progressive change. Through a case study of *Heathers* (dir. Michael Lehmann, 1989) and *Freeway* (dir. Matthew Bright, 1996), we see how the violent femme is able to expose injustices and inequalities, but also the limits of this borrowed power. The bitch manifesto has caveats.

Chapter 6 looks at the iconic subcultural phenomenon of the rave scene that was to the 1980s and 1990s youth what Woodstock and the hippie movement was to the youth of the 1960s. The focus is twofold. First, it discusses the politics of the scene and the milieu that gave rise to it. Second, I explore the role women play in rave. The case of the invisible woman questions the egalitarian ideals of the rave community and comments upon gross inequalities based on gender, age, and class that underpin many youth subcultures. I look at Doug Liman's *Go* (1999) with reference to *Human Traffic* (dir. Justin Kerrigan, 1999) and *Groove* (dir. Greg Harrison, 2000).

As a retrospective study of post-1980s youth iconography is a project in time travel, it is appropriate that Chapter 7 takes as its subject the teenager in the time travel genre. The journey through time is an analogy of the rites of passage from youthful naiveté to wisdom. I juxtapose *Donnie Darko* (dir. Richard Kelly, 2001) with *Back to the Future* (dir. Robert Zemeckis, 1985) to gauge the ideological disparity between Generation X and the Baby Boomer generation, arguing that such films articulate dramatic social, political, and cultural changes. They elucidate the relationship between history, power, and identity through the actions of the teenage protagonists. As a composite figure who documents the present as he (re)lives the past, only to eerily forecast a dystopian future, what cultural anxieties does the character of Donnie Darko represent? And what hope do we have of redemption in such troubled times?

Chapter 8 concludes with the oeuvre of director Richard Linklater, whose films provide micro-narratives of the experiences of the so-called slacker generation. Linklater's body of work provides a tangible, visual trace of the narrative progression of Generation X to post-youth culture. The films function as popular culture signposts, drawing attention to a journey for a generation whose end signifies a return to the beginning. As with Linklater's characters, we too are seeing the philosophic musings and nostalgia of a generation that has now begun poaching from its own iconographic database, as is evident from its self-referentiality and kitsch merchandising. The 1980s has replaced the "old skool" of the 1960s and 1970s—Atari t-shirts are the new vintage, dancing to remixes of "Smooth Criminal" is "so bad, it's good," and Generation X boasts its own bona fide cult figures, from Bart Simpson, Kenny, and Cartman, to Silent Bob and Jay. The deaths of 1980s icons Michael Jackson, John Hughes, and Patrick Swayze in 2009 literalized the passing of an era and generation. This final chapter raises that age-old question: when the party ends, where do we go from here?

Chapter 1
The Subcultural Style of Generation X

Generation X means a lot of things to a lot of people. We are a culture, a demographic, an outlook, a style, an economy, a scene, a political ideology, an aesthetic, an age, a decade, and a literature.

To some, belonging to GenX is a cop-out. To us, it is a declaration of independence. We exist. (Douglas Rushkoff 1994a: 3)

Sometime, somewhere along the way after the turbulent 1960s and 1970s, the American public began (and not for the first time) to bemoan the state of youth. This time around, the younger generation was charged with being apathetic, confused, disillusioned, and shallow. Branded like barcodes, they were christened a deadbeat "Generation X." While some turned to this cohort to understand changes in public attitudes, values, and beliefs, for others it was the answer to the age-old question: what's wrong with society? Notwithstanding the relative ease that many found in identifying Generation X, *what* constituted this group remained less obvious—a point clearly signaled by Douglas Rushkoff's opening quote. The trope of Generation X—unemployed, unkempt, parked on the couch, one hand on the remote control and the other holding a can of Coke, and listening to "that awful music"—was enough to convince any person over 40 that Generation X youth were in need of a good cuff behind the ears. Boxed and labeled, they were going nowhere fast, or anywhere at all.

Generation X is a genealogical conundrum. Popular definitions perpetuate an image of pathological aimlessness and dysfunction that not only indicates generational elitism and misconception, but more significantly the awkwardness in discussing Generation X as a unique historical experience. This book shifts beyond conceptualizing Generation X simply as a market demographic with a precise start and end date. Youth subcultures cannot be so easily bookended. Instead, I turn to representational practices as a strategy for identification, for it is impossible to comprehend Generation X without reference to ways of reading culture. As with the elastic category of youth itself, Generation X has a plurality of meanings. In this chapter, I explore this idea further through a discussion of the politics of subcultural stylings and symbolism, and how media reappropriation became a means for Generation X's articulation of their ideologies and shared identity.

In conversational vernacular, "youth" has become interchangeable with "teenager," "adolescent," and "juvenile" at various stages of history. These have become commonsense phrases that naturalize an idealized trajectory from childhood to adulthood. The obviousness of these terms would at first appear an unnecessary subject for discussion, but pulled apart and relocated into different discourses and contexts, they become as ambiguous as they are slippery. The definition of youth, according to the law, is a prime example of this. In legal parlance in the United States, the classification of a juvenile depends upon an individual's region of residence and state legislation, and is further complicated by the severity of the offense if a crime has been committed. The complexities of distinguishing minors from adults need not refer exclusively to cases of juvenile delinquency. For instance, according to the West Annotated California Family Code: Emancipation of Minors Law, an adolescent may be classified as a legal adult if the person fulfills various criteria, such as entering into a valid marriage (prior to 18 years of age) or is on active duty with the national armed forces (Champion 1992: 15–17, 212). Attempts to reduce youth to a singular definition are problematic as they have a homogenizing and alienating effect. As Allison Whitney argues, "The use of biological and psychological theories to explain the teenage phenomenon serves to pathologize the terrifying and violent transformations of the teenage body while seeking to establish a new set of rationalized social boundaries that might contain and regulate the teenage experience" (2002: 57). This, however, does not imply that existing definitions of youth in public discourse are redundant. What it does suggest is that youth itself is an historical formation that is culturally and temporally specific, rather than an inherently natural one. This is apparent in records that show how visual and literary representations of youth have changed over the ages. Philippe Ariès (1962) argues that until the 12th century, childhood as a stage in life was not recognized. Infants and children were often portrayed as little men and women. Children's attire, pastimes, games, and hobbies were largely indistinguishable from those of their elders as conveyed in sources such as art, school records, and journals. Inspired by religious iconography of the Infant Jesus, the 13th century saw these subjects more closely resembling the modern conceptualization of childhood. It was not until the 17th century that the young were considered important and different enough to be featured alone in artwork as opposed to being a part of the family portrait (Ariès 1962: 31–44, 48, 65).

Transformations in artistic impressions indicated that the social imaginings of youth were influenced by evolving religious beliefs and socioeconomic shifts, for instance, the industrial revolution of the late 18th century. David Bakan ascribes three significant movements in modern American history that made adolescence a social fact (1971: 979–95). These were the introduction of child labor legislation, separate legal procedures for juveniles, and a widespread, structured schooling system. The massive growth in industry witnessed increasing numbers of young people in the workplace. As a result of the Evangelical movement, which saw children's welfare as the responsibility of society, child labor laws were implemented to protect children. In the legal system, young people were deemed vulnerable, and therefore to be separated from older offenders and to be administered corrective, rather than punitive, treatment (Bakan 1971: 981–2, 984, 988). In the late 19th century, compulsory public schooling in America for those aged between six and 18 years created a population of young people who were postponing entering the adult world of work.[1] Hugh Klein summarizes how major developments have been influential in characterizing youth, "industrialization occurring during the later 1800s created the *need* for a stage of adolescence; the Depression created the *legitimized opportunity* for adolescence to become differentiated from childhood and adulthood; and the mass media influence/blitz of the 1950s *crystallized* this life stage by giving it a reality all its own" (1990: 456). It is Klein's final point— the crystallization of youth as a result of mass media influence—that brings us back to contemporary times. The concept of youth as consumer radically altered perceptions and propelled them into the public eye as an identity and group in their own right.[2]

Mixing Politics with Pleasure: The Style of Subcultures

Archetypes and familiar narratives of youth are maintained and propagated through the circulation of texts in media, spaces of consumption, and sites of production. Whether switching on the television, visiting the Cineplex, turning on the radio, logging onto the internet, or perusing through a magazine rack at the newsagents, we cannot avoid images geared towards youth, from preteens to twentysomethings. Popular television programs especially have become particularly adept at packaging the youth experience into products. For instance, during its six-year run on the Warner Bros. network, *Dawson's Creek* (1998–2003) was responsible for placing a bevy of songs in the top ten playlist on commercial radio and creating a soundtrack of teenage life. Even the short-lived science fiction series, *Roswell* (1999–2002), made its mark in popular culture. Aside from the usual merchandising, it inspired publications in the tradition of fanfiction, which continued the saga of its characters long after the show had been cancelled, and spawned an exclusive fashion line by Levi Jeans in the Spring 2000 collection. More recent shows geared towards a *Young Vogue* readership, such as the CW

---

1   Here, David Bakan is referring to the refined, well-structured schooling system that the education system today most closely resembles. Hugh Klein, however, notes that as early as the 18th century, schools referred to as academies, colleges, pensions, or little schools were founded where children could be sent to "further their tuition in life and manners" (1990: 449).

2   While the 1950s has often been cited as the decade that the "teenager" was born, Jon Savage (2008) argues that the basic attributes of post-war youth, such as rebellion, restlessness, and rituals, were already established by the time of the Beatniks and rock 'n' roll. In *Teenage*, Savage offers a prehistory of youth culture where the identifiable character of the teenager can be seen even in the mid-1800s. G. Stanley Hall's seminal book, *Adolescence* (1904), was already paving the way for the study of adolescents as a distinctive group prior to the 1950s. The book itself generated popular discussion and further study in the decades to follow. The 1950s milestone is notable because of its intense concentration on teenagers by the media and the market that, while not new, was unprecedented in terms of sheer scale. See Savage (2008) and Hall (1904).

Television Network's *Gossip Girl* (2007–) and Warner Bros.' now-axed *The O.C.* (2003–2007), boast designer looks—from preppy, J-Crew Manhattanite to boho So-Cal—that generate their own fashion trend, with or without endorsement. Heavy cross-promotion and merchandising is now de rigueur when it comes to youth culture. CD soundtracks sidle up beside baseball caps and action figures. While it is yet another opportunity to cash in on the hype for promoters, for the fans the very act of consumption involves an active *production* of meaning and an important interplay of politics and pleasure. To elaborate on this further, I turn to subcultural theory as a way of understanding the importance of culture and style as markers of identity. While subcultural theory has, since its inception, attracted criticism, its emphasis upon style still remains profoundly influential.

Subcultural theory, as expounded by the Birmingham Centre for Contemporary Cultural Studies (BCCCS), stemmed from the observations of working-class youth in post-Second World War Britain. The Centre itself, established in 1964, would come to define the study of spectacular subcultures that included the Teds, Mods, Rockers, Punks, and Skinheads. The impacts of social upheavals were tracked through the symbiotic relationship between youth, style, and identity. The BCCCS developed an innovative, interdisciplinary approach that shifted focus from sociology and ethnography (as was popular in the American tradition of qualitative empiricism, such as that of the Chicago School) to social semiotics. The Centre advocated that subcultures are a mediated response by youth to counter prevailing social problems. Subcultures expose a fundamental tension between the political, cultural, and economic elite, and the subordinated underclass. They were seen as physical manifestations of the general contradictions of their time, and attempts to resolve intergenerational and class paradoxes (Cohen 1972: 25).

The formation of the Teddy Boy subculture in the 1950s is one example of how youth responded to post-war tumult and expropriation of land. The development of new towns and high-density estates destroyed important communal spaces—the local pub, the corner shop, the street corner—and irrevocably damaged the dynamics of the traditional neighborhood structure (Cohen 1972: 16). Workforce reform and economic restructuring further added to a state of depression, while the widespread introduction of automated techniques made many in semi-skilled occupations redundant. It would have the effect of robbing many of their livelihood, pride in the job, and denying people the "artificial paradise of the new consumer society" (Cohen 1972: 21–2). In this climate, the Teds poached from the style of 1950s Saville Row high fashion that was originally designed for affluent young men. Their flouting of flamboyant hairstyles and the Edwardian-style outfits, more theatrical than practical, such as the jackets draped with flaps and velvet collars, "knitted ties, plain or flowery waistcoats, tight-fitting trousers or 'strides,' and—incongruously at first—blunt shoes with enormous crêpe soles," flew in the face of their status as low-paid, manual labourers (Fyvel 1961: 41). As part of the Teds' arsenal to signify and reaffirm an exclusive membership, fashion "represented a symbolic way of expressing and negotiating with their social reality; of giving cultural *meaning* to their social plight" (Jefferson 1976: 86). Within the context of an aristocratic heritage, the Teds established a status that recognized style as the singular sign of belonging (Stratton 1985: 215). By transforming new-age dandyism into the masculinist reclamation of territory, this group solidarity was a protest against dismal conditions.

Rituals and style win back space for marginalized groups and invest them with agency and resistance (Widdicombe and Wooffitt 1995: 16–19). This becomes particularly evident when we look at bricolage, a process whereby the original meaning of a text or action is subverted or erased. Take, for example, Dick Hebdige's account of 1970s British Mods, "pills medically prescribed for the treatment of neuroses were used as ends-in-themselves, and the motor scooter, originally an ultra-respectable means of transport, was turned into a menacing symbol of group solidarity. In the same improvisatory manner, metal combs, honed to a razor-like sharpness, turned narcissism into an offensive weapon" (1979: 104). In other instances, the Union Jack became a hijacked sign which was reappropriated to decorate the backs of shoddy anoraks or made into stylish tailored jackets. During a protracted period of high youth unemployment, the original signification of the suit—ambition, efficiency, and compliancy—was turned into an empty fetish and a parody of the situation in which the Mods found themselves (Hebdige 1979: 104–5).

Despite a preoccupation with symbolic stylings and a coded language, it must be stressed that subcultures are not free-floating, autonomous agents. They do not operate outside structures of power. As Michel Foucault writes, multiplicitous points of resistance "play the role of adversary, target, support, or handle in power relationships" (1978: 95). For instance, try as they might to buck the system, the 1960s Hippies and 1980s Ravers could not escape capitalist culture and the market economy. But as oppression is always met with resistance, identity and power are always in an unstable state of struggle and negotiation. This argument is maintained throughout this book.

While the Birmingham (BCCCS) approach was certainly progressivist for its time, it was not without shortcomings. Subcultural theorists maintained that the stylized form of subcultures resigned them to being dead-end formations. John Clarke writes,

> Sub-cultural strategies cannot match, meet or answer the structuring dimensions emerging in this period for the class as a whole. So, when the post-war sub-cultures address the problematics of their class experience, they often do so in ways which reproduce the gaps and discrepancies between real negotiations and symbolically displaced 'resolutions.' They 'solve,' but in an imaginary way, problems which at the concrete material level remain unresolved. (Clarke et al. 1976: 47–8)

This overemphasis upon symbolic gestures and imaginary resolutions questions the effectiveness of subcultures, as well as shortens their lifespan. Once its moment is over, it becomes an historic artifact that can only be revived via poor imitations or going back nostalgically to ogle its preserved remains. In arguing that "subcultural empowerment is empowerment without a future," subcultures are denied of any capacity to evoke real social change (Gelder 1997: 87). Any possibility of resistance is further nullified by its commercialization, which is itself a defeatist logic. Pertaining to 1970s punk subculture, Hebdige laments its appropriation into the mainstream,

> as soon as the original innovations which signify 'subculture' are translated into commodities and made generally available, they become 'frozen.' Once removed from their private contexts by the small entrepreneurs and big fashion interests who produce them on a mass scale, they become codified, made comprehensible, rendered at once public property and profitable merchandise. (Hebdige 1979: 96)

Subcultural theory is premised on the notion that subcultures, like any meaning system, mobilize their own language and codes. When a subcultural text is dislodged from its context, it loses its original meaning. Transformed into a fashion accessory, a passing fad, or gimmick, it is supposedly emptied of political agenda. Incorporation of subcultural style into popular culture industries has a neutralizing effect that renders it benign (Baron 1989: 208–9). In short, the tokenistic nature of subcultures dooms them to failure, with their obituaries written the very instant they start appearing in all manner of forms on the shelves of Wal-Mart or the catwalks of Milan. The inbuilt flaw in subcultural theory comes to the fore when we apply it to post-1980s youth subcultures such as Generation X. What if the politics is in the packaging? How can we account for the interplay between subcultures and commercial culture? And why, even after it has been surpassed by a new cohort (Generation Y? iPod Generation?) does Generation X still hold cultural currency?

Putting the (wh)Y in X

In studying Generation X, an understanding of its unique sociotemporal context unavoidably takes us over familiar terrain. As a disclaimer, while this often reproduces contrived versions of the past and reductive stereotypes, as a starting point it enables us to write an alternative narrative of Generation X that brings together the political with the popular, and social practice with symbolic meaning. Backtracking to the Baby Boomers, this was a generation that, after two world wars, benefited from a renewed post-war idealism and readiness to return to a state of normality, stability, and productivity. The affluence and confidence of these halcyon times, despite the looming threat of nuclear annihilation, manifested itself in the unabashed culture of consumerism. From Elvis Presley to the Pontiac, Tupperware to television, and luxury stockings to the suburban paradise, the times had never been better. Charging into the modern age, Jim Heimann aptly captured that gilded chapter in contemporary American history, "after saving the world from Axis aggression the American public looked beyond their pre-World War II days and gazed to the future. And the future looked great" (2003: n.p.). Gaining much of its formidable clout by way of sheer numbers, the Baby Boomers—born between the mid-1940s to the early 1960s—attended colleges in unprecedented numbers and exerted enormous pressure in political arenas in a general milieu of economic and political optimism (Gare 1999: 228).

If the Baby Boomers were hailed as the proud leaders of a new and improved nation, their successors—born between the mid-1960s and early 1980s—were viewed as a lame sequel. As a result of readily available birth control and feminist intervention in the 1960s, the marked downturn in births would see the rather unfortunate label of Baby Busters shadow them. Refusing to pop out a baby or two for the country did not bode well in the push for progress and productivity. Not only were they fewer in numbers in a time when the motto was more, but they were also seen as somewhat, if not outright, defective. Statistics indicated that children of this generation were twice as likely as their parents to be the progeny of divorce (Ritchie 1995: 36–9). The family-centered fabric that the Baby Boomers had advocated so hard for was beginning to fray at the edges. The honeymoon period was indeed over. Generation X had arrived.

The phrase "Generation X" first appeared in the early 1950s, when Robert Capa captured in a photo-essay project the life experiences of a group of 20-year-olds after the Second World War. He called them "The Generation X," the unknown generation. In 1964, *Generation X* was the title of a book by Charles Hamblett and Jane Deverson that documented interviews with British youths, most of whom identified themselves as belonging to a subculture such as the Mods or Rockers. In 1976, "Generation X" was the name of a punk band fronted by Billy Idol—the name supposedly poached from Hamblett and Deverson's publication (Ulrich 2003: 3–13). However, it would be Douglas Coupland's fictional narrative, *Generation X: Tales for an Accelerated Culture*, in 1991 that would put Generation X on the cultural map. The novel followed the lives of three twentysomethings who abscond to a desert town on the fringes of Palm Springs, California to escape a vacuous, middle-class mentality and to ponder the meaning of life.

> We live small lives on the periphery; we are marginalized and there's a great deal in which we choose not to participate … Our systems had stopped working, jammed with the odor of copy machines, Wite-Out, the smell of bond paper, and the endless stress of pointless jobs done grudgingly to little applause. We had compulsions that made us confuse shopping with creativity, to take downers and assume that merely renting a video on a Saturday night was enough. (Coupland 1991: 14)

Overeducated and underpaid, Andy, Claire, and Dag take up Mc-Jobs—described by Coupland as service sector jobs that are "low-pay, low-prestige, low-dignity, low-benefit, no future"—and spend their days telling disturbing stories and ruminating on seemingly facile subjects (1991: 6). They live in the Now, but muse about the past and theorize the future. It is a transient existence where nothing is seriously planned. The future is watching a nuclear mushroom cloud on the horizon, sunglasses on, a cheap beer in one hand, and a cigarette in the other. Despondent, angry, and deeply ironic, the novel was quickly adopted by the mass media as a veritable dictionary of the brats of the Baby Boomers. The image of a generational takeover was reinforced by the theatrical release of Richard Linklater's independent feature, *Slacker* (1991) (which will be discussed in detail in Chapter 8). Overloaded with Texan left-wing "losers and schmoozers, conspiracy buffs, angry romantics, vanishing poets, and wacky philosophers," *Slacker* depicted a youth subculture that had turned its back on a regular nine-to-five in favor of philosophical roaming (Pierson 1995: 187). Cynical, indolent, and with an anti-establishment philosophy, "slacker" became a household label symbiotic with Coupland's Generation X.

The simultaneity of Coupland's book, Linklater's movie, and the distinctive grunge music scene in Seattle, Washington was sufficient validation that the Baby Boomers' time had reached its end. With two being coincidence, three being a trend, the various terms surrounding Generation X were latched upon, categorized, packaged, and retailed to become an industry unto itself (Coupland 1995: 72). The frenzied media response endeavored to demystify this generation, bandying around the catchphrases with reckless abandon and inciting bouts of moral panic. However, it was not a case of a top-down effect, whereby an unwitting group is defined solely by external agents. In his study of deviants and subcultures, Stanley Cohen argues that "the process of identifying deviance, necessarily involves a conception of its nature" (1987 [1972]: 74). The labeling participates in the act of becoming. Labels place and distinguish individuals and events, and they assign events to a context that gives them meaning within and outside the subculture (Hall et al. 1978: 19). Subcultures are neither immaculately conceived nor are they the effluvial byproducts of mainstream culture. As with all subcultures, Generation X was present at its own conception, forged out of circumstances that create appropriate technologies and spaces for expression—a type of evolution in fast-forward if you will. In the case of Generation X, an involved and complex engagement with mediated forms enabled them to make sense and meaning from a giddily transforming landscape. The analog technology of television specifically would have a formative influence upon Generation X, functioning as the training ground that would shape, and be shaped by, a generation.

I Want My M(e)TV: Media Saturation

Over and above all else, the determining feature of Generation X was its relationship with popular culture and media texts. Despite the paucity in numbers compared with the Baby Boomers—Xers born between 1965 and 1977 constituted only 45 million of the general American population—they possessed an imposing annual purchasing power of $125 billion, which made them a lucrative target market (Hornblower 1997: 58). All manner of products and images would be peddled, eventually reaching peak saturation with media technology that was advancing at an ever-accelerating rate. The improved quality and decreasing price of television sets meant that the entertainment box was found in a high proportion of households, often with multiple sets under the same roof. The proliferation of VCRs in the 1980s, along with cable and satellite services, personal computers, video game players, and new visual formats, had the effect of dramatically altering viewing patterns (Dorr and Kunkel 1990: 6). The impressive range of electronic devices available in the home granted access to information unparalleled in previous decades. By the time they had even completed school, a startling proportion of Xers had already encountered personal computers and rudimentary electronic games. Growing up as a child, I recall that whenever problems or operational issues with the VCR arose, my parents would turn to my younger brother. He was an electronics guru and computer whiz at age six. Born at the tail end of Generation X, he exemplified a new breed of youth who knew how to set the timer on the video or conquer kingdoms in a computer game before they could even tie their shoelaces. While the American public of the 1950s experienced a television revolution, the 1980s and 1990s were marked by a multimedia explosion and the information superhighway (Dorr and Kunkel 1990: 5–6). This was the way of the future, and Generation X had its finger on the pulse.

The significance of technology to contemporary life is depicted in the film *Electric Dreams* (dir. Steve Barron, 1984). A young urban architect, Miles (Lenny von Dohlen), buys a personal computer in an effort to organize his life. Hooked up to the main electrical system, the computer, Edgar, is the ultimate in scientific engineering. It not only makes the perfect coffee, operates all the lights and security system among a multitude of other domestic duties, but also helps Miles win over his attractive neighbor, Madeline (Virginia Madsen). No mere modern appliance, Edgar is the next stage in human evolution, as is clear when it assumes human traits and emotions. The potential nihilism of the computer, as shown by Edgar's jealous rage of the budding relationship between Miles and Madeline, is resolved only after the technology is shared with the rest of the San Francisco Bay community. Edgar hijacks the air waves of a local radio station and transmits one of its musical arrangements over all frequencies to the jubilation of the masses. The film closes with Miles and Madeline blissfully driving off into the sunset as people at the beach, in the city streets, on rigs, in aerobics classes, and in shopping centers are compelled to dance with joyous abandon to Edgar's song.

In a trend analogous to television sets, the improved technology and reduced cost of the VCR ensured that Xers either owned or had access to one from a relatively early age. One study reported that by the end of the 1980s, approximately 75% of American households owned remote control devices (Ainslie 1988: 127). By the middle of 1989, the penetration level for cable subscription was 54.8% of American homes, showing a subsequent annual growth rate of two to three percentage points (Broadcasting 1989: 14). Generation X was the impetus for pushing home entertainment beyond multiple sets to multiple channels and multi-range devices. At the same time, VCR use fostered an individually-oriented rather than communal viewing practice (Grant 1988: 14). Increased unsupervised time in front of the tube, coupled with network restructuring, redefined the function of television as entertainer and educator.

Prior to the mid-1960s, most networks were regulated by advertisers who sponsored programs by paying for air time and production costs. As program integrity was an indicator of the reputability of advertisers and their endorsed products, image became paramount, thus reproducing family-oriented, conservative values. The invention of the "scatter plan" in the early 1960s meant that program structure and content would be forced to adapt to a free market of supply and demand economics. Under this system, networks were to cover production costs with advertisers simply purchasing a segment of broadcasting time. By alleviating sponsors of their responsibility for content, networks could generate higher profits from selling air time (Ritchie 1995: 86–90). Fierce competition among rival stations saw networks expand into subjects previously considered too risqué or off-limits to the sensibilities of middle-America. Family shows of the 1950s and 1960s, such as *Leave It To Beaver* (1957–1963), *The Brady Bunch* (1969–1974), and *The Partridge Family* (1970–1974), which were once the staple, quickly become vapid and irrelevant in a climate of escalating fears of crime, political corruption, and an AIDS epidemic. The televised ideals of the romantic 1950s could no longer sustain itself, and the ills of the world could not be resolved by the end of a 30-minute episode.

Weaned on a culture of capitalism and hypermarketing, television for Generation X became a gateway to the greater global community. Television would often contradict their lived experiences, or give expression to their worst fears. Public scrutiny of a fallen Nixon Administration, the bloodiness of Vietnam beamed live into living rooms across the nation, the poverty of third world countries that media events such as *Live Aid* brought under the spotlight—these historical events entered the public imagination and remained there through the circulation of images via various media platforms. For Generation X the television set became, as Karen Ritchie describes it, the surrogate "babysitter, their entertainment, their teacher, and their night light" (1995: 86).

The collective cynicism and despondency was exacerbated by recessions in the early 1980s and 1990–1991. The crash of the stock market in 1987 capped a dismal decade of economic hardship, which saw massive corporate downsizing and some 43 million jobs being terminated between 1979 and 1995 in America. The youth entering the employment sector during this period labored longer hours for considerably less pay. For those who opted to stay in school, there were also signs that the education system was also failing them. In a *Time* article, Margot Hornblower cited one study that showed cutbacks in federal grants were forcing one in three students into the workforce in order to support themselves (1997: 60). The plight of a dispossessed generation is echoed in David Baerwald's song "I'm Nuthin'."

I'm sick of people talkin'
About American dreams
That's all gone
Ain't nothing there for me
Cause you see
I'm nuthin'. (Baerwald 1994)

Devoid of their parents' idealism and aspirations, the American Dream was but a bitter nostalgia for a long gone and foreign past for Generation X. Even the benefits of a two-income household provided little comfort, greatly outweighed by the high probability that Xers would be less financially successful, or even on par, with their parents (Corbo 1997: 58). The great expectations of the 1950s and 1960s had, by the mid-1980s, been traded in for expectations of great disappointment.

The appropriation of media texts would become a way of life, a resistive response, and coping mechanism. Aided by the VCR and remote control, for Generation X television became an interactive medium that allowed them some control over their surroundings. Channel surfing and rearranging the order of material with the VCR (via editing or extracting a program from its intended context) allowed texts and their meaning to be played with and manipulated. The significance of this interplay can be illustrated in Sean Cubitt's (1991) discussion of timeshifting. Cubitt argues that television attempts to create reality by capturing, or at least simulating, the present as happening right before the viewer's eyes. What videotape accomplishes is that it "forces back on to broadcast its own incompletion ... Through video, TV can cease to be a slave to the metaphysics of presence" (Cubitt 1991: 36). This is most evident in news-of-the-hour segments, where events claimed to be current may in fact be several minutes, hours, or days old. The video recorder dissolves the aura of live television and its ubiquitous present. Any notion of its uniqueness and immediacy (which we subconsciously translate as objective and unmediated—"it is happening before my very eyes, therefore it must be reality, not a representation") surrenders to the fact that what we are witnessing is really a replay of the past (Cubitt 1991: 35–7). In the age of mechanical reproduction, we are only privy to replications where time is not fixed.

The volatility and dynamism of time, space, and history allows logics and narratives to emerge where the search for truth becomes irrelevant. This relies on establishing a distance from "the real," or rather conceding that reality itself is a loaded and relative term. Instead, as Lawrence Grossberg states, "only one's affective commitment, however temporary or superficial, matters. Authentic inauthenticity refuses to locate identity and difference outside the fact of temporary affective commitments" (1989: 265). Authentic inauthenticity represents a willingness to admit to its own superficiality, with intrinsic value residing in the investment we have in something, whether it be a person, a place, an object, or event.[3] While I do

---

3   The rejection of depth models has resulted in a variety of tactical strategies such as "anti-advertising" to sell to a generation whose first language is irony. Carolyn Hicks cites

not agree with Grossberg's vision of "ironic nihilism" and ultimate disappointment, his observations of the surface and affectivity are nevertheless insightful (1989: 264). Loosened from the constraints of linear time and the quest for absolute truth and reality, fragmented entities and free-floating signs no longer signify lack, but may be reappropriated into texts of personal and collective relevance.

The postmodern sensibility of Generation X, with its self-referentiality, irony, and pastiche, finds heightened expression in Quentin Tarantino's *Pulp Fiction*. Released in 1994, the film is a product of its times. Its appeal is largely dependent upon its proud exploitation of "hackneyed stories, stereotyped characters and general genre clichés" (Woods 1998: 100).[4] Intertwining several narratives, the film switches from one storyline to another with the ease of switching channels to create a type of collage culture. The characters participate in a type of time travel, where "a 40s film noir meets 50s and 70s celebrities with 1990s sensibilities" (Hopkins 1995: 16–17). The salvaged imagery of bygone eras comes to the fore when hitman, Vincent Vega (John Travolta), takes his boss' wife, Mia (Uma Thurman), to a diner called Jackrabbit Slim's which is decked out in the nostalgic style of the 1950s. There they drink milkshakes in booths shaped like convertibles, while wait staff dressed as pop icons of the past, such as Marilyn Monroe, Buddy Holly, and James Dean, work the floor around them. When the couple take to centerstage for a dance competition, they twist to Chuck Berry's "You Never Can Tell." Vega himself is a recycling of a 1940s *film noir* gangster depicted by the 1970s icon of cool—John Travolta. Here, time has not simply been stopped but looped, grafted over itself several times over until it is difficult to distinguish where (or when) in time they are located at that precise moment. Symptomatic of Generation X, the film exhibits a "detached appreciation for consumer culture" that celebrates the depthlessness of the image in contemporary culture without succumbing to it (Hicks 1996: 74).

---

a Sprite advertisement that relies on its smug knowingness of what is real and fake for its campaign,

> Macaulay Culkin is sitting in front of a house with a cute little girl, who leans over to kiss him but is thwarted when he declares 'I'm not really your boyfriend, I'm an actor. And this house isn't real, it's a set.' He pushes over the house façade, revealing the set behind it, and exposes two more actors backstage: 'And these aren't really your parents, they're just extras.' Offering the girl a Sprite, he comforts her with the words 'The only things that aren't fake are you, me and Sprite,' at which point the girl turns into a cardboard cut-out and is carried off stage. (Hicks 1996: 77)

4   Quentin Tarantino himself professed that cinema and television cultures were his main influences and salvation growing up in an uneasy period in American history. Tarantino recalls, "The Vietnam War and Watergate were a one-two punch that basically destroyed Americans' faith in their own country … The attitude I grew up with was that everything you've heard is lies. The president is a monkey" (quoted in Woods 1998: 13).

Figure 1.1   Generation Xploitation of collage culture: Hitmen, Vincent Vega (John Travolta) and Jules Winnfield (Samuel L. Jackson), in *Pulp Fiction* (1994)

Source: The Kobal Collection, The Picture Desk

I've Got You Under My Skin: The Subversiveness of Media

Douglas Rushkoff argues in *Media Virus: Hidden Agendas in Popular Culture* that power is no longer marked by physical territory and material acquisitions, but by images, ideologies, and data, which have become the most valued currency—all hail the mediascape as the final frontier (though we could also add cyberspace to this) (1994b: 3–4). Considering the disastrous effects of online viral outbreaks, capable of wiping out billions of dollars in lost revenue (we need only look at the ILUVYOU virus of 2000), and the power of a front page, scandalous image to topple a government, this is no understatement. For a generation brought up on multimedia, it is of little surprise that rallies and picket lines have been replaced with protest enacted through virtual sites. Echoing Rushkoff, Iain Chambers argues that the final bastion to be conquered is the "shadowy traces, images of a composite world, languages of potential sense" (1990: 8). By accenting the point of electric connection between text, reader, and producer, every text, memory, and moment becomes a potential site of struggle and meaning. Andrew Hultkrans' acerbic commentary that Generation X was "so goddamn media-savvy that the phrase 'The Medium is the Message' has for us the cozy familiarity of a nursery rhyme" wryly points to the subversive potential of a well-honed media literacy (1994: 298).

Rushkoff likens media events that provoke social change to biological viruses. Using the multitudinous networks available in mediaspace, media viruses spread rapidly and easily over an extensive populace. The "protein shell" that attracts attention—be it "an event, invention, technology, system of thought, musical riff, visual image, scientific theory, sex scandal, clothing style or even a pop hero"—affixes itself onto the recipient, and from there the virus injects its viral code to transform or even destroy the existing genetic code (Rushkoff 1994b: 9–12). Media viruses work beneath the skin of the host, rather than against it, and have the ability to alter the social DNA. Rushkoff's viral agent is a useful metaphor to explain how audiovisual texts and formats can be slowly affected/infected to take on new meanings, and to conceptualize the feedback loop between a text and an audience. To illustrate, I turn to the influence of MTV.

Conceived in 1981 as the brainchild of Robert Pittman, the Executive Vice President of Warner Amex Satellite Entertainment Company (WASEC), MTV had an immense impact on popular television programming. A commercial cable channel broadcasted via satellite, MTV was devoted to rock music videos which aired 24 hours a day, seven days a week (Kaplan 1988: 1–2). The prioritization of visual style over narrative within the video clips was a dramatic departure from the stock standard content of the time. It demanded new modes of engagement to make sense from the stream of disparate and seemingly unintelligible images. As one 18-year-old interviewee commented in a study, "It's an art to catch just enough of different story lines to follow all of them. My parents can't take it. I usually end up alone in front of the television" (quoted in Ainslie 1988: 127).

In MTV, conventional narratives were de-narrativized and coded in a lexicon that reveled in its "discontinuity as an opportunity for instantaneous transformation" (Rushkoff 1994b: 134). The fragmented aesthetics and "frequent raids upon the past" were characteristic of a postmodern ethos of textual poaching and reappropriation (Goodwin 1987: 47). Like a virus, its very existence relied on its act of spreading, infecting, and mutating. MTV required its audience to participate actively in the process of making connections and meaning. The visceral and transitory nature of the image meant that it could not be reduced to a singular interpretation of a singular reality, making its trajectory highly unpredictable. Its slick veneer made it difficult to hold down. This is further accentuated by the speed at which MTV moves. As Hugh Gallagher writes, "6:11 P.M. It's 'Classic MTV' and they're showing a video from three years ago. That's how fast this operation moves—three years and you're in the fucking archives" (1994: 188). Blink, and you might miss it.

Prior to MTV, the shortest edit utilized by filmmakers was approximately two seconds. Anything less was considered incomprehensible to the audience (Rushkoff 1994b: 130). With the arrival of MTV, edits became dramatically shorter with one third of a second not uncommon. It was a metaphorical IV-push of visuals into the viewer's system. The speed of the media text and the speed at which it was read refuted the prosaic complaint that Generation X had a limited attention span. As quickly as a text was processed, it was as rapidly superseded by its replication and recycling. As with any stage of evolution, accelerated culture demanded not only the ability to keep pace with the rapid deluge of information but also to adapt.[5] Flitting on the borders—too fast and always out of the grasp of those who cannot comprehend it—MTV is the perfect analogy for a generation manipulating the rules of the game and using pop culture as their battleground. The subcultural style of post-1980s youth extends beyond rituals and practices alone to encompass reading strategies to navigate through a continually metamorphosing environment of technological progress and information overload.

---

5   Douglas Rushkoff explores this acceleration of technology, information transmission, and nonlinearity of social narratives in *Children of Chaos* (1997).

Chapter 2

Rebels with a Cause: Popular Youth Cinema, Unpopular Politics

> When the causes of the decline of Western civilization are finally writ, Hollywood will surely have to answer why it turned one of man's most significant art forms over to the self-gratification of highschoolers. (Review of *The Breakfast Club*, in *Variety* 1985: 19)

> The problem with casting an impressive British actor like Helen Mirren in a teen-oriented American film is it raises expectations.

> But the teen genre is not known for producing many intellectual gems, so it should not come as a great surprise that *Teaching Mrs Tingle* … fails to deliver. (Sue Yeap 1999: 112)

The teenpic is either loved or loathed. No prisoners are taken. I have but a handful of friends who will entertain a suggestion to see the latest Hollywood high school offering on a Saturday night, but always with the disclaimer that they are expecting to leave their brains at home for this exercise in frivolous indulgence. Others would not be caught dead laboring through 90 minutes of puerile, tits-and-ass jokes, and all-too-predictable prom night antics, preferring the meaningful adult drama or a brooding French import of the *noir* genre. These indicators of personal taste implicate a host of binarisms that demarcate the integrity and value of highbrow art from the vulgarity of mass-produced texts, and suggest a clean break between youth and adulthood. However, such divisions tend to overlook the important cultural work that popular culture, in this case youth cinema, performs. This chapter looks at the construction of adolescence as a liminal space and experience. Cultural anxieties are manifested through fears of "anxious bodies" that threaten to transgress the limits of social acceptability. I pay particular attention to the representation of youth as rebel. The rebel functions ideologically as a warning of the dangers of youth in the context of the 1980s and 1950s. However, it is also through this figure that the unpopular politics of contemporary society's perennial folk devil can be funneled.

Jonathan Bernstein's *Pretty in Pink: The Golden Age of Teenage Movies* (1997) is symptomatic of a longstanding tradition that continually debases youth cinema, specifically those films released during the 1980s. On the one hand, it is a nostalgic fondness for the happy (teenage) days (in the way that we recall posters of rockstars and actors plastered on our bedroom walls), but at the same time this look-back is pilloried as being trite and somewhat embarrassing. Bernstein jibes,

"The eighties was the period when parents were away for the weekend for an entire decade, leaving the kids in charge of the movie industry. Suckers" (1997: 221). His grievances ricochet haphazardly from the adolescent desires of an audience he identifies as "Mr. Dumb Horny 14 Year Old," to the opportunistic studios pandering to this audience base, to the desideratum of an industry dominated by an aged population attempting (unsuccessfully) to recapture its lost youth (Bernstein 1997: 4). Efforts to tackle relevant social issues derail into acerbic diatribes or dismissive statements, typifying a "not another teen movie" knee-jerk reflex.

The wrath of critics, whose benchmark for "good cinema" relies upon realism and broaching issues of adult importance, is pervasive. Disparaging reviews of teen films, as can be seen in the opening quotes, tend to be the rule, rather than the exception. For instance, in the same breath, Elayne Rapping praises the rarefied "pure art" of *Badlands* while berating *Reckless* and *American Graffiti* as "too absurd to discuss" (1987: 17). Similarly, Armond White laments, "John Hughes' confessional comedy *The Breakfast Club* is so obviously, miserably fake—the characters don't even talk like teenagers. (And who ever heard of Saturday detention?)" (1985: 9). The standoff between cynics and supporters of popular youth cinema is captured in the two-way riposte between Noel King and Adrian Martin as they deliberate the merits of the teen movie. King profiles Martin as a populist culture crusader who is prone to wanton bouts of misguided enthusiasm and over-intellectualization of "the dynamic, the energetic, the volatile" (1992: 46). King scathingly writes,

> Martin's discussion of teen movies, after all, is a very sophisticated ethical/ rhetorical exercise (though he would never call it that), one enabled by a range of education, reading and research. Which is to say that Martin's own distinctive 'critical gestures' separate *him*, as an 'intelligent critic,' from *them*, the 'mass audience.' It is a fantasy to imagine it could be otherwise. After all, what social group is going to agonize about whether or not the teen pic is being given its critical due? (King 1992: 46)

King's abrasive reproaches point to a generalized resentment towards the serious study of youth cinema, and from which a host of flawed assumptions surfaces. King (mis)aligns teen films with slavish populism and anti-intellectualism while tacitly elevating high culture to the point where its social and cultural relevance need not be questioned. This political division is masked by relocating blame onto Martin's personal style and elitism. Martin's sharp rebuttal exposes King's biased posturing,

> 'writing the popular' as a critic has little or nothing to do with reaching 'the people,' as that mob is feverishly imagined by troubled intellectuals, while it has everything to do (and this is what's positive about it) with marking out and travelling down new lines of social exchange, and finding new connections and networks that cut across previous socio-cultural divisions. Writing about

popular culture, then, isn't doomed to be merely regressive or circular; it's more like a 'mutant' form of critical activity for a changing cultural terrain. (Martin 1992b: 48)

Martin's assertion widens the scope and possibilities in critical cinema and cultural practice. Just as film cannot portray real life—even the modest documentary cannot claim to be a truly objective account of events—our interpretations cannot exist simply at the level of the literal. The intentions of the filmmaker, as expressed through form and style, are negotiated through the reading strategies of the audience. Critiques that cordon off those "'precious' films from that hideous, amorphous 'mass' of objects branded teen movies" fail to address *why* a film resonated so deeply with its audience members, no matter how implausible the storyline (Martin 1989: 12, 14).

While youth cinema is generally resigned to the slums of celluloid culture in film criticism, the popularity and pleasure principles of the genre warrant critical engagement. Dealing with the politics of the everyday, popular culture holds intense meaning for its readership. As Paul Willis states, "Culture is not artifice and manners, the preserve of Sunday best, rainy afternoons and concert halls. It is the very material of our daily lives, the bricks and mortar of our most commonplace understandings, feelings and responses" (1979: 185–6). The intensity of youth and its nostalgic evocations in popular culture can be explained through the idea of affectivity. Lawrence Grossberg roughly translates affectivity as a "feeling of life" (1992: 56). He writes, "Affect always defines the quantitatively variable level of energy (activation, enervation) or volition (will); it determines how invigorated we feel in particular moments of our lives. It defines the strength of our investment in particular experiences, practices, identities, meanings and pleasures. In other words, affect privileges volition over meaning" (Grossberg 1992: 57).

Affect can explain our intense reaction to a stimulus—be it a scent, a picture, or the memory of a childhood friend—to the point that it threatens to spill over, to overcome us because of the vested interest we bring to a text. The sensation of ecstasy is a personal and collective immersion that not only marks the experience as relevant—it matters—but also signifies the construction of difference and identity (Grossberg 1992: 57–8). For instance, *Stand By Me* (dir. Rob Reiner, 1986) opens with a saddened man (Gordie, played by Richard Dreyfuss) sitting in his car on an empty road. He looks down at the newspaper in the seat next to him. A story headline reads, "Attorney Chris Chambers Fatally Stabbed In Restaurant." When two young boys ride past on their bicycles, the camera zooms in and Gordie's voiceover (as an adult) takes us back to when he was the age of twelve. The article and the boys provide the triggers for Gordie's nostalgic musing of his youth and three boyhood friends, one of whom was Chris Chambers. At the end of the film, Gordie types on his keyboard, "I never had any friends later on like the ones I had when I was twelve. Jesus does anyone?" His resigned acceptance of Chris' tragic death and the protagonist's own middle-agedness accentuate the instability and ephemerality of youth. It is intensely personal, but simultaneously smoothed over by the passing of time and the much altered circumstances from which he recalls the events of that unforgettable summer of 1959. When Gordie's son (Chance Quinn) remarks to a friend that his dad "gets like that when he's writing"— referring to Gordie's obliviousness to the immediate surrounds—it is clear that newspaper clippings and passionate stories of youth passed from father to son will never capture the emotional gravity of Gordie's experiences and memories. Words become a poor substitute. It is this emotional profundity of youth—the intensity of a fleeting moment that feels like a lifetime—that makes youth cinema a fascinating subject of study.

Criteria that demarcate crude commodity from high art, and the ordinary from the extraordinary are informed by existing relations of power. As the Pop Artists of the 1960s exposed, with their fiberglass-encased urinals and painted cans of Campbell soup, markers of objectivity and fine taste are arbitrary and actually work to privilege certain forms of knowledge. Take, for instance, the furor created by the introduction of popular culture texts, such as films and magazines, into the Australian secondary school curricula by the Victorian Certificate of Education (VCE) in the early 1990s. Traditionalists were swift to denounce this move a desecration of "cultural heritage" (Martin 1992a: 37). But whose cultural heritage was being threatened? Who was speaking, and who was silenced? Exclusionary practices disadvantage those lacking the literacy to engage with high-cultured (read: valued) texts, relegating them outside of power and credibility.

While the asymmetrical distributions of cultural capital favor an elite minority, disenfranchised communities are able to use the disempowered sites of popular culture to negotiate their social position (Brabazon 2002: x). As Simon Frith and Jon Savage argue, "The 'accessibility' of popular culture … describes the fact not that 'everyone' can understand it, but that everyone can use it, has a chance to be heard, to develop their own language, however difficult or *unpopular* what they say may be" (1997: 15). Popular culture is able to tell narratives of social experiences that may otherwise be passed off as banal or dangerous, giving voice to marginalized groups and actualizing social tensions through cultural representations. As history has shown us, popular culture has been instrumental in not only placating, but also heightening and articulating, cultural anxieties during times of great change. World wars see a rapid proliferation of propaganda, while a post-9/11 environment has witnessed all manner of displays of patriotic bravado to patch over the constant fear of invasion. A homeland under attack is almost always accompanied by a call to its citizens to remain vigilant of the sanctity of borders between "Us" and "Them." This reference to terrorism is not coincidental or overstated. Youth have, time and time again, been demonized and targeted as a menace to society—alien, foreign, monstrous, the Other. The metaphor of youth as the Other has been capitalized on in popular culture, as can be seen in television series such as *Roswell* (1999–2002: the three lead actors are extraterrestrials who look like regular high school students), and films such as *Teen Wolf* (dir. Rob Daniel, 1985: the hero is a basketball-playing lycanthrope), *The Lost Boys* (dir. Joel Schumacher, 1987: a gang of rebel youths are murderous vampires), and *The*

Faculty (dir. Robert Rodriguez, 1998: high school staff and students are one by one turned into alien beings).[1]

During the boom in popular youth culture (specifically cinema) in the 1950s and 1980s, cultural anxieties and tensions of the foreign body would often be played out through the representation of the unruly rebel. I cite these two decades because of their striking similarities (a theme that is continued in Chapters 3 and 7). In America, both periods immediately followed a decade of massive, post-war upheaval that was immediately compensated by a post-war optimism, decadence, and delusion that teetered on a knife's edge. The 1950s boasted the convenience and modernity of technological progress (its potential was summed up by push-button technology—the efficiency of a household appliance and the supposed ease of nuclear annihilation), a thriving industry and economy, the stability of the nuclear family, and Dwight Eisenhower's assurance that the future never looked so good (Wójcik 1997: 102–3). The 1980s, in a bid to forget Richard Nixon's indiscretions and the failure of American armed forces in Southeast Asia, was an almost mirror-like image of the 1950s. Under the leadership of Ronald Reagan, the laissez-faire economy and meritocratic ideals fostered a culture of capitalism and materialism (paralleled in the United Kingdom under a Tory government). During this time, America's influence upon its former political opponents was palpable (the disbanding of the Soviet Union in 1991, three years after Reagan's term ended, would officialize America as the leading superpower) and the nation would once again experience a boom in technological advancement (computers, video, and so forth). However, beneath the composed surfaces of these decades stirred a constant paranoia. In the 1950s, it was the steady threat of the Red Menace abroad, the possibility of nuclear attack, the dangerous black body in desegregated schools, and a violation of the American way by Communists, which reached fever pitch during the McCarthy era. In the 1980s, the power of nuclear energy once again was seen as a real peril, as was the rampant drug trade, AIDS, and the dissolution of the nuclear family. Additionally, the dominance of the youth demographic in consumer culture and in the media was met with a general mentality that saw youth as a problem to be solved. The 1950s and 1980s were both defined by ultra social and political conservatism. Youth cinema of the 1980s reappropriated the popular memory of the "rebellious teen" that was crystallized in the 1950s to represent the cultural anxieties of its context of production.

Social unrest and tension were filtered through cinematic representations. Pertaining to the 1950s, Timothy Shary (2005) argues that American movies in general were starting to undermine images of a victorious nation. Films began to adopt darker tones and foreboding narratives (as seen in *film noir*) that perpetuated an air of anxiety. These were traits that also ended up becoming the stylistic and narrative template of much teen cinema of the period (Shary 2005: 20). At the same time that these teen films exploited a culture of fear, concerns surrounding the

---

1   For a discussion of the teenager as alien in *Roswell*, see Badmington (2004: 166–75).

exploitation of youths were also gathering momentum in light of the entertainment industry's rush to make a quick buck from this group. As Thomas Doherty writes, "even as editorial writers, law enforcement officials, and parents were shoring up the barricades against teenagers the business community was welcoming their arrival at the gates, and with good reason: there was a fortune to be made selling trinkets to the invaders" (2002: 40). The paradox of the dominant culture industry needing this demographic, while at the same time patronizing them, has remained consistent even to this day.

The size of the Baby Boomer cohort and their purchasing power made them a formidable force and major cog driving the film industry. When their parents were at home watching television, young people were traveling in droves to the movies for a number of reasons. One of these was that post-war teenagers were the first generation to use cars not just for work purposes, but also for leisure. This mobility was conducive to a teenage culture that was becoming increasingly autonomous of the parent culture (Shary 2002: 3). "Parking" at the drive-in signified the ultimate freedom, and it is no coincidence that this tableau has become a mainstay in nostalgic evocations of the 1950s.

While images of youth were not uncommon prior to the 1950s—juvenile actors such as Elizabeth Taylor, Judy Garland, Mickey Rooney, and Frankie Darro were already household names—their burgeoning roles in films led to what Doherty terms the "juvenilization" of American cinema. This stood in stark contrast to the period prior to the mid-1950s when the American cinema-going public was assumed to be heterogeneous and multigenerational, as was reflected in the broad appeal of the storylines (Doherty 2002: 1). A feel-good Shirley Temple narrative or a moralistic Andy Hardy-production would be a reliable crowd pleaser for the young and geriatric age groups alike. However, with the explosive popularity of rock 'n' roll, and loosened regulations surrounding the production of films that allowed more risqué issues to be broached, it would be inevitable that young audiences would demand films with narratives and characters that more closely resembled their own experiences. This is why James Dean's character of Jim Stark in *Rebel Without a Cause* (dir. Nicholas Ray, 1955) is the prototype of the rebellious, male teenager. While Elvis Presley was making a name for himself in music, and Marlon Brando on a motorbike was already impressed into the public's imagination, Dean's depiction of teenage angst would sear the image of disenfranchised youth into the popular culture landscape. Jim Stark's anguish and disillusionment with middle-class society was a critical commentary on the breakdown of the nuclear family, narrativizing the loss of an American utopia through intergenerational conflict. As Jerold Simmons muses, "In the era of *Father Knows Best*, *Rebel* was the first motion picture to express our world rather than theirs. More than any other, it captured our youthful torment, our restless natures, our craving for acceptance" (1995: 63). Thomas Leitch argues that the film valorized the adolescent perspective by restricting adults to one of two types—they were largely ineffectual, or threatening figures to be avoided (1992: 46). In *Rebel Without a Cause*, adults are absent from the life-altering decisions made by teenagers who must also bear the responsibility for their own actions. The narrative's defining moments do not take place within the usual scenario of the family home but in the town streets, in chickie races, in abandoned buildings, and knife fights. The rebellious youth was a dramatic statement of the presence of a distinctive community and a point of identification for young people. So popular was the image of the young rebel that from the mid-1950s onwards, the motion picture industry was actually going out of its way to establish delinquency among American youth as the norm (Considine 1985: 182). However, not all representations were as sympathetic as in *Rebel Without a Cause*.

Incarnations of the juvenile delinquent as the morally-devoid folk devil often served as cautionary tales, warning of the consequences lest a society let down its guard against undesirables. The "teenage terror" posed an easily identifiable assailant and target. The proliferation of popular youth culture in the 1950s would be consonant with the nation's priority to keep its youth in check, where pandering to this group would be matched with punishment and discipline (Tropiano 2006: 22). This would be exemplified in *Blackboard Jungle* (dir. Richard Brooks, 1955), a film that was controversial for its high level of violence. It was the story of an idealistic English teacher's struggles in a rough, inner-city high school. As the heroic protagonist, Richard Dadier (Glenn Ford) doggedly refuses to give up on his students even though they appear to be dead-end, urban urchins. While Ford's performance as the empathetic teacher was laudable, it was the antics and dissonance of the pupils, described in the film's original theatrical trailer as "teenage savages," that stole the show. They were the source of fascination, vexation, and fear. For instance, the students openly taunt and threaten teachers in class and resort to violent beatings. One particularly nasty hoodlum, Artie West (played by Vic Morrow), harasses Dadier's pregnant wife, and another student attempts to rape a female teacher. The film commences with a public awareness notice voicing concern over the causes and effects of juvenile delinquency, before cutting to the opening credits as "Rock Around The Clock" plays over the sequence (also the track closing the film). *Blackboard Jungle* was the first film by a major motion picture studio to tee up the juvenile delinquent with the youth-driven rock 'n' roll scene. Violent responses during screenings by a small minority fueled speculations of the immorality and belligerence of a generation out of control. Cultural anxieties, however, could be allayed by the end of a 90-minute screening. At the end of the film, the tension of teenage savagery is resolved when Dadier gains support from his students to turn in to the authorities the worst teenage offenders who are beyond saving.

The release of the film *Rock Around The Clock* (dir. Fred F. Sears, 1956) added to the escalating moral panic surrounding youth. In cities from America to Europe, conservative parties were again crying out against the corruption of impressionable adolescents by the hypnotic rock 'n' roll craze. Cashing in on the success of the hit single by Bill Haley and His Comets, and the song's appearance in *Blackboard Jungle* a year earlier, it would be inevitable that *Rock Around The Clock* would follow in the contentious footsteps of its predecessor. When occasional disputes broke out between youths and theater staff during screenings, and juvenile vandals took to "trashing lobby displays, slashing seats, and, at drive-ins, speeding off with speakers," it was seen as evidentiary of a very real threat of the juvenile delinquent (Doherty 2002: 113). The rising adolescent crime rate in the late 1940s and 1950s in the United States brought under tight scrutiny and censorship those films depicting juvenile delinquency. This had the effect of stirring curiosity and publicity. Not only were the films regarded as having a negative impact upon youths, but they also raised concerns about the unflattering image being conveyed to audiences abroad. Simmons (2008) details how *Blackboard Jungle* was shadowed by controversy with protests and bans in several American states, while *The Wild One* (dir. Laslo Benedek, 1953) was banned in Britain in 1954 and only approved for general release 13 years later. The high-concept nature of such films, with their familiar plotlines, character types, and cinematic style, made them extremely marketable, exploitable, and transferable to later decades (Wyatt 1994: 19, 30). The generational divide—youth versus everyone else—would endure.

Popular youth culture of the 1980s saw a reappropriation of the rebel. At times, it borrowed directly from the iconography of 1950s films that in a way was nostalgic for what seemed a less complicated, romantic era. This again perpetuated the myth of the glories of the past and the redemptive qualities of community and family for disorderly, angst-ridden youth. Examples in film included *The Outsiders* (dir. Francis Ford Coppola, 1983) and *Cry Baby* (dir. John Waters, 1990). In television programs, the token bad boy resembled James Dean's rebel in mannerisms and visual style, from the stormy countenance and trademark quiff of Luke Perry in *Beverly Hills, 90210* (1990–2000), to Johnny Depp in *21 Jump Street* (1987–1991).[2] In tandem with the free-market ethos of the 1980s, youth cinema started to see a new breed of rebels emerge in films typified by the likes of *Ferris Bueller's Day Off* (dir. John Hughes, 1986), *Risky Business* (dir. Paul Brickman, 1983), and *Real Genius* (dir. Martha Coolidge, 1985). Often popular, middle-upper class, Anglo-American teenagers—a sharp contrast to the ethnic, working-class minorities who were seen as the juvenile delinquents in the past—these privileged youths seemed hardly the type to have reason to buck the system. Take, for example, the cult classic and quintessential teen film *Ferris Bueller's Day Off*. Ferris (Matthew Broderick) plays truant, takes without permission a Ferrari owned by the father of his friend Cameron (Alan Ruck), spends a day in Chicago with two friends—they fine dine, visit tourist sites, catch a ballgame, and join a street parade among other activities—and manages to evade being caught at the end of it all. To the ire of his elder sister, Jeanie (Jennifer Grey), and the odious school dean, Ed Rooney (played with delicious insidiousness by Jeffrey Jones) who is out to get him, Ferris even has the entire community convinced he is either a hero or a saint. In one scene, he gatecrashes a parade on a main street, mounts a float, and then lip-syncs to Wayne Newton's "Danke Schoen" to a crowd of adoring onlookers. A group of

---

2   Johnny Depp played Tom Hanson, an undercover police officer who infiltrates high schools and colleges.

Figure 2.1   License for thrills: Sloane (Mia Sara), Cameron (Alan Ruck), and Ferris (Matthew Broderick) on a mission for serious fun in *Ferris Bueller's Day Off* (1986)

Source: The Kobal Collection, The Picture Desk

young people begin to spontaneously dance in the streets in perfect synchronicity (which later films would borrow and spoof). The perfectly choreographed routine flaunts the film's detachment from reality, with promotional posters pegging the film as, "Leisure Rules. One man's struggle to take it easy." The whole street parade scene, and the entire film for that matter, is a splendidly ridiculous exercise in unadulterated indulgence. Living the grand life, Ferris is an arrogant egotist. A rebel without a *real* cause?

While it would be easy to pan *Ferris Bueller's Day Off* as a teen comedy going for gags, this undervalues the meaning and significance the film held for youth, especially those who lived through the 1980s. In fact, the intergenerational and cultural tensions that were treated with seriousness in the 1950s find heightened expression through the film's humor, itself a mode of delivery that allows the unspeakable to be represented. *Ferris Bueller's Day Off* recreates the façade of the perfectly well-adjusted, nuclear family—father, mother, and two children living in a palatial home in middle-upper class suburbia—with many of the jokes deriving from Ferris' absurd, but ultimately triumphant, efforts to maintain this exterior image. In the opening scene, we are already made aware that beneath the surface, all is not as it seems. For starters, Ferris has an unhealthy disregard for authority (he provides a checklist on how to play hookey from school in the opening scene), his only sibling loathes him with a vengeance, the parentals are blissfully ignorant, and the school staff members are moronic, out of touch, or plain vengeful.

Ferris manipulates the system and those around him, and indulges in the opulence and excesses of the 1980s like a pig rolling in warm mud. *Ferris Bueller's Day Off* encapsulates the Reagan era's near solipsist worldview and insatiable appetite for immediate gratification—of living in and for the moment—with the protagonist's reverence for that dirty F-word ... fun.[3] However, there is more at work here than just play and pleasure. Reclaiming "fun" from its otherwise derogatory, depoliticizing connotations, R.L. Rutsky and Justin Wyatt state that it "makes fun of that which takes itself too seriously, of that which cannot laugh at itself. In its essence, then, fun is parodic, ironic" (1990: 10). As it has no regard for boundaries, fun performs the politics of that which is considered absurd, hedonistic, profane, and/or marginal. Occupying liminal spaces, Ferris continually transgresses physical and symbolic boundaries, and has an uncanny ability to evade being pinned down and punished.

Border Raiders: Transgression and Liminality in Youth Cinema

Liminality and transgression are characteristics that define the cultural construction of youth. Citing Arnold van Gennep, cultural anthropologist Victor Turner described the *rites de passage*—the rites of transition that accompany all major, socially acceptable changes—as distinguished by three phases: separation, margin (*limen*), and aggregation (1967: 94). Within the margin phase, the subject becomes ambiguous for it is in a phase of transition and transformation. While this is a necessary phase before arriving at the final, stable state (in this case, competent adulthood), bodies in liminal zones are potentially dangerous for they fall "in the cracks of social structure, that is, in between socially sanctioned roles," and exist beyond the governing myths of a dominant culture (Rothenbuhler 1988: 68). As a result, the behavior of these offending liminal bodies must either be denied of their meaningfulness or interpreted within the dominant social structure.

The liminal phase articulates the ambiguity and paradox of youth. As Adrian Martin argues, it is an "intense, suspended moment between yesterday and tomorrow, between childhood and adulthood, between being a nobody and a somebody, when everything is in question, and anything is possible" (1994: 67,

---

3   This obsession with the accelerated times of the 1980s was not only prevalent in cinema and television, but also in literature. Authors such as Douglas Coupland, Bret Easton Ellis, Katherine Texier, and Susanna Moore, whose works were dubbed "blank fiction," often explored the hyper-consumerist culture of the decade. They focused on urban youth and their disillusionment, confusion, and sense of marginality in a world of fast cars, fast money, fast drugs, and fast youth. As James Annesley writes, blank fiction spoke in "the commodified language *of* its own period" (1998: 2, 7).

68). The abject nature of the liminal body is translated into (monstrous) biological manifestations during puberty—the onset of menstruation, acne eruptions on the face, the sprouting of hair, hormonal imbalances, ejaculation of bodily fluids, and so forth.[4] These excessive bodies need to be contained. Julia Kristeva's definition of abjection—that "which does not respect borders, positions, rules" and "disrupts identity, system, order" (1982: 4)—perfectly captures the notion of the potentially dangerous, liminal body during puberty. Moving beyond the biological, the disruption to order and system can also be seen in the movements of youth through physical sites. They often hover in spaces that can be classed as liminal—the street corner, the mall, the park, the high school—all of which are characterized by continual movement, and are outside of direct control. Although such locales may be under surveillance, for example, the privatized space of the shopping mall, youth are still accorded a high degree of autonomy from adult supervision. In summation, we may argue that youth—liminal subjects occupying liminal spaces—are transgressive. By default, they are all rebels who offend sanctioned boundaries. Social order can only be maintained by interpreting them as such to retain the "natural order" and hierarchy.

Picture the scenario. It is a school night in the middle of an Arizonan suburban sprawl, the heart of "white-bread land." The parentals are watching the late-night news, reading their books, and planning their kids' futures. Graduation, Yale, and then, of course, marriage. Just a typical evening, and no one would think otherwise. But instead of sleeping or studying, teenagers all over the district are tuning their radio sets because somewhere on a low frequency channel, a pirate disc jockey is giving them directives. And he means serious business.

> *Harry Hardon*: Doesn't this blend of blindness and blandness wanna make you do something crazy? Then why not do something crazy? Makes a helluva lot more sense than blowing your brains out. You know, go nuts, go crazy, get creative. Got problems? You just chuck 'em, nuke 'em. They think you're moody? Make 'em think you're crazy. Make 'em think you might snap! They think you got attitude, you show some real attitude. Ah! I mean, go nuts! Get crazy! Hey, no more Mr Nice Guy!

In *Pump Up the Volume* (dir. Allan Moyle, 1990), the words of DJ Happy Harry Hardon (Christian Slater), the alter ego of the bookish outcast Mark Hunter, provide an anarchic set of instructions. They are directed to a disempowered group turning against systemic oppression in a community that straitjackets its youth but expects them to keep on smiling. All hell is about to break loose. No more Mr Nice Guy. When one girl exclaims "Hallelujah!" to the DJ's suggestions, it is clear that Harry Hardon is not just another average Joe with a microphone and

---

4 It is a theme that has been explored time and again in the teen slasher film. Promiscuous teenagers often face the most gruesome deaths. Their sexual transgressions, that is, their failure to control their bodies must be punished (Clover 1987: 187–228).

a foul mouth. As a modern-day messiah, Harry Hardon is a martyr on a mission. What ensues is mayhem. Paige Woodward (Cheryl Pollak), the model student bound for Yale, ditches her hair drier, cosmetics, and pearls in the microwave, and blows them up. Teenagers all over the district stand up, shout out, and dance in revolt and celebration to a common tune from Harry Hardon's musical repertoire. A crowd gathers at the school field, culminating in a frenzied atmosphere akin to a freakish carnival. It is the middle finger salute to authority. Over the course of the narrative, Harry Hardon uncovers that the school has an unjust policy of suspending, expelling, or harassing students seen as problematic, such as a pregnant teenager and students failing classes. Under the auspices of its iron-fisted principal, Loretta Creswood (Annie Ross), the school retains its leading average SAT scores in the state by denying an education to those it considers unworthy of being taught. Instilling an atmosphere of fear and paranoia, where questioning authority results in swift punishment for both students and staff members, the actions of higher management are professionally dubious and morally suspect. As Harry Hardon muses in the film, "everything is polluted" and they are "living in the middle of a totally … exhausted decade where there's nothing to look forward to and no one to look up to."

Pump Up the Volume easily attracts slurs of being yet another innocuous teen film with the usual suspects—pissed off, pimple-faced high schoolers and villainous authoritarians who are as clueless as they are conservative. The film cannot claim to be an epic tragedy, nor can nostalgia be used as a trump card to elevate it above that all too common charge of shallow teenage escapism. *Pump Up the Volume* unapologetically oozes cool with its attractive cast (Slater was at the peak of his career as a teen idol), a hip MTV-style soundtrack, and self-aware repartees. The film's reveling in the anarchy of (having and creating) fun alone provides arsenal for its trivialization in film critiques. However, this anarchic fun plays an important function.

As the transformative potential of the carnivalesque is evident in *Pump Up the Volume*, it is useful to draw upon Mikhail Bakhtin's writings of the carnival. In medieval European folk culture, carnival was, for a brief time each year, a period of sanctioned disruption to social order. The strict protocols of an ecclesiastical and ascetically-driven community gave way to a festive period that rejoiced in satire and counter-representation, with marketplaces the teeming center of public humiliations, mock scenarios where sacrosanct rituals were made a farce of, and masquerades (men dressed as women, women as men, humans as grotesque figures) (Bakhtin 1994: 196, 200). Importantly, the body of the grotesque was "never finished, never completed; it is continually built, created, and builds and creates another body" (Bakhtin 1994: 233–4). Its orifices, convexities, and protuberances were open for all to see, and glorified rather than concealed. Peter Stallybrass and Allon White state, "given the presence of sharpened political antagonism, [carnival] may often act as *catalyst* and *site of actual and symbolic struggle*" (1986: 14). Within the short timeframe and space of glorious pandemonium, the most scathing commentaries could be made, and hegemonic practices exposed and ridiculed

**Figure 2.2   Rebel with a cause: Pirate DJ, Happy Harry Hardon
(Christian Slater), in *Pump Up the Volume* (1990)**

Source: The Kobal Collection, The Picture Desk

without reprisal. During this state of volatility, new modes of public intervention became possible. Carnival deliberately distressed the binary oppositions that organize society, turning the world topsy-turvy (White 1993: 170).

Like the subjects of carnival, the teenagers in *Pump Up the Volume* exhibit certain grotesque features. They are bodies in the act of becoming—gangly limbs, hormonally imbalanced, and libidinally charged—that threaten to spill over. Some of these bodies do. Malcolm Kaiser (Anthony Lucero), a student suffering bullying and depression, ends up committing suicide by shooting himself. Although we never witness the act, we can imagine the bloody gore of the scene. Paige, the straitlaced princess, goes ballistic at a PTA meeting, spewing criticism at the school board before shrieking at the news crews outside. At another point, the "Eat Me-Beat

Me Lady" (the alter ego of Nora Diniro [Samantha Mathis] who is one of Mark's classmates) composes a poem that Harry Hardon reads on air, "My insides spill on your altar and tell your future. My steaming, gleaming guts spell out your nature." While these bodies are read as deviant and festering like open sores by authority figures in *Pump Up the Volume*, their difference is extolled by the teenagers. When they rebel, they forge a space—a modern-day marketplace—where their bodies become intentionally visible and open for all to see. This culminates in the teenagers assembling en masse at the school field where, regardless of social standing, economic stature, and race, they join in concerted protest and revelry to dance and scream profanities under the patronage of Harry. Openly criticizing the authorities, their plight is aired over the news. There is a method to the madness.

The student body, however, signifies more than a simple inversion of binaries. It indicates the transformative possibilities of transgression. Stuart Hall articulates this subversive potentiality of transgression,

> The low invades the high, blurring the hierarchical imposition of order; creating, not simply the triumph of one aesthetic over another, but those impure and hybrid forms of the 'grotesque'; revealing the interdependency of the low on the high and vice versa, the inextricably mixed and ambivalent nature of all cultural life, the reversibility of cultural forms, symbols, language, and meaning; and exposing the arbitrary exercise of cultural power, simplification, and exclusion which are the mechanisms upon which the construction of every limit, tradition, and canonical formation, and the operation of every hierarchical principle of cultural closure, is founded. (Hall 1993: 8)

The carnival and the grotesque create a liminal space. Carnival's transgression of tightly policed borders is both outward-looking at the Other, but also forces an inward gaze at the self. For example, the nom de plume of "Happy Harry Hardon" is a parody of the institution—Hubert H. Humphrey High School. The DJ hijacks this sign, inverts it, and makes a travesty of it. In doing so, a new meaning for the acronym HHH is produced. When the authorities attack Harry Hardon for his bad behavior, it is an inadvertent attack against their own selves. They cannot blame Harry Hardon without acknowledging how they are also to blame for the dire state of affairs. The pirate DJ exposes the hypocrisy of public institutions that continually penalize youth without recourse.

In *Pump Up the Volume*, carnival laughter performs the dissonance of the youth because it debases official discourse. In one scene, two students wire a boom box to the school's loud speaker system. It broadcasts a voice recording of David Deaver (Robert Schenkkan), the school's hypocritical guidance counselor, that has been remixed and dubbed into a rap version. At the same time, it speaks the language of the student body while making a mockery of their opponents. Carnival laughter is also directed at the self. When Harry Hardon laments Malcolm's suicide on air the night after, the tragedy is turned on its head when the DJ, realizing there is nothing to be gained from wallowing in self-pity, subverts it into a comic situation. His obituary turns to the subject of "shit[ting] your shorts" before death, and crass jokes about heaven. It is a case of laughing in the face of, and in spite of, danger. Above all, carnival laughter is about unison and inclusion (Bakhtin 1994: 200). The spasmodic release may be an individual expression, but it is bound to a wider populace. When the teenagers take to destroying public property, wild dancing, and retaliation against the disciplinary institutions of school and family, a distinctive community is formed. Everyone—from jocks to punks, yuppies to stoners—congregates at the field. The separate cliques of the high school morph into a conjoined mass, which contrasts with the aggressive adult world. This student cohesion is even more pronounced after we witness Miss Emerson (Ellen Greene), a young English teacher, being jeered at by her colleagues and fired after daring to question her superiors. Maintaining strained power relations, the dynamics between the adults are destructive, exclusive, and divisive.

In *Pump Up the Volume*, the youth create a shared space to air their grievances. Their visible bodies and loud voices become marked signs of disruptive transgression, and also the sites of multiple narratives of social experience. In the closing scene when he reveals his true identity, Mark's/Harry Hardon's final words are "Talk hard!" It is a fitting decree for a generation doggedly forced into silence. These words are reappropriated by his listeners who each interpret what it means to go crazy and get creative. The graffiti on a wall at the high school—"Truth is a virus"—becomes a self-fulfilling prophecy. After Harry Hardon has been arrested, teenagers throughout the country begin to set up their own radio channels to query the legitimacy of previously accepted social truths, and as a way for the disenfranchised to band together. Instead of feeling ashamed of being dejected and rejected, they claim it as their own. Their symbolic struggle has metamorphosed into real action. The film, and by extension the genre of youth cinema, gives voice and visibility to the teenage experience, acknowledging the serious work in their play and pleasure. As the youths in *Pump Up the Volume* talk hard, they also keep on dancing and laughing long after Harry Hardon has gone. The fun is not yet over.

Chapter 3

Taking Out the Trash: The Politics of Remembering (and Forgetting) Molly Ringwald

Don't you forget about me
Don't, don't, don't, don't.
(Simple Minds ["Don't You (Forget About Me)," 1985])

Each generation is remembered via seminal icons that seem to capture the zeitgeist of an era and community, with youth culture contributing an impressive catalog of key personalities. The canonized likes of Ritchie Valens, James Dean, Sid Vicious, and Kurt Cobain continue to be memorialized and shrouded in a cloak of mystery, romantic tragedy, and myth; with books, movies, and television programs functioning as a type of prolonged eulogy to the dead and buried. While they have entered history as notable figures, this chapter takes as its subject American film actor and youth icon Molly Ringwald who is of the present but remains firmly, and problematically, entrenched in the past. Under the auspices of filmmaker John Hughes, Ringwald would be hailed as the quintessential teen queen in the mid-1980s. By the time her face graced the front cover of a 1986 edition of *Time* magazine, she was already a household name for a market that had crowned her the "model modern teen" and was the poster child for teenage angst (Corliss 1986b: 67). The Molly Ringwald phenomenon, during the actor's three-year reign at the multiplex, instigated a media feeding frenzy that spilled onto the streets, with devoted fans—the Ringlets—imitating Ringwald's punk-flapper fashion and flaming mop top. Ringwald's fame began to descend into obscurity in the late 1980s. This coincided with her attempt to break into what many considered more adult roles. While it may appear a case of yet another child actor's unsuccessful transition to adulthood—their novelty and endearing cuteness having worn thin—Ringwald continues to be prolific in film, television, and stage productions, and has achieved considerable acclaim; even appearing in Jean-Luc Godard's 1987 film adaptation of *King Lear*. However, there remains the incessant need to lock the actor in a 1980s time capsule. This nostalgic fixation with Ringwald as the eternal youth associated with the decade is symptomatic of contemporary preoccupations and anxieties in which the past is understood "not as a given 'thing' which we must preserve, but as a force constantly resonating in the present, producing new layers of sound and meaning" (Popular Memory Group 1982: 243). Where is Molly Ringwald now? And does anyone really care?

The fear of being forgotten is perhaps matched only by the paralyzing anxiety of being trapped in the past and unable to escape. As an ideological compression of events, it is history at its most efficient and ruthless. History positions the temporal and spatial into orderly compartments where it "clarifies, tidies, and elucidates" (Lowenthal 1985: 234). What is inevitably lost in this lockdown is the fundamental basis of time, that is, the intensity of the ephemeral. As history handles excess awkwardly, it often replaces the liminality and emotive gravity of an experience with measurable facts and figures, especially those that do not fall into the category of official history. In its fixed state, authorized narratives occupy the center while marginalized narratives are ignored or pushed so far to the edges that they disappear altogether. In studying the cultural body of Ringwald—a figure who is regularly exhumed from a nostalgic necropolis in popular remembrances—this chapter broaches the politics of memory and history, and the role of film in facilitating the restoration of what history has omitted or buried.

Exhuming the Past and Historical In(ter)vention

Zygmunt Bauman states, "Identity sprouts on the graveyard of communities, but flourishes thanks to the promise of the resurrection of the dead" (2001: 17). This resurrection conjures up ghosts that reiterate and reinstate dominant histories. The social relevance bestowed upon an event, a period, a people, becomes incumbent upon its ability to be defined via the tangible artifacts and verifiable information encased in books, museum exhibits, documents, and the records from authority figures and dignitaries. It forms a type of archival history. The result is an often static and petrified narrative permanently etched in relics and monuments, stored in dusty vaults where the clock has stopped. As Greil Marcus writes,

> History is written as we speak, its borders are mapped long before any of us
> open our mouths, and written history, which makes the common knowledge out
> of which our newspaper reports the events of the day, creates its own refugees,
> displaced persons, men and women without a country, cast out of time, the living
> dead: are you still alive, really? (Marcus 1995: 17)

The stories of displaced persons—the "living dead"—are erased the very moment the experiences are surpassed by the chronometer of modernity. By relegating them to the domains of myth, hearsay, rumor, fiction, and folklore, this leaves little or no vestige of their existence. One need only turn to political demonstrations, such as coordinated protests against the Iraq War and refugee detention centers in east Australia, to witness the privileging of sanctioned government and media reports, even when factually incorrect, over public opinion and even the experiences of those involved in the actual event. The inability to anchor an identity to a validated past writes out disempowered groups from their own histories, perpetuating their dislocation from the cultural memoryscape.

Alternative and oppositional narratives and ideologies are to be found in other forms, such as oral history, and in popular or mass mediums (Dyer 1998 [1979]: 2–3). These modes expand the possibilities of (re)thinking about the past, and contribute to a collective process that can be described as the "social production of memory" where everyone is a potential historian (Popular Memory Group 1982: 207). Cinema provides one such implement for recording, and later recalling, events that may otherwise be ignored. Considering the visual and aural spectacle of youth culture, it is of little surprise that cinema, with its ability to capture sight, sound, and movement, has become integral in providing a kind of unofficial documentation of the youth experience. More importantly, it is the *affective* threads in cinema—its ability to re-spark certain corporeal responses— that reconnects the past to the present. It creates not only meaning, but furthermore a sense of *meaningfulness*. The diegesis of film bestows youth a time and space that can be named and claimed as their own. It allows them to play out positions of subordination, dominance, and struggle that speak in the language of the disempowered. As Patrick Wright asserts, it is the periphery "where the disorders of the centre are most manifest and ... where the future must be found" (1992: 357). Here, the stories of the unpopular players, in a history not of their own making, become salient and purposeful. When fashion, the graffiti on a wall, the local street-corner hangout, or the parochial colloquialism associated with a fad means more than the contents of a published register of events and invokes a collective consciousness, then the rules of coercive interplay between history and identity begin to buckle under the weight of memories liberated from the past.

Too often has history been equated solely with a complete, inert past and unquestioned truth. Time is tidily categorized as past, present, and future in dominant historiography, like separate checkpoints on a disconnected overpass. History creates the illusion of objectivity, stability, and distance. It maps a "symbolically serviceable past" that allows us to derive an explanation of *where* we are now, the final destination, in a linear and naturally unfolding narrative (Lowenthal 1985: 228). The paradox is "that the proper object of history is not the past but the past–present relationship" (Popular Memory Group 1982: 240). The interstices between past–present become an ambiguous space where memory and nostalgia hover, regarded as an offence to the empirical logic of archival records with its exactitude/precision of dates, key figures, and locations of importance. However, as argued by Andreas Huyssen, it is precisely this fissure in time that makes memory powerfully alive and critical in our understandings of the past (1995: 3). The image banks of bygone days do not function as storage systems or passive receptacles, but rather partake in the dynamic, reciprocal shaping of current times (Samuel 1994: ix–x).

Popular memory is one means of investing the past in the present. It retrieves throwaway slivers from what Marcus describes as "the dustbin of history," that is, alternative stories, flows of time, and space that reveal the struggles and paradoxes that shape social organization and knowledge (1995: 13). It challenges the notion of a monopolistic, singular remembering. The bridging of gaps reinserts those rendered invisible and silent by modernity into the landscape of the Now, thus providing the opportunity to revise, rewrite, and reinterpret previously untouchable truths of societal antiquity generated by (oftentimes nationalist) myth. Popular memory is both an object of study and a political practice (Popular Memory Group 1982: 205). It enables the disenfranchised to negotiate an identity from their fragmented and fractured subjectivities, and to intervene in historical narrative (Giles 2002: 24). Svetlana Boym's (2001) concept of reflective nostalgia is worth considering here as an adjunct to popular memory. Boym contends that restorative nostalgia attempts to recuperate a sense of historical truth by evoking national narratives through a return to origins and intentional monuments. On the other hand, reflective nostalgia is more concerned with the "meditation on history and passage of time" and the "imperfect process of remembrance" (Boym 2001: 41, 49). Boym writes,

> If restorative nostalgia ends up reconstructing emblems and rituals of home and homeland in an attempt to conquer and spatialize time, reflective nostalgia cherishes shattered fragments of memory and temporalizes space. Restorative nostalgia takes itself dead seriously. Reflective nostalgia, on the other hand, can be ironic and humorous. It reveals that longing and critical thinking are not opposed to one another, as affective memories do not absolve one from comparison, judgment or critical reflection. (Boym 2001: 49–50)

Popular memory and reflective nostalgia wedge the past into the discursive and ideological framework of the present, in which remembering becomes political. They fill in the holes in official historiography where the adage of "gone but not forgotten" holds steadfast. In making this statement, it is important to point out that both popular memory and reflective nostalgia are hegemonic enterprises. Like history, they are intrinsically interlocked in constant negotiation with dominant discourses and also seek validation and a legitimate status. This does not negate their significance as historical interventions, but provides the opportunity for critical reflection.

Remembering Molly: Moving Memories

Molly Ringwald, in collaboration with John Hughes (in varying capacities of director, producer, and scriptwriter), churned out three seminal films in succession about, and for, youth—*Sixteen Candles* (dir. John Hughes, 1984), *The Breakfast Club* (dir. John Hughes, 1985), and *Pretty in Pink* (dir. Howard Deutch, 1986). *Sixteen Candles* was the simple story of a girl whose 16th birthday is forgotten by her family. It proved hugely successful financially and marked Ringwald's debut into teendom in the lead role as the angst-ridden Samantha Baker. The narrative of misunderstood youth struck an emotional chord with its primarily teenage viewers. It secured an audience for Hughes' future projects and shot Ringwald into

Figure 3.1   High school confessions: Bender (Judd Nelson), Andy (Emilio Estevez), Allison (Ally Sheedy), Claire (Molly Ringwald), and Brian (Anthony Michael Hall) in *The Breakfast Club* **(1985)**

Source: The Kobal Collection, The Picture Desk

instant fame.[1] She was metamorphosed into an adolescent ingénue whose name alone became, as Hughes described, a "bankable box-office attraction" (quoted in Corliss 1986b: 67).

The second film, *The Breakfast Club*, took as its premise a torturously boring Saturday detention that brought together five students from the various echelons of the high school hierarchy. The tropes of the "brain, an athlete, a basket case, a princess, and criminal," as defined by one of the principal characters in the film, are interrogated and deconstructed. By the film's conclusion, each character has undergone a life-altering revelation of the injustices of social stereotyping and confronted their own personality flaws. As the prom queen, Claire Standish, Ringwald's portrayal of vulnerability and stoicism solidified her as an icon of her times (and age). *The Breakfast Club*'s reception hailed a rising generation of young actors dubbed the "Brat Pack" (it included the likes of Ally Sheedy, Demi Moore, Emilio Estevez, Rob Lowe, and Robert Downey Jr.), and testified to the dynamism of the Hughes–Ringwald partnership. As Andrew Pulver writes of the Brat Pack,

---

1   Although Molly Ringwald had been performing since early childhood, it was *Sixteen Candles* that put her in the Hollywood limelight as a starlet.

"it's impossible to underestimate the emotional charge that much of their work carried for the serried ranks of teenagers who saw themselves, heightened and idealised maybe, flashing across the screen" (2000: 5).

The last of the triptych was *Pretty in Pink*, the vehicle to showcase Ringwald's acting prowess and celebrity power. Although promotional material alluded to the onscreen chemistry of the trio comprising Ringwald, Andrew McCarthy, and Jon Cryer in the roles of Andie, Blane, and Duckie respectively, it was Ringwald's name in the credits that drew the crowds and her performance that became synonymous with the film. As a student from a blue-collar background and situated on the lower rungs of the social pecking order, Ringwald's character continued to portray the stubborn determination, confusion, and optimism that had become her trademark range of emotions in the Hughes oeuvre. The trials and tribulations of being young attained a sense of seriousness and validity that had been immortalized in the 1950s films about youth, especially the juvenile delinquent genre, but had become somewhat diluted with a spate of late 1970s and early 1980s gross-out movies, such as *National Lampoon's Animal House* (dir. John Landis, 1978) and *Porky's* (dir. Bob Clark, 1982). Leading the 1980s resurgence in the genre of youth cinema was John Hughes who, according to Stephen Tropiano, "set the tone for the eighties teen films" (2006: 177). The auteur would be known for his "deft touch for teens' cultural concerns and personal interests," and his ability to convey the dimensions and depth of his subjects (Shary 2005: 71). Hughes made six teen films in the decade, three of which starred Ringwald as the lead actor.

The moral centers of the Hughes–Ringwald films addressed the insecurities associated with teenage life. They juxtaposed the struggling working class with the progeny of wealthy Baby Boomers, and explored the guilt and pain associated with hallway harassment. The movies presented a mixture of the innocence and craziness typical of the genre, grounded in the very real experiences of "teendom's silent majority of average, middle-class suburban kids" (Martin 1994: 67). The actors were propelled into the public sphere as archetypal teenagers, enabling Ringwald to reach the pinnacle of her popularity. Ringwald's stardom is a phenomenon of production (a filmic construction) and consumption by the audience. Her characters were markedly different in her three Hughes films—a disgruntled and cynical 16-year-old, an uptown preppie, and a working-class loner—and each movie was distinctive in terms of genre. For instance, *Sixteen Candles* was outrageous screwball comedy, *Pretty in Pink* fell into the category of "serious drama," and *The Breakfast Club* vacillated between the two. However, there were common threads running through all the movies which allowed for recognition and identification across texts. One of these was the vulnerability of Ringwald's characters. This trait was capitalized on through narrative and the aesthetics of film style, such as the camera's lingering close-ups, which privileged moments of pensive contemplation and confusion as conveyed through Ringwald's signature pout and elfish facial expressions. The films additionally offered quasi-utopian resolutions to teenage existential crises—being ignored on one's 16th birthday, the dream of seemingly impossible romances, being misunderstood, and a quest for self-identity. This was the glue that bonded Ringwald not only to her ardent fans, but also to an audience of youth who experienced the 1980s wave of American teen cinema. As Pauline Kael wrote, Ringwald's appeal was her "charismatic normality" and ordinariness (quoted in Agger 2004). There was nothing remarkable or spectacular about the situations she was in, compared, for instance, with the outlandish narratives of *Weird Science* (dir. John Hughes, 1985) and *Ferris Bueller's Day Off* (dir. John Hughes, 1986). Coupled with the intensity and intimacy of the big screen, this ordinariness was transformed into something quite extraordinary—an extraordinariness that refers to the aura surrounding celebrity status and the audience's own identification with an actor's performance and familiar scenarios. In Ringwald's characters, youth saw inflections of their own growing pains. At her pinnacle, the actor had become the poster girl for a generation of youth. Studio executives were quick to take advantage of her favorable position among the adolescent set. At 18 years of age, Ringwald had signed a lucrative contract with United Artist that allowed her virtual freedom for development and creative control of projects (Hutchings 1986: 87). Sought after by some of the film industry's most influential personalities, it seemed the actor was destined to continue her career into the 1990s.

Molly Ringwald could do no wrong; that is, until she grew up. First, she lost her virginity, fell pregnant, and then got married. I am referring to the films *The Pick Up Artist* (dir. James Toback, 1987), *For Keeps* (dir. John G. Avildsen, 1988), and *Betsy's Wedding* (dir. Alan Alda, 1990) respectively. Ringwald had matured from young love and prom dresses to dealing with the mafia, battling post-partum depression, and wedding gown dramas. Even when still portrayed as a teenager, the roles the actor pursued placed her outside of the insulated high school zone. In *Fresh Horses* (dir. David Anspaugh, 1988), Ringwald was cast as a teenage bride who has an affair with a college student (played by her *Pretty in Pink* co-star Andrew McCarthy). The setting was a barren, rural wasteland that removed the characters from the customary pink bedroom or the grand ballroom of the annual prom. Ringwald and McCarthy reprised the parts of disadvantaged girl from the wrong side of the tracks and privileged preppie. The film went so far as to make a direct reference to *Pretty in Pink* when Matt gives Jewel a pink scarf as a gift. Jewel, however, is not the same sweet 16-year-old that was Samantha Baker. Her backstory unveils the incestuous advances of a drunkard stepfather and a marriage of convenience to a wholly detestable older man, played by a seedy-looking Viggo Mortensen. Jewel does not attend school, and her days are squandered wandering around dilapidated buildings and sites. Thrust into a premature adulthood, Jewel's experiences and knowledge isolated her from the majority of youths who watched the film. Molly Ringwald was no longer the model teenager.

After *Pretty in Pink*, Ringwald's films tended to be marginally profitable. None were embraced with the same fervor that had greeted the Hughes–Ringwald repertoire. A bitter parting from Hughes after *Pretty in Pink* signaled Ringwald's severance of the umbilical cord from the man who had made her the face of misunderstood adolescence in the 1980s, thus completing the actor's impatience to graduate from the teenage years (People Weekly 1996: 48). Just as rapidly as her ascension to fame, three years later she was pronounced as past her prime. Ringwald no longer seemed to be making history. She appeared to have *become* history. With hindsight, the promotional poster's catchphrase for *Sixteen Candles*—"It's the time of your life that may last a lifetime"—sounds like an ominous premonition of arrested adolescence.

There are sociopolitical implications involved in the rendering and remembering of Molly Ringwald as the personification of an era. In our private reminiscences and popular culture, Ringwald's past has been scrawled over the pages of her present to perpetuate a myth of the way things never really were, doused with nostalgic affection. The actor, Sandra Dee, provides a useful point of reference in gauging Ringwald's importance as a teen icon as both share several uncanny resemblances. Achieving star status for her roles in clean teenpics (1950s–1960s), Dee was dubbed the "role model of choice … Her wide appeal to her own generation as well as adults doubtless stems from the fact that she seems to epitomize that nice 'girl next door' … relying on decent instincts and common sense," according to a 1959 popularity poll in *Motion Picture Herald* (quoted in Doherty 2002: 160). She was famous for her wholesome characters of Gidget and Tammy in such films as *Gidget* (dir. Paul Wendkos, 1959), *Gidget Goes Hawaiian* (dir. Paul Wendkos, 1961), *Tammy Tell Me True* (dir. Harry Keller, 1961), and *Tammy and the Doctor* (dir. Harry Keller, 1963). However, Dee's public image was a façade that concealed a troubled private life scarred by incest from the age of eight, alcoholism, anorexia, ill health, and a troubled adulthood (Dee 1991: 87–94). Even though later films would cast her as the sexual tease or nymphet, the Dee mythology of the chaste adolescent stubbornly persisted even after the actor's personal traumas were leaked to the media.[2]

Roland Barthes' definition of myth is relevant here. Barthes describes myth as the naturalization of history through the distortion (not concealment) of the meaning of a sign. It is interpreted as the reason, rather than the motive, for an existence (Barthes 1972 [1957]: 129). The "function of myth is to empty reality: it is, literally, a ceaseless flowing out, a haemorrhage, or perhaps an evaporation, in short a perceptible absence" (1972 [1957]: 143). Representations of Sandra Dee, purified of her real life circumstances, functioned to signify the ambitions and dominant values of a society that prided itself on its newfound stability after the Second World War. This resolve would only be fortified after the upheavals in the following two decades, which included the turmoil of the Vietnam War, the sexual revolution, and the shaken confidence of the American public after the Watergate debacle.

---

2   Georganne Scheiner (2001) points out that the Tammy films which propelled Sandra Dee into the public eye as an innocent were not representative of her career. In fact, the actor was portrayed more often than not as a troublesome youth with sexual innuendo inflected in her performances.

Dee's embodiment of cultural contradictions poses a dilemma that necessitates an airbushed image of a 1950s of drive-in movies and soda fountains. The story of a dysfunctional, middle-aged woman who was lonely, depressed, and psychologically damaged has no place in endorsed rememberings. As Svetlana Boym writes, "Revelation of mortality is of no use for group identity—it is precisely what has to be suspended" in order to stave off acceptance of "physical and human frailty, aging and the unpredictability of change" (2001: 78). Sandra Dee of the Now never existed. Instead, she has been replaced by the perpetual image of a beautiful, uncorrupted girl who replays in time like a record on a continuous loop. The all-American sweetheart is a cultural construction that acts as a buffer against the actuality of social malaise, and is representative of a symbolically serviceable past. Giorgio Agamben astutely observed that, "The real subject of history is the State" (1993: 99). It was never really *about* Sandra Dee. Although the actor may have entered anthologies of cinema as a figure of the times, the erecting of a metaphoric memorial of Tammy appears more as an early tombstone in retrospect. Although her career was going somewhere, Dee herself was going nowhere.

Similar to Dee, Ringwald was the vessel for an impossible vision of social order that had already begun to crack during the 1980s and would worsen throughout the 1990s. For instance, where the 'Yellow Peril' once threatened the nation-state, the paranoia of the AIDS epidemic transplanted this terror of invasion onto the individual body. The legacy of political and economic restructuring by the Reagan Administration had fostered an ethos of mass gluttony, fueling rampant consumerism in the face of societal denigration (Cannon 2000: 1189). The relentless individualism and pursuit of wealth had taken precedence over more pressing national and international issues that included,

> the Iran-Contra scandal; the staggering annual budget deficits; the government's slow response to the AIDS crisis; the crack cocaine wars that turned inner cities into shooting galleries; the debacle in Beirut, Lebanon, that left 211 U.S. Marines dead; the growing gap between rich and poor; the doubling of the nation's incarceration rate. (Cannon 2000: 1187)

The spiritual emptiness of the go-go 1980s and dictum that "greed is good," so perfectly captured in Oliver Stone's *Wall Street* (1987), extended beyond the world of executive mergers and acquisitions to deepen into the sanctuary of the family and home. This theme was explored in the timely film adaptation of Bret Easton Ellis' novel *Less Than Zero* (dir. Marek Kanievska, 1987). In direct contrast to the idealism in Hughes' films, *Less Than Zero* plunged its youth into a world of opulent Beverly Hills mansions, expensive convertible cars, fatalistic orgies of drugs, empty sex, and the dark underbelly of gold-cufflink crime. The series *21 Jump Street* (1987–1991) similarly capitalized upon the fears of the accelerated aging of the young. The episodes revolved around a team of undercover police officers who infiltrated high schools and colleges by posing as students. They exposed all manner of serious problems, such as homosexual beatings, teenage prostitution, gang-related violence, and homicide. Youth were no longer in danger, but more likely the ones to be dangerous. The menace had crossed over enemy lines and was now on domestic soil.

As the virtuous teenager in the Hughes oeuvre, Ringwald was the corporeal collateral against the widespread ethos of nihilistic consumption, corruption, and hedonism that had become associated with the 1980s. In a time when sexual intercourse ran the risk of disease, emotionless trysts, or even death, Ringwald's characters were interested in romantic love and relationships (Hentges 2006: 42–3). In the context of widening disparities between the prosperous few and economically-disadvantaged many, Ringwald's characters reconciled the gaping chasms through social mobility in which, as Jim Leach writes, "the mystical prescience of the loser-outsider and *her* victory over a corrupt and corrupting society, engages a restoration and realization of the American ideal of a classless and egalitarian society" (quoted in Lewis 1992: 139). When the collapse of the nuclear family continued to burgeon, Ringwald was the voice of reason. In *Sixteen Candles*, the chaotic environment of the home differentiates between Samantha's rationalism and her scatterbrained family members as they prepare for her older sister's wedding. In *Pretty in Pink*, Andie lives with her unemployed father Jack (Harry Dean Stanton). From the film's onset, she is established as the steady center of the family and assumes an almost maternal role. It is she who must urge her father to seek work, to accept his wife's desertion several years prior, and to meet his responsibilities as a parent. In *The Breakfast Club*, as the majority of the narrative takes place within the school premises, Claire's interaction with her family is minimal. However, from the brief discussion the character has with her father (Tim Gamble) in the film's opening sequence, he is portrayed as ignorantly detached from his daughter and an unsound authority figure. When Claire complains to him that her consignment to Saturday detention is absurd, Mr Standish retorts, "I'll make it up to you. Honey, ditching class to go shopping doesn't make you a defective. Have a good day." The apathetic response is telling. There is no interest, nor time, in listening to the experiences of youth.

The Time of Your Life: Stretching the Moment

An important aspect of the role of cinema in contemporary society is to articulate the memories that are effaced in the construction of dominant cultural narratives. This has implications not only for extending the parameters of history, but also the notion of time itself and the articulation of cultural spaces. To illustrate this, I turn to *Some Kind of Wonderful* (dir. Howard Deutch, 1987) which was written by John Hughes. The protagonist, Keith Nelson (Eric Stoltz), spends his college fund savings on a pair of diamond earrings for the most desirable girl at his school after she agrees to accompany him on a date. His father, Cliff (John Ashton), reprimands his son for this decision and attempts to reduce Keith's actions to that of an ignorant teenager.

Father: You're only eighteen years old for Christ's sake!

Keith: Then I'm nineteen, then I'm twenty. When does my life belong to me? ... See, in the eyes of most people around here, I'm a nothing ... I want to show this girl that I'm as good as anybody else ... Dad, didn't you ever have guys at your school that didn't fit in? ... Well, I'm one of those guys.

Father: I thought things were going okay for you.

Keith: Yeah, well I like art. I work in a gas station. My best friend is a tomboy. These things don't fly too well in the American high school.

Keith's work and leisure interests result in his social alienation. His greasy work overalls and fondness for painting are signifiers of his second-class citizenship. He is excluded from the dominant center of the influential school clique. The oppressive hierarchies between the powerful and marginalized are played out within the realm of the confessional date and high school. These are sites of negotiation and contestation where youth do have a degree of power in effecting change. For Keith, the sensory and emotive assumes a significance more *real* than the dream of a future manufactured by his father. It marks a radical, political agenda to live in the Now. The culmination of teen movies at the all-important keg party, prom, or clandestine rendezvous for the meeting of lovers, do not just capture a fleeting moment but a splinter of time that lasts a lifetime because of its gravity. Here, cinema functions as a form of "interpretive truth" which captures moments, mimicking the candidness of a Polaroid picture. As cultural constructions that blur the boundaries between personal recollection and public knowledge, films are able to investigate "cultural patterns of fantasy and denial" (Giles 2002: 24). Popular media and memory reclaim the discredited private and collective sources of information, practices, and expressions that are not considered wholly credible, and imbibe them with a cultural currency and means of contribution to an historical narrative.

Popular memory gives legitimacy to evanescent moments that are lost in the translation of experience to historiography where there is no adequate, nor appropriate, linguistic modality for its expression. This notion is supported by Stewart Brand's propositions in *The Clock of the Long Now* (1999). Brand argues that memory is sensory as it moves faster than our current thoughts can process. As a result, the industrial time imposed on the working body lacks a perfect synchronization with the personalized sense of time that memory imposes on our recollection of events. The Long Now testifies to the mutability of time, its multidimensionality, and the role of corporeality in the interpretation of past events. Brand's theorizations imply that the relevance of a narrative becomes less contingent upon its correspondence to the actualities of an objective world than upon "its ability to describe a possible world that one lives and experiences" (Roberts 1997: 135). This *sensory history* permits recollections of the past that need not be merely surgically retrieved from a repository, but are manifested in the physical sensation during the act of recall. The seductive myth of history as logically-derived outcomes of past events can no longer displace experience "as far as possible outside the individual: on to instruments and numbers" (Agamben 1993: 17). When it is relocated onto the individual, the authority granted by scientific certainty and verification becomes suspect and accepted truths begin to fray at the edges. When the illusion of a centrifugal stability and hegemonic mask becomes transparent, relations of power are at their most volatile and vulnerable.

Popular memory and the cinematic apparatus clearly have significant application for recording and recalling the experiences of youth that have often been deemed unworthy of serious discussion. The exceptions to the rule occur under highly specific conditions, such as the tragic dramas and moral panics that saw the Columbine and Virginia Tech shootings occupy headline news, and cultural revolutions that include the rave phenomenon and third-wave feminism. This raises the question of whose history is really being told and by whom; a sentiment expressed by Jon Savage who wrote, "there's a whole history being constructed here, but I'm not sure that it's mine" (1997: 2). The direct transcription of artifact to fact and vice versa cannot always account for the more personalized interpretations of an event. A more flexible paradigm is one that integrates representational politics into (re)constructions of the past. Michael Schaffer wryly remarks that,

> thanks to Hughes and his colleagues, I knew exactly what to expect when I moved home [to the United States] at age 14. High school would be big and crucial; my standing in its hierarchy of jocks and brains and losers would determine my happiness. Like any true, red-blooded American kid, I knew I would care desperately about the football game, the dance afterwards, and the big, drunken party to follow. Hey—I'd watched the instructional video. (Schaffer 2001: 28)

Whilst Schaffer later admits that his high school experiences resembled little of the "instructional" Hughes movies, the statement emphasizes the currency of the films and the pedagogy of popular culture. The shared space of the high school is often where fantasy and reality collide in such a way that they become indistinguishable. The films work as a type of animated high school year book. In a way, they are anthologies of collective memories. The excessiveness of intense moments in teendom—the ecstasy of the first kiss, the anxiety of graduation, fears of gym class bullying—are granted a mode for representation and interpretation through cinematographic techniques; for instance, the intimacy of a close-up shot, the accompaniment of image with musical score, and montage sequences. These moments are invested with a profundity and importance that cannot be adequately relayed by conventional historical documentation. Youth ceases to be a phase to be simply thumbed at. The problems and politics of youth are acknowledged as very real.

In Hughes' films, a micro-politics is practiced in which the high school functions as a microcosm of society. The central agency is transferred from adults to adolescents. This traversal and dissolution of boundaries enables an ideal mobility and "reconciliation of diverse bodies" (Speed 1998: 104). Here, the nerds can be hailed the heroes (*Weird Science*), the stifling bureaucracy as embodied by the pompous, vindictive school dean can be subverted in the name of freedom (*Ferris Bueller's Day Off*), and the artistic recluse can befriend the most popular girl at school (*Some Kind of Wonderful*).[3] Like the glorious pandemonium of the carnival, the boundaries between authority and the oppressed are transgressed. The malleability of the high school structure is a precursor of social change. In a memorable scene from *Pretty in Pink*, Andie confronts Blane to discuss the senior prom. When she demands an answer as to whether he will escort her or not, he feebly mumbles that he had forgotten a previous engagement. It is obvious that this is an outright lie.

> *Andie*: You're a liar. You're a filthy, fucking no-good liar! You don't have the guts to tell me the truth … You're ashamed to be seen with me … You're ashamed to go out with me. You're afraid. You're terrified your god damn rich friends won't approve!

Beating Blane against the locker, Andie is the vision of the frustration of the disempowered. In her rage, she acts as a siphon of social truths. Prom politics becomes a point of reference for global politics.[4] Meaghan Morris rightly states that culture has "supplanted politics and religion as the dominant heading under which the social and moral issues of the day are played out" (quoted in Davis 1997: 30). In a decade of excessive consumption and capitalism, *Pretty in Pink* is an emotive purging and commentary of the times. Music and fashion are not just consumer products, but metaphysical skins grafted onto the body. It is significant that Andie dresses in clothing that layers the vintage over the modern. After having been stood up by her partner, she resolves to attend the prom solo as an act of self-empowerment to show that she has not been defeated. Her presence alone, however, is not enough. Andie's actual prom dress must speak words for her. She "takes Iona's prom dress and the lurid pink gift from her father and, with her artistic bent, converts them into something that is less a garment than a statement: a cool, pink, fuck you, a sexy suit of armor" (Bernstein 1997: 77). The character's wearing of fragmented pop couture from various eras is derived less from financial necessity than self-determinism and agency. In this decade of meta-cultures, the past and present congeal into an eclectic bazaar of styles, where in(ter)vention of commodity culture allows infinite possibilities for transformation and subversion.

---

3 Although Howard Deutch directed *Pretty in Pink* and *Some Kind of Wonderful* (which John Hughes wrote), Hughes is still credited as the auteur of these films.

4 Amy Best's *Prom Night* (2000) provides a cultural critique of the struggles, resistance, and relations of power that exist in the organization and experience of the prom.

The prom gown is a hybrid creation of outdated, second-hand garments (one of which is clearly from the 1960s) that refuses to be comfortably categorized as definitively of the 1980s, or classically stunning. When Andie enters the grand ballroom in her homemade ensemble, the moment crystallizes the oppressive class structure. More importantly, there is overwhelming pathos in the scene. It acts like a snapshot in time that has not only been captured, but also vicariously (and cathartically) experienced by the audience.

The Ringwald phase of the 1980s carries such emotional gravity for the youth of then and now that the actor has transcended her own existence to become a rare phenomenon—an image that encapsulates a moment so deeply that it has literally shaped pop culture history, and is crucial to how it is remembered by the youth of that era. Nostalgic strolls down the 1980s memory lane are traced through the trajectory of a Ringwald–Hughes plot like a geographical map. Molly Ringwald *meant* something more than just a teenage takeover of the multiplex. Popular culture, popular memories, and fandom have grounded the actor's identity (fictional and real) in time, and her place within it. She is no longer just an abstraction of the 1980s. Molly Ringwald *was* the 1980s.

While popular remembrances of the actor ensure that she will not be forgotten or lose her iconic status, there is always the potential danger of inadvertently historicizing memory. Where Molly Ringwald is *now* illuminates the trade-off for being heralded the model teen of an era. Ringwald's fountain of youth, "laced with citric acid," is a stalemate that condemns her to relive her teenage years over and over again (Corliss 1986a: 83). In an interview, John Hughes commented in relation to the character of Ferris Bueller, "You don't want to see him today. You'd hate him. He'd either be a bum or a politician" (quoted in Daley 1999). Ringwald, as with Matthew Broderick as Ferris, represents that transitory, but seminal, moment of optimism that the future holds unbounded potential, before the disappointment of adulthood descends. The ephemerality of Ringwald's high school days are intentionally stretched, pulling her past over the present. In short, Ringwald had not only been typecast. She had been *time*cast.

Homecoming Queen: Back to School

Molly Ringwald's projects in recent years underscore her cauterization in the 1980s in which she wears the decade like the scars from a third-degree burn. In *Teaching Mrs Tingle* (dir. Kevin Williamson, 1999), the actor portrayed a timid administrative staff member at Grandsboro High School who converts into a farcically foul-mouthed substitute teacher—appropriately for History class. In the Australian production *Cut* (dir. Kimble Rendall, 2000), she was cast as a B-grade Los Angeleno soap actor. Fourteen years prior, Vanessa Turnbull starred as a teenage victim of a slasher film. Production was halted when a murder was committed during the film's shooting. The actor returns to fill in as the dead girl's mother, only to discover that the past has literally come back to haunt her as the killer is a paranormal phantom that materializes into corporeal form each time the original reel is revisited. Despite the film's black humor and Ringwald's acerbic impression of the diva which poked fun at her own infamous, fiery temper, *Cut* failed commercially. It seemed the audiences were still not ready to see the actor grown up.

In arguably her most memorable part in recent years, Ringwald was required to return to high school. *Not Another Teen Movie* (dir. Joel Gallen, 2001) parodies the popular American teen films of the 1980s and 1990s, with particular reverence paid to the Hughes opus. Ringwald's cameo appearance as a flight attendant reflects upon her integral function within this discursive framework. At the film's climax, Jake (Chris Evans) attempts to convince Janey (Chyler Leigh)—who is partially modeled on Ringwald's character of Andie Walsh—not to leave him for France. Incidentally, Ringwald had defected to France in 1992 after her popularity in American cinema bottomed out. Struggling to express his feelings, Jake plagiarizes identifiable lines from other teen movies, including *Pretty in Pink*, only to be reprimanded by Ringwald for his lack of originality and hyperbolic sentimentality. When the two lovers resolve their differences, ready for the kiss that will cue the rising swell of inspiring music and the credits, Ringwald's character cynically rebukes them. Directing her comments to the camera, she complains, "We all know where this is going. Fucking teenagers."

For that brief moment in time, Ringwald stepped out of the 1980s. The "adult Molly" brought her present into the past, enabling her to resist timecasting as the perennial adolescent. In that transient window of opportunity, Ringwald's importance to youth culture, popular memory, and middle-America in the 1980s convene in a perfect synchronicity and clarity. The irony of knowing "where this is going" was that she was never allowed to go beyond "there." It is relevant that Ringwald's much hyped role was to take place within borrowed plot lines from her Hughes projects, where the school is called John Hughes High, and the cover track over the closing titles is "Don't You (Forget About Me)" by Simple Minds, as quoted in the epigraph. The song was, of course, the anthem for *The Breakfast Club*.

Sandra Dee, the personality, only existed in and for the 1950s and 1960s. The person behind the mediated public image was superseded by the greater narrative of a myth. Her final performance would cast the last(ing) impression in popular culture of a still-life portrait and homage to the dead. Molly Ringwald, however, has not experienced this finale. She continues to have a presence in the entertainment industry. She has moved from the 1980s, through the 1990s, and into the 21st century. While her impressive performances in post-Hughes productions have garnered critical attention and acclaim, for instance, her role as Frannie Goldsmith in the television miniseries *The Stand* (dir. Mick Garris, 1994) and as Sally Bowles in the Broadway production *Cabaret* in 2001 and 2002, the past maintains an uneasy stranglehold over her. Reviews and articles tend to hark back to Ringwald's Hughes heydays in much the same way we cannot resist forlornly reminiscing about the once-brilliant child prodigy who has stepped into mediocrity in adulthood. It signifies a loss that is both theirs *and* ours. In a particularly scathing commentary on her fashion sense in a *People Weekly* issue, critics wrote, "'I think she's having an identity crisis because she's outgrown all her clothes' says Ilene Beckerman. Adds costumer Penny Rose: 'She's confused. She'll have to go back to the '80s'" (People Weekly 1999: 92). A decade later, and the 1980s throwback still remains. During an interview promoting *The Secret Life of the American Teenager* on talkshow *The View* (episode: February 6, 2009), the female hosts could not help but gush about Ringwald's films from the 1980s. After being shown clips from *Sixteen Candles* and *The Breakfast Club*, Ringwald responded that it was akin to looking at baby pictures—they were fond memories, but tempered with cringe.[5] Ringwald resists inertia, always chasing the dream of social mobility. We loathe to release Ringwald into the world beyond graduation because the dream of *that* 1980s is not yet ready to be over. A critical examination of nostalgic and populist memories of this actor reveals our complicity in her timecasting, and forces a reflective gaze upon the self. Whom we yearn for provides an intimation as to *what* we long for. While Samantha Baker, Claire Standish, and Andie Walsh are tactically remembered as the darlings of a decade, Molly Ringwald herself may yet hitch that elusive ride back to the future.

Note

An earlier version of this chapter was first published in *Cultural Studies Review* (March 2007), vol. 13(1), 89–104.

---

5   In *The Secret Life of the American Teenager* (2008–), Ringwald plays the mother of a pregnant teenager. Ringwald herself was four months pregnant with twins at the time of the interview on *The View*.

Chapter 4
Girl Power: The Politics of Pop

Silence is golden but shouting is fun
Freedom fighters
Future is female
Spice Revolution.
>   (The Spice Girls [liner notes from the *Spice* album, 1996])

Pushed up against the barriers, hundreds lined the boulevard. Thousands more behind them brought the gathering to a teeming swell. With traffic stopped and security tight, the atmosphere crackled with tension and nervous anticipation. Already amassing from the early hours of the day, youth had taken to the streets once again to rally for their cause. Then, from the outskirts, came a tremor of activity. Like a tsunami it stirred and undulated, multiplying tenfold by the time it reached the barricades. Voices roared as bodies surged towards the main thoroughfare, going for the jugular. The air was a sonic boom of hysteria.

Six o'clock: a double-decker bus painted with a gigantic Union Jack ambled around the boulevard corner, and with it traveled the adoration of thousands of fans. The world's media was witnessing the power of popular music, celebrity fame, and fandom. One of the century's most recognizable musical ensembles, a ragtag group of youths hailing from Britain, had crossed the Atlantic to the Americas bringing their brand of revolution. No mere promotional tour, this was history being made. But this cultural moment did not take place in 1964, nor was it four mop-topped lads from Liverpool inciting the commotion. The year was 1998, and from the roof of the double-decker it was five fabulous lasses instigating the scene of mayhem. In their matching white pant suits, they glowed under the spotlights and frantic flashing of cameras. Perched high above the hordes, they were the vision of deified divas.

That day in 1998, I had been in the vicinity of Hollywood Boulevard when the Spice Girls launched the world premiere of *Spice World: The Spice Girls Movie* (dir. Bob Spiers, 1997) at Grauman's Chinese Theater. While familiar with their first album *Spice* (1996), I was certainly no devotee. After making the admission that I did not even know their real names, I was given a hasty education by the enthusiastically obliging, prepubescent girls and a twentysomething male who surrounded me. I was, as with many others, of the ilk that regarded the music of the Spice Girls as a highly successful strain of bubblegum pop, and was skeptical of their Girl Power mantra. After all, they were carefully constructed personalities—caricatures with a fondness for outrageous outfits and dangerously high platforms—pandering to a teen and preteen demographic, and whose popularity was driven by capitalist ventures and well publicized gimmicks with a girly spin. Arguably their most infamous incident was during their presentation to Prince Charles at the 21st anniversary Royal Gala in Manchester on May 9, 1997, during which the group broke protocol to hug and kiss the Prince of Wales. While Charles was left smiling sheepishly at the cameras with lipstick marks on his cheek, the Spice Girls grinned and winked their way into the headlines with their trademark victory hand signs (Rolling Stone 1997: 76). Aside from a few catchy jingles and naughty media moments, their claim to fame seemed to be their faces being plastered on everything from potato chip packets and pencil cases to Pepsi cans. Right?

How very wrong I was. In the company of frontline aficionados, the verve of the crowd—a fury of noise and movement—was testament that this was no mere fluffy kids' entertainment, and beyond the glitter and glamor something more was going on. Hemmed in by preteens dressed as mini Spice Girls, young boys, and men shouting with approval, the sense of camaraderie was undeniable and infectious. With hindsight, I was witnessing a microcosm of a cultural phenomenon much greater than I could have fathomed at the time.

As is typical of most pop music groups, the once formidable presence of the Spice Girls has disappeared. Yet the very mention of the quintet still provokes impassioned debate as to whether they represented a dynamic feminism or a musical farce. Riding their descent from superstardom into musical mediocrity, scathing criticisms of their solo careers by connoisseurs of "serious music" replay ad nauseam. Discussions inevitably end up returning to the Spice Girls as old news, dredged up as a topic of lowbrow 1990s pop pap. As for yesterday's Spice supporters, even though they have packed their platforms away, there is a residue of the Spice experience that lingers. It was evident in the anticipation of the much hyped Spice Girls reunion and world tour in 2007 that saw closet fans coming out in droves for a nostalgic trip down memory lane. While history holds a special place for the men of rock—we need only look at The Beatles, the Rolling Stones, and AC/DC—it does not easily grant the same honor to the antics of five feisty women (this extends to female pop groups in general) and their fans. Where were you when you first heard "Wannabe" or when the Spice Girls landed in America? The most likely response is: who cares? For many, however, singing and dancing to the *Spice* album with a hairbrush for a microphone, pledging Girl Power with friends in school yards, and standing with thousands of others at a Spice Girls concert (or premiere) were defining moments in *their* history. The relationship between cinematic and musical mediums provides a powerful trigger for their recall, sparking what Will Straw describes as an "'extrasomatic memory' (memory stored outside the body)" which transforms fleeting moments into personal and collective history (2001: 58). This is particularly important in a culture where the proliferation of images and sounds in the media has rendered popular culture texts redundant at an ever-accelerating speed. This chapter employs the explosive phenomenon of the iconic Spice Girls as a case study of a postmodern feminist politics, reinforcing the tight connection between cinema and music through the construction of the (intertextual) star persona.

Fighting Feminism(s): Breaking the Waves

> Maybe the third wave will lead the way to a calmer and more reconciled future.
> I just wish they'd get started. (Summers 1995: 30)

In 1995, Anne Summers' contentious article "Shockwaves at the revolution" made the damning accusation that a younger generation of women had failed to carry on the women's movement, thus setting in motion a vicious slanging match among feminists. That same year, Helen Garner's *The First Stone: Some Questions about Sex and Power* painted a dismal picture of young feminists as "punitive girls" who had turned their backs on issues of radical and liberal feminism (1995: 100). Such sentiments echoed a concern that the victories and social liberties won for, and by, women were being squandered by the daughters of feminism (D'Arcens 1998: 106). This inheritance allowed them to experience the fruits of their predecessors' labor, but in their apathy and ignorance, they had purportedly forgotten the painstaking hardships of those efforts. Anita Harris argues that criticisms of a naïve, self-centered Generation X were being filtered through criticisms of young women who were seen as abandoning social causes and disregarding historical memory, social critique, and collectivist politics (2004: 135). This feminist backlash turned the spotlight on an issue that had been fermenting for some time, exposing a generational friction that would find its way into discussions of women in popular culture (especially in the 1990s). What follows is a discussion of dominant narratives of feminism to illuminate the problems of its current conceptualizations and to probe the terrain of women in popular culture. By unraveling the ideologies that surround young, female artists, the politics of labeling them comes to the fore.

The progression of feminism in contemporary western society has been traced through three distinct phases. The first wave dates back to the mid-19th century and was mapped up until the early 20th century. In the United States, it was characterized by the struggle for basic legal and liberal rights, including women's right to vote, to own property, and to sit in the Senate (O'Neill 2002: 20). With their demonstrations and protest marches, first-wave feminists made considerable headway against the blatant socio-sexual inequalities, creating a hairline crack in the monolithic wall before them. The 1960s saw the emergence of second-wave feminism that was augmented by the new left and the Civil Rights movement in America (Peraino 2001: 693). The maxim that "the personal is political" challenged conservative values and beliefs of women's roles in the private sphere while opening opportunities for them in the public sphere. Milestones included reproductive rights to legalize birth control and abortion services, a conscious effort to eradicate workplace discrimination (which introduced a discourse of sexual harassment into the judicial vernacular), the introduction of anti-rape laws, the equal division of property upon divorce, and the vocalization of equal pay for equal work (O'Neill 2002: 20). A third wave identified feminists who came into consciousness in the 1980s and 1990s. They were characterized by their

Do-It-Yourself (DIY) ethic. With its reappropriation of popular cultural texts, Judith Peraino described third-wave feminism as an approach to gender that was postmodern and paradigmatic (2001: 693). At its most favorable, it was regarded as fervently creative. At its most damaging, it was seen as an adverse reaction to the second wave. Vitriolic dialog between the two groups continued to have a polarizing effect. It encouraged the misconception of "feminism as an empire that is either falling prey to an adolescent *coup d'état* or covetously ruled over by rapacious matriarchs" (D'Arcens 1998: 115–16).

Although useful, these dominant narratives paint two centuries of women's social history in broad brushstrokes that overlook major contradictions and complexities. For example, while the second wave was championed for its rejection of abstract individualism in order to build a cohesive feminism to protect all women, this claim was inherently flawed from its inception (Nelson 1995: 23–40). It would not only reformulate, but furthermore perpetuate, existing oppressive power structures. The loudest of feminist voices emphasized the race and class privileges of a largely bourgeois, Anglo-Saxon populace (hooks 1984: 6). As Anna Julia Cooper observed, "when and where I enter, in the quiet, undisputed dignity of my womanhood, without violence and without suing or special patronage, then and there the whole *Negro race enters with me*" (1988 [1892]: 31). Although penned over a century ago in response to African-American liberation, the declaration still holds validity in current discussions of crises of identity in feminist politics. Cooper's statement elucidates the problematic position of being a gendered, black body. Just as her femaleness cannot be rendered invisible, her blackness cannot be overlooked. This underscores the difficulties of establishing a feminist subjectivity for marginalized communities. Even Cooper's own assertions inadvertently reiterate this predicament. The position of education and privilege from which she spoke could not reconcile the distance between herself and the disadvantaged colored women in shanty towns whom she claimed to speak for, but never directly to (Washington 1988 [1892]: xlix). What is evident from Cooper's *A Voice from the South* is that voices of disenfranchised groups are drowned out by the dominant.

It was not surprising that the image of second-wave feminism as an exclusionary club would compel third wavers to hastily distance themselves. However, failure to acknowledge the continuities between feminisms results in self-defeating, empty dialog. In their analysis of the book *Listen Up: Voices from the Next Feminist Generation*, Allison Howry and Julia Wood studied the major concerns expressed by third-wave feminists in relation to the second wave and found considerable overlap and congruity, rather than outright opposition (2001: 332). The many values shared by both arms of the movement included resistance to societal devaluation, acknowledgment, maintenance of connections among women, the urgency to claim and use their feminist voices, and the general continuation of struggle over gender inequalities (Howry and Wood 2001: 332–3). The coining of catchphrases such as "victim feminism" and "power feminism" made famous by Naomi Wolf have further oversimplified the complicated nature of the movement, weakening the position from which women are able to speak. Where they were once seen to be fighting against the patriarchal institution, women were now seen to have turned against each other. Feminism now conjures the impression of a political catfight. This only adds fuel to a fire that continues to burn potential bridges.

Sisters are Doing It for Themselves: DIY Feminism

> Riot grrrls, guerrilla girls, net chicks, cyber chix, geekgirls, tank girls, supergirls, action girls, deep girls—this is the era of DIY feminism. (Bail 1996: 3)

The 1990s witnessed an explosion of self-professed, young feminists in the media, from magazines to music, comics to cartoons, and television to the silver screen. The cultural landscape would be marked in particular by the caustic music of the Riot Grrrls, the stoic female hardbody in action films, and the cheeky flavor of the Spice Girls. Although competent and influential women were no strangers to popular culture—Charlie's Angels, Honey West, Emma Peel, and Wonder Woman from the 1960s to the 1980s are quickly invoked in popular memory—the images of powerful females in the 1990s were significant in terms of sheer volume and visibility, the type of feminism they proclaimed, the modes of activism, and their origins.[1]

Taking the male-dominated, underground subculture of punk as its grassroots, the Riot Grrrl Movement defined a new feminism distinguished by a postmodern sensibility. Building on the headway made by their 1970s female predecessors, such as Debbie Harry, Patti Smith, and the Slits, the DIY ethos of punk offered the opportunity to rewrite women's roles. As Rebecca Daugherty points out, the "rock epiphany of punk ethics and aesthetics opened the door for women to trade in their eyeliners and hairspray for electric guitars and the authorial pen" (2002: 29). If the punk masculine objected to populist culture and boredom, the punk feminine upped the ante to include a reordering of gendered space (Daugherty 2002: 31). One particularly notable incident illustrating this was Ludus' final performance at the Hacienda in Manchester on November 5, 1982. The lead singer, Linda (Linder) Sterling, wore "a dress of discarded chicken meat sewn onto layers of black net" (Nice 2002). The all-female group strung tampons from the balconies and

---

1   Julie D'acci provides an illuminating account of one of the lesser known heroines in 1960s television, that of private eye, super sleuth Honey West. In post-Second World War America, the so-called crisis of masculinity that arose from women's accomplishments in the wartime labor market, the aftershock of the Cold War, the success of the Soviet-launched Sputnik (mobilized as evidence of America's own technological impotence), the prominence of African-American men during the Civil Rights movement, and the changing roles of middle-class white men, enabled characters such as West to enter popular discourse. Touted as a "sportscar driving, martial-arts wielding, pet-ocelot toting 'female dick,'" West broke down conventions that relegated women to the roles of the sensible, good woman or the voracious harlot (D'acci 1997: 74–5).

distributed giblets wrapped in pornography to audience members. At the climax of the act, Sterling ripped off her skirt to display a black dildo strapped to her groin, turning the phallic symbol into a ludicrous appendage (O'Brien 1999: 196–7). The negative reactions to this confronting vision of womanhood betrayed cultural expectations that women are objects for viewing pleasure. This was summed up by Sterling's recollections of the night 15 years later,

> I remember the audience going back about three foot. There was hardly any applause at the end. And that was a crowd who thought, nothing can shock us, we see porn all the time, we're cool. When that happened, when they stepped back, I thought, that's it, where do we go from here? (Quoted in O'Brien 1999: 197)

The aggressiveness of women in the 1970s punk music scene would gather momentum with the arrival of the Riot Grrrl Movement in the 1980s and 1990s. With its principal beginnings on the north-west coast of the United States in cities such as Seattle, Olympia, and Portland, the movement grew from a localized, national subcultural scene into an international countercultural phenomenon. Often aligned with third-wave feminism, the Riot Grrrl Movement enabled young women to engage with, redefine, and remake cultural texts.

One of the most famous Riot Grrrl punk groups was Bikini Kill, an all-female band hailing from Olympia, Washington that advocated a feminism with a distinctly punk politics agenda. Their music overtly addressed issues surrounding violence directed towards women, with taboo topics such as rape, incest, and domestic abuse taking centerstage (Temple 1999: 17–28). The shock factor of their performances was an abrasive representation of women and young girls. It was not unusual for the band's singer, Kathleen Hanna, to appear onstage topless with the word "slut" scrawled on her midriff (Hirshey 2001: 160). If the image of the classic female beauty had been constructed in the media as a commodity to be gazed at through a one-way mirror, the Riot Grrrl offended with its anti-glamor, kinderwhore aesthetics, and smashed the mirror to return and challenge the gaze. The general ethos was, "Get angry, get even, have fun—or all of the above—is the rowdy M.O. of the smart slut set. Cuisinart your femininity: Dress like a baby doll and cuss like a stevedore" (Hirshey 2001: 160).

"Grrrl" reclaimed the word "girl," stripping away its childish naivety and reinscribing it with a suggestive growl. Derogatory gendered terms, such as "bitch," "slut," and "cunt," were written on the skin as a form of crude body-art that transformed the female figure into the ultimate text. Irony and contradiction became the tools of the Riot Grrrl trade, as was seen in the quasi-uniform of second-hand baby doll dress, clunky Doc Marten boots, body piercings and tattoos, and smeared lipstick. By appropriating the "accoutrements of girlhood, femininity, and alternative youth culture for an ironic (dis)play and disruption of the signifying codes of gender and generation," the Riot Grrrl refused to be invisible, ignored, and relegated to the anonymity of the screaming fan or the disembodied chanteuse (Kearney 1998: 158).

Despite becoming an international cultural movement, the Riot Grrrl Movement remained in the underbelly of popular culture and operated outside most mainstream channels. This intentionally refused the external agents of major recording studios and publishing houses the right to sanitize and package the proudly aggressive femininity. Borrowing from Lynda Nead, this denied the regulation of the body by removing the boundary separating the traditional female beauty (in Nead's case it was the poised, classical nude) from an unruly, pornographic nakedness (1992: 12–16). The body of the Riot Grrrl was like an open wound, a grotesque titillation that spilled out fluids and exposed its devouring orifices like the vagina dentata. As with the punks who spat at their audiences, the Riot Grrrl body broke down the hierarchical structure of the subject–object relation by blurring the boundary between the watcher and the watched. This went beyond returning the gaze to literally pulling the audience out of its comfortable facelessness in the mosh pit. For instance, during Hole's 1999 Australian tour, Courtney Love gave away a guitar to a female audience member at the climax of each concert as an invitation to DIY.[2] Music-making became a metonym for a wider cause—make noise, be seen, and be heard. At one concert, her instruction to the recipient captured the philosophy of her forceful feminism, "play it loud and DON'T give it to your boyfriend" (Hopkins 1999: 11). Devoid of a slavish adherence to a presumably masculine, white-collar management, Riot Grrrls played the music they wanted in the way they wanted.

The Riot Grrrl Movement was not limited to the domain of the concert or garage gig. Music was just one facet of a wider movement characterized by its technologics. Ednie Kaeh Garrison describes technologics as the blurring of boundaries between human and machines in which technology is not merely an extension of the human experience but an integral component of it (2000: 144). Garrison argues that contemporary feminists have a symbiotic interfaced-connection with technology that, albeit not freely available, is becoming increasingly accessible (2000: 144). With the trend towards the digitalization of communication in leisure and industry, this has opened a floodgate of alternative modes in which women can travel along the information superhighway and contribute to the production and circulation of texts. These texts include videos, magazines, and compact disk booklets, all of which embrace a "low-tech, amateur, hybrid, alternative" style (Garrison 2000: 150–1). With its rejection of the refined appearance of professional publications, the most basic of technologies—a computer, modem, and photocopier—became the weapons of choice, as could be seen in the burgeoning internet and fanzine culture.

As with any subcultural movement, the Riot Grrrl Movement became a target for mainstream appropriation. Try as they might to keep it underground, the

---

2   Although Hole is not an all-female band, the prominence of Courtney Love as the definitive Riot Grrrl resulted in the group being identified according to her politics.

antics of angry women would bubble to the surface in a very public manner. It would be inevitable that much brouhaha would be made of Courtney Love's numerous public outbursts, such as assaulting airline staff and paparazzi—the vitriolic harpy for the 1990s and 2000s had a poster girl. As Catharine Lumby xaptly observes, within a postmodern context the meanings of images reside in their rapid circulation, rather than within the text itself (1997: xxv). While many female bands failed to reach the popularity of groups such as Hole, Bikini Kill, 7 Year Bitch, and Huggy Bear, and Riot Grrrl websites and fanzines have come and gone, longevity would not be the benchmark that their importance would be measured against. The political praxis instigated by the Movement constructed a lived, intense experience that transcended its transience. In the same way that "Punk was about being looked at, creating a temporary celebrity," the Riot Grrrl Movement unsettled the surface of popular culture and left behind a permanent scar of an angry female agency (O'Brien 1999: 191). It rebutted any claims that the accomplishments of the first two waves of feminism had paved the way for a post-feminist society. Judith Peraino argues that the very idea of "post-feminism" is a hegemonic device that camouflages a U-turn back to tidy gender roles (2001: 692). It is a precipitate claim that major gender inequalities no longer exists, and problems are dismissed as minor creases in the social fabric that are easily ironed out. Attempts by Riot Grrrls to separate their culture from male-dominated commercial ventures, and women's continued struggle in the masculine terrain of post-punk music indicated that the battles of the first and second wave feminists had been fought, but the war had not yet been won.[3]

Space Invaders: The Politics of Pop

> Picket signs alone are not enough, as they will be cast with residual modes
> and rendered ineffectual and impotent—quaint signposts from another era
> demanding a different kind of intervention. (Zimmerman 1993: 52)

If the Riot Grrrl was the iconoclasm for a femininity that was vehemently anti-establishment, political, aggressive, and subversive, the Spice Girls appeared the

---

3   Gender-based discrimination has been an enduring quality in punk and alternative rock music since the 1970s. Despite their free-for-all maxim, which permitted anyone the opportunity to pick up an instrument and form a garage band, this did not translate into a gender-blind solidarity. The fact that female bands are still a minority and remain the target of derogatory slurs that debase them as unskilled musicians and psychotic "bitches" still serves as a reminder that a wide gap persists. Rebecca Daugherty points out that in punk mythology, "girls were portrayed as a hazard to the integrity of the all-male band," and cites Nancy Spungen as the female wedge responsible for the demise of the quintessential male punk rock band The Sex Pistols (2002: 33–4). Such bias is also reinforced by the relative absence of accounts of female bands in music journalism.

polar opposite. Championing mass appeal, the pop sensations opted for a polished and pretty exterior that reinscribed an aesthetically pleasing femininity back onto the body. Dominating the international music charts in 1997, the face of Spice materialized into a frenzied circulation of their image that was imprinted on everything from coffee mugs, fanzines, lunch boxes, accessories, and shampoo, to their own customized Barbie-like dolls. It illustrated Andrew Goodwin's point that, "The commodity form of pop has always needed other discourses of visual pleasure that are unavailable on disc" (1992: 9).

The most vehement criticisms against the Spice Girls arose from their clean image compared with the jagged edges of the Riot Grrrl. Ellen Riordan goes so far as to say that the popularization of Girl Power overshadows "genuine Riot Grrrl values," creating a monstrous Frankenstein of "commodified fashion statements" (2001: 294). Susan Hopkins concurs,

> In today's late capitalist marketplace, popular music stories and styles are more powerful and profitable than ever. Girls and young women are playing an increasingly important role in these image-based economics. But 'Girl Power' has more to do with the construction of identity commodities than with commitment to any substantive feminist politics ... Behind the staged 'statement' is only the perfect vacancy of the pop music 'star.' (Hopkins 2002: 73–4)

Girl Power supposedly gave the illusion of empowerment through consumption, suggesting that feminism could be bought, mixed, matched, and tailored to taste. It epitomized Karl Marx's (1887) notion of commodity fetishism, in which supporters/consumers are oblivious to their slavish adherence to the capitalist machine. According to critics, the Spice Girl flavor of feminism was superficial and served only to satisfy the capitalist pocket by feeding off the desperation of young girls filling voids of juvenile insecurity.

Although feminism is in danger of losing its political edge when reduced to the mere production and purchase of commodities, dismissing the Spice Girls simply because of their status as commodified agents is equally troubling as it ignores the complex cultural function of celebrity, discredits the fan base, and rejects popular culture as a potential site of struggle. In fact, the Girl Power and Riot Grrrl Movement share more in common than they do differences. Take, for example, the division between commercial and noncommercial ventures. Kylie Murphy argues that, in fact, an artistic space that is purely precapitalist is a social and economic myth (2001: 141). To demonstrate this, Murphy refers to punk as an alternative mode for the construction, selling, and distribution of an image. In spite of its proud anti-establishment and anti-corporatism declarations, punk was a commodified lifestyle. At the same time as eschewing authority, participants would also closely follow trends in fashion by wearing the accepted punk couture. In other words, slapping punk with a label of authenticity works as a marketing device to sell the idea of "originality" and "truth." Applying this to Riot Grrrl, the Movement would not have been as widespread had it not been dispersed through the mediums of music albums, internet technology, magazines, and videography. It was already part of a commodity culture.

A credibility based on a presumed authenticity and exclusivity (based on its underground status) is itself a double-edged sword. The minute something is appropriated by the commercial market, success becomes automatic failure. Slandering a celebrity a "sell-out" has an undermining effect as it detaches a text from its politics. When Courtney Love traded in her tattered dresses and smeared makeup for a Versace gown and personal stylist—transmuting from "an exhausted heroin-using outcast into a beautiful, respected film star and model"—it signified more than an image overhaul (Hopkins 1999: 13). The artist was accused of shamelessly selling her soul for a saunter down the commercial red carpet and swapping politics for prettiness. At around the same time, Hole had reshaped its earlier brute edge for a more harmonized sound that seemed to fit the image of a new, and less confrontational, Love. Although Love had gained credibility as a starlet and model (roles emphasizing physical beauty), there was a consensus that she had done so by forfeiting what made her the fearsome virago. What is forgotten is that Hole and Love were, from the very beginning, already capitalist formations. Criticizing the artist for having lost her street credibility are really attempts to confine her in a manageable space. It was clear Love had become too big for her Doc Marten boots.

By trespassing onto the center(stage), Love posed a threat. It was no surprise that she attracted harsh censure that nullified, or at least diluted, her dangerous feminist politics. Labeling her as a cheap mouthpiece of the popular culture machine, however, is too simplistic. Draped in her designer wardrobe, beautified, and mainstreamed, there still lurked an angry woman who declared, "You want a piece of me? / Well I'm not selling cheap" (Hole 1998). With a shrewd smirk, Love flaunted the masquerade that had delivered her fame. In his review of Hole's third album, *Celebrity Skin*, Brian Dillard astutely notes, "the melody and accessibility are actually subliminal secret weapons—pretty masks that, like the Dorian Gray faces of the Hollywood elite, hide something altogether more sinister" (1998). Exploiting the system that sought to manipulate her, the artist deftly navigated within the terrain of the dominant, wearing the artificial celebrity skin over her scarred Riot Grrrl body.

The co-imbrication of politics and style is even more obvious when discussing the Spice Girls. While blatant consumption was encouraged, buying a Girl Power look, attitude, and lifestyle was less sales pitch than strategy. Girl Power illustrated Ednie Kaeh Garrison's argument that within an historical period defined by late capitalism, intertwining style and politics is a necessary tactic against hegemonic enterprises (2000: 143). In spite of their entourage of stylists, personal trainers, public relations managers, and accountants, and beneath the glossy veneer and glamor, the Spice Girl manifesto was no benign vision. The opening line in their debut single "Wannabe"—"Yo I'll tell you what I want, what I really really want"—was a militant pledge of musical and social world domination (Spice Girls 1996). Their philosophy of Girl Power as a "new age feminism" advocated the rights of all females to vocalize their valued opinions (Aplin 1997: 29). Geri Halliwell, otherwise known as Ginger Spice, candidly admitted, "Ok, so a lot of people think it's just cheese ... but if we can give anyone a bit of motivation, make any girl just sit up and go: 'I'm strong,' then that beats any No. 1 or meeting any star" (quoted in Syson 1997). While the sloganeering proved to be an overly idealistic promise that women could, and would, attain success in life, its ability to incite confidence and passionate campaigning was a cultural milestone.

The Spice Girls yanked young girls out of their bedroom-based fan culture and constructed an unusual synergy between the celebrity and supporter that is often an undervalued relationship. The "Spice Squad" were the very embodiment of the fans that Henry Jenkins describes, that is, "poachers who get to keep what they take and use their plundered goods as the foundations for the construction of an alternative cultural community" (1992: 223). Purchasing merchandise permitted the fans to participate in the Spice Girls' self-empowered negotiation of identity. The exchange of money for the latest publication of a Spice Girls magazine shook itself loose from the stranglehold of commodity fetishism, making the consumers' relations to the commodity paramount, conscious, and not hidden. Fans were urged not to simply identify with a Spice Girl, but *as* a Spice Girl (Driscoll 1999: 175). It exemplified how meaning is generated from the dynamic interplay between the viewer, text, and intertext (Tulloch 1990: 238). For example, one unofficial guide entitled *All About the Spice Girls and Me* (Wyllyams et al. 1997) interjected the group's profile page with room for readers to slot in their own personal details to simulate a sixth Spice member. A rudimentary quiz fortified this direct identification by telling readers which Spice Girls' personal style they most resembled (all the profiles stressed a confident, positive personality). The result was a quasi-DIY scrapbook of the reader's investment and interaction with the group.

By dissolving the boundaries between the star and fan, the Spice Girls opened a virtual floodgate for young females to reorder the space around them and their positions within it. In their authorized book, *Real Life—Real Spice: The Official Story* (Spice Girls 1997), the Spice Girls' rise to superstardom is depicted as if five of our closest friends had by chance infiltrated the world of show business in a real-life dreams-come-true narrative. The prologue begins with its own wish-fulfilling scenario, "Once upon a time there were no Spice Girls. Just five little girls, each very different, but each with their own special talents and dreams and a touch of star quality" (Spice Girls 1997: n.p.). Complete with exclusive portraits capturing them in private moments, commentary by the girls and various family members, and a diary-like address to the reader, *Real Life—Real Spice* reads like an intimate family album negotiating their groundedness as ordinary girls and as international idols. Despite their fame, we are frequently reminded of humble beginnings and links to the real world of family, friends, school days, memories of a childhood spent in working-class council estates (as was the case for Melanie "Sporty Spice" Chisholm), and their first menial jobs. Encompassing the mundaneness of the everyday and the mystique of stardom, representations of the Spice Girls capture the complexities of a postmodern feminism that could not be rendered static and therefore pinned down. Patricia Zimmerman states,

> The days when political activity focused solely on the streets, aiming to change the world and make it a better place are gone, looking more and more like a painted Volkswagen bus without an engine ... activist politics needs a different kind of vehicle, one with more power and an ability to maneuver over multiple terrains—real, discursive, and representational. (Zimmerman 1993: 52)

Rejecting the outdated modes of political activism, that engineless "Volkswagen bus," the Spice Girls employed the vehicle of popular culture for the mass promulgation of their feminist agenda. There was nothing mindless about their image circulation, nor their infiltration into the public and private realms of the city billboard, classroom, and bathroom. The face of Spice commanded attention with, and to, its gaze (who can forget the Union Jack, knickers-exposing mini-dress worn by Halliwell during the BRIT Awards evening in 1997). Their peppy pop lingo resonated the Riot Grrrl directives to be noticed, acknowledged, and reckoned with. Both advocated that all females be liberated from a stuffy definition of conservative femininity. It was no coincidence that the Spice maxim, "Silence is golden but shouting is fun" that was captured in the liner notes of their debut album, echoed the Riot Grrrl's "A loud woman is a good one." Refashioning the disruptive, unruly woman into one wearing four-inch platforms and microskirts, Girl Power attempted to critique systems of power while toying with them at the same time. In a society that limits the social, political, and economic influence of confident, young women, the Spice Girls worked the system while always remaining out of reach of critics. As Gary Susman notes, their self-titled film is essentially critic-proof because "the Spice Girls, who have cannily marketed themselves through shameless overexposure, are just as shrewd at deflecting the critical backlash by anticipating it" (1998). Like the spectacled garishness of a bikini-clad, mud wrestling competition, the Spice Girls retained center-ring but were too slippery to be handled by those on the outside.

Female Bond(ing): It's a Spice World

Spice World: The Spice Girls Movie expands the group's projected image in music and the media. Like a press conference, the film is "question and answer" time in a narrative completely under the control of the Spice Girls. It is a brilliant take on the media circus, and is not afraid of turning the laughter back on themselves. Merging fact and fiction, the film mixes the glamor of fame and fantasy with the common experience of female friendship. Following the madcap antics and adventures of the group in the lead-up to their first live concert at the Royal Albert Hall in London, their numerous escapades (including bootcamp dance school and encounters with aliens) give the impression that we have been granted a backstage

**Figure 4.1   Space invaders: The proud, loud, and popular feminism of the
Spice Girls in *Spice World: The Spice Girls Movie* (1997)**

Source: The Kobal Collection, The Picture Desk

pass into their hyperreal world. The film relies upon a knowledge of "vital Spice
stats" and in-jokes as a type of membership into the Spice club—you are in if you
get *it*. Those who have no idea (the critics) need not apply.

Borrowing from the familiar docudrama style of The Beatles' *A Hard Day's
Night*, *Spice World* blurs the boundaries between public and private lives but
pushes its excessiveness to carnivalesque proportions. Law and order have given
way to a topsy-turvy state where anything goes. The Spice Girls stomp around the
sets in their platforms (and trainers), mingling with superstars playing themselves.
Among the illustrious list are Sir Elton John, Elvis Costello, and Bob Hoskins.
The movie comically upsets the hierarchy of celebrity royalty with pop sensation

by making fun of both. At one star-studded publicity party, Posh Spice (Victoria Beckham) is chatting with Jennifer Saunders of *Absolutely Fabulous* fame. When Posh asks if Saunders knows anything about manta rays, the latter is so eager to impress that she foolishly bumbles that it is one of her favorite designers. This fashion faux pas has not been lost on Posh, and Saunders becomes the butt of the joke. Meanwhile, Scary Spice (Melanie Brown) is berating Sir Bob Geldof for his unkempt tresses. Later in the scene, we cut back to the duo and Geldof is sporting one of Scary Spice's trademark hairstyles. The crux of the scene is the willingness to abandon decorum for disorderly fun. Dusting off the snobbery of blue blood, celebrity power, the Spice Girls maraud this privileged space and inject cheeky audacity and color into an industry of black power suits and haughty profiles. The message is simple—a bunch of girls can make a difference. No one is immune from them.

Playing with the idea of fame, the film continually reminds us of the artifice of the Spice Girls' projected personas and the media. Celebrity status is laid on the table from the onset, questioned, and poked fun at. At one point aboard their insanely decked out tour bus, Sporty Spice remarks to the others, "I don't get it. Why do people stereotype us all the time?" At that very moment she is riding an exercise bike, Baby Spice (Emma Bunton) is sucking on a lollipop and holding a stuffed toy, Posh Spice is posing on a miniature catwalk in her signature little black dress and reading a fashion magazine, Ginger Spice peers down and quickly crosses her arms over her well-endowed chest, and Scary Spice is terrorizing fish in the aquarium. Each reacts with an expression of guilt at Sporty's comment. Their response is to give each other new alter egos. In the following scene, the Spice Girls are at a photoshoot where they volley between them ideas for new images while largely ignoring the irritating remarks of their photographer (Dominic West).

Posh: What about Bricklayer Spice?

Photographer: Sexy. Come on, energy.

Baby: Or, um, Trainspotting Spice.

Photographer: Smashing.

Sporty: What about Sporty-but-I-am-actually-interested-in-other-things Spice?

Photographer: Go for it girls. Go for it. Come on.

Ginger: Or Cheesed-off-with-cheesy-photo-sessions Spice.

After abandoning their photographer, the girls set about reinventing themselves by donning the clothing and wigs of icons, such as Twiggy, Marilyn Monroe, Charlie's Angels, and Wonder Woman. They then take turns adopting the appearance and attitude of a fellow Spice member, acknowledging that their celebrity skins are as changeable as their outfits. Rather than apologizing for their manufactured personas, they claim it as their own. Graeme Turner defines celebrity as a genre of representation—a commodity traded by media industries and a cultural formation with certain social functions—and argues that, "a significant component of [the Spice Girls'] appeal to their audiences was both their explicit acknowledgement of their commodification *and* their refusal to allow this to de-legitimise them" (2004: 9, 55–6). The Spice Girls shrug their shoulders, but it is with a knowing wink.

To look for depth in *Spice World* is a pointless exercise, and that is intentional. When the documentary filmmaker, Piers (Alan Cumming), tells his crew, "Now, remember, the camera is the window to the soul ... what I want to do is take my audience on a journey into the mind's eye of the Spice Girls, and focus on their deeper subconscious," we get the punch line. In the public's eye, the Spice Girls are nothing but surface. For the fans, however, this is enough. They are aware that they must fill in the remainder of the incomplete picture like a scrapbook exercise if it is to make sense. This exemplifies John Tulloch's assertion that meaning is constructed through the negotiation of textual ambiguities by the interpretative fandom community (1995: 113). The role of the fan is made clear when two preteen competition winners, Jack (Devon Anderson) and Evie (Perdita Weeks), spend an afternoon with the Spice Girls in London. It begins as an uninspired, and stifling event dictated by insurance policies and a public relations agenda that puts up a wall between the fan and performer. When the Spice Girls break protocol—they escape with the children from their road manager, Clifford (Richard E. Grant), and spontaneously jump aboard a speedboat on the River Thames—the audience is reassured of *their* place in the picture. It only becomes meaningful when they have become a part of it, and are not just observers.

The relationship between fan and celebrity is reinforced at the film's mockumentary conclusion which, although scripted, is the most truthful part of *Spice World*. Actors assume their real names, discuss their roles in the movie, and air their concerns as the camera tracks past them. Speaking on a cell phone to his manager, Richard E. Grant complains, "What? They want me to play their road manager while I'm on a mobile phone getting angry all the time. I don't want to end my career." Moments later, the camera rests on Cumming venting his frustrations to two other actors also out of character. Reverting to his native Scottish accent, he whines, "Okay. They want me to lose my Scottish accent, that's fine. Fair enough, I'll do a silly posh accent. But the chestwig. I mean this comedy chestwig!" The Spice Girls also tell Claire Rushbrook (who plays Deborah, Clifford's assistant) that they are relieved to have a "serious" actor in the film to give it depth. Funnily, it is Posh who finishes Ginger Spice's sentence about not wanting the film to be superficial. The candid sequence ends with the Spice Girls approaching the camera and directly addressing the audience. They wave, they point at the audience, and they make individual remarks. Posh points out "the two snogging in the back" of the theater and comments on one person's fashion, Baby makes a joke about the mess of popcorn that the audience has made, and when Sporty ponders why people sit at the end of a film to watch the credits, Ginger ironically replies, "It's probably the sad anti-climax. It's all over. Back to reality." It is a reminder that the film operates as a cog in the wider Spice world system where borders separating fact from fiction, the diegetic world of the narrative from our non-diegetic position as viewers looking in, and star from commoner, are no longer sacred.

For all its superficiality, frivolity, and light humor, *Spice World* is a parable of the significance of girl power and camaraderie. While we witness the Spice Girls dominate glamorous gala events and concerts, their passion and zeal to perform is surpassed only by their dedication to maintaining a close-knit circle of personal relations. It is a saccharine, but poignant, moment towards the film's end when they realize they have compromised their integrity and are in danger of losing sight of why they started out in the music industry in the first place. They jeopardize their concert at Royal Albert Hall when they wait in hospital for their friend, Nicola (Naoko Mori), to give birth (the baby's father has long gone). The bond between girlfriends is prioritized over professional careers. The Spice Girls have become one of *us*. Accomplishing what Superman and Spiderman were never able to do, they do not hide behind disguises to distinguish the Clark Kents from their alter ego caped crusaders. They are the every-girl *and* superheroine at the same time. This is apparent from the textual poaching from the world of 007 throughout the narrative. For example, as *Spice World* opens, a seductive song ("Too Much") is played as female silhouettes dance against a psychedelic, swirling background that is reminiscent of a Bond film. Later, during a pitching session between Clifford and two Hollywood filmmakers, played by George Wendt and Mark McKinney, a cringe-worthy idea for a script entitled *Spice Force Five* is put forth. It is, as the Hollywood duo sell it, a story of "crack operatives in their own field: they're the martial arts expert [cut to Baby Spice sucking on a lollipop and flipping three assailants], counter-espionage agent [cut to Sporty descending from the ceiling *Mission Impossible*-style and scoring a goal on a miniature soccer board game], the explosives expert [cut to Scary accidentally blowing up an entire building], the master of disguise [cut to Ginger entering a telephone booth as a saucy redhead and exiting as Bob Hoskins who says direct to camera, "Girl power, equalization of the sexes" while giving the victory hand sign as the *Wonder Woman* theme song plays in the background], and Victoria [cut to Posh looking seductively into the camera]." During the photoshoot, Posh even gears up as Ursula Andress' character from *Dr. No* with a blonde wig, trademark bikini, and brandishing a hunting knife. Roger Moore himself makes a cameo as Chief, a spoof of the mastermind M, who sprouts nonsensical advice and sayings with a bizarre barnyard theme. The effect is a parodic homage to one of the world's most recognizable heroes. But this time, the misogynistic leanings of the Bond films have been hijacked. Adopting the commanding presence and heroics of 007, and the über-feminine, but also independent, ways of a Bond Girl, the Spice Girls are James Bond *and* Honey Ryder at the same time. It encapsulates the Spice Girls' ethos that it is possible to be female and powerful.

Recalling my experience at the *Spice World* premiere in 1998, I was surrounded by (and complicit with) the representational politics of the Spice Girls. It was discernible in the throngs of fans around me. Aside from the obvious desire to see, hear, and touch their idols, the fans were caught up in a ritual of celebrity worship that implicated their own integral involvement in being a part of something greater. They were not there just to see the Spice Girls. The Spice Girls were just as eager to see *them*. As hokey as it seemed at the time, the female fans inserted themselves into the 'imagineered' world of the Spice Girls as activists and took to the streets that day in support of a cause. While they wore the attire of their favorite Spice member (their own celebrity skins), accessorized with a Spice backpack, and waved posters, their deep investment was manifested in the wholly corporeal nature of the experience—their laughter, screams, and surging bodies. More than mobilizing a market, the Spice Girls attempted to formulate an identity politics for a younger generation that would make feminist aspirations more accessible and ratifying. Validating the experience and existence of the fans, Girl Power celebrated its space invasion.

Coinciding with Geri Halliwell's departure to pursue a solo career, support for the Spice Girls waned by the end of 1998. Their fame had run its course. The tremendous force and influence of their fleeting conquest in popular culture has been conveniently forgotten over time. In popular memory, however, we are left to salvage and remember it as an experience of camaraderie, a collaborative effort between fan and celebrity, and the feeling of an era. It meant something. Their ephemerality and embeddedness in popular culture allows understandings of the Spice Girls to shift over time and across context to survive the deadening effects of historical erasure. More than a decade after their global domination, the ongoing fascination and derision of the Spice Girls stubbornly attests to their continued, animated existence. Even after the moment is gone, they have not.

As with Courtney Love, the Spice Girls were a problematic paradigm of feminism. And perhaps that was part of their appeal. Susan Hopkins writes, "there is something magic in that moment when Courtney Love reaches out to her young female audience and passes on her guitar. There is a fleeting sense that anything is possible" (1999: 14). When the Spice Girls stepped away from the red carpet to clasp the hands of their fans, sign autographs, and incite vocalized outbursts of Girl Power, there was a magic to *that* moment. In that brief period, the crowd's verve and positivity, and the Spice Girls' reciprocity were saturated with the feeling that anything was possible. The intensity seared itself into popular culture and popular memory. It was befitting that the lyrics of one of their songs was "Live forever, for the moment" (the song held the number one spot in the UK charts despite Halliwell having left the band two months earlier) (Spice Girls 1997). There is a life beyond Warhol's 15 minutes of fame. Viva Forever.

Chapter 5
Violent Femmes: Angry Girls in Youth Cinema

I'm sexy, I'm cute,
I'm popular to boot!
I'm bitchen! Great hair!
The boys all love to stare!
I'm wanted, I'm hot,
I'm everything you're not!
I'm pretty, I'm cool,
I dominate the school!

(Toro Cheerleaders in *Bring It On* [dir. Peyton Reed, 2000])

I cannot help it, but I get a grim satisfaction when I see another bitch bite the dust. The teen film provides a veritable smorgasbord that indulges this guilty pleasure. When the leader of über popular clique "The Plastics" is hit by a school bus in *Mean Girls* (dir. Mark S. Waters, 2004), our reaction is less shock than amused laughter. When Kathryn's (Sarah Michelle Gellar) scheming is exposed in *Cruel Intentions* (dir. Roger Kumble, 1999), her public humiliation reduces the socialite to a social leper that is cathartic and wholly gratifying for the audience. Her character is modeled upon the villainess, Marquis de Merteuil, from Pierre Choderlos de Laclos' novel *Les Liaisons Dangereuses*. In *The Craft* (dir. Andrew Fleming, 1996), vengeance is sweet when the demented teen witch, Nancy (Fairuza Balk), is incarcerated in a psychiatric ward, and left screaming and writhing in her straitjacket.

Teen films hold a special place for the bitch. While a film may occasionally leave out the token bullying jock or the socially incompetent chemistry geek, the absence of the bitch—the quintessential prima donna—has a far more resounding impact as she demands the glare of the spotlight with her acerbic words and actions. Popular Hollywood cinema demands that her stinging words and wicked ways repulse, serving to justify her inevitable punishment. She is no Mona Lisa for there appears to be no mystery behind her cunning smile, or so it would appear. Even the heroine who has played the girl-next-door throughout the narrative must often resort to becoming somewhat of a bitch, or exhibit bitch-like qualities, in order to bring about narrative closure and a sense of victory. I allude not to an Olivia Newton-John pseudo transformation at the end of *Grease* (dir. Randal Kleiser, 1978), where Sandy Olsson benignly exchanges her pastel ensembles for black Lycra, red lipstick, dangerously high heels, and attitude. Instead, I am referring to the "good girl" playing nasty and enacting justice in the way that

Carrie White (Sissy Spacek), in the film *Carrie* (dir. Brian De Palma, 1976), embarks on a homicidal prom night mission, seeking retribution upon all those who have tormented her. After a vindictive prank by several students sees her drenched in pig's blood and humiliated in front of her peers at the prom, Carrie uses her telekinetic powers to bring down the building in a rain of fire, killing all the students and staff in it. This is, however, not a simple case of beating the bitch at her own game. While the heroine acting the bitch is often misconstrued as going against character, hence her return to the girl-next-door role by the film's end, this paradox diametrically pits the fashionably evil against the virtuous good in a far too simplistic binary.

Although youth cinema, the teen film in particular, often paints cartoonish caricatures, the bitch is often one of the most complex of its constructed personalities. This figure possesses not only the propensity for destruction but also the power for potential change, rather than functioning merely as a necessary evil or foil in the plot. This chapter explores the transgressive qualities of the bitch within a post-1980s neoliberal, historical context, broadening the parameters to encompass the angry girl underdog in youth cinema. As she is an adaptation of the violent femme, this requires the backtracking to cultural narratives of the dangerous woman. Major changes and continuities in the bitch icon in youth cinema are traced through case studies of two seminal films that proudly boast the angry cattiness of its heroines—Michael Lehmann's satire *Heathers* (1989), and Matthew Bright's postmodern fairytale/nightmare *Freeway* (1996). Crossing boundaries of acceptable gender roles, the violent femme expands the narrative possibilities for young women and the venting of female aggression as political intervention. However, the outcomes of the narratives indicate a cultural unease surrounding problematic women, and expose the limitations of a bitch politics on the periphery.

Queen Bitch: The Femme Fatale

Barracking for the underdog—the new girl, the unattractive nerd, or the independent spirit with a heart of gold—and gleefully anticipating the downfall of the vile teen dominatrix is a response already shaped and swayed by cultural history. The teen film is no exception. The genre hooks into an already established tradition of "bad women" in visual art and literature. In the late 1980s and early 1990s, a spate of fatal femme movies was unleashed in commercial cinema. Spearheaded by the controversial *Fatal Attraction* (dir. Adrian Lyne, 1987), and followed by the likes of *Basic Instinct* (dir. Paul Verhoeven, 1992), *Body of Evidence* (dir. Uli Edel, 1993), and *Jade* (dir. William Friedkin, 1995), the manipulative, intellectual seductress became a prominent personality that has solidified into a stock character type. Speaking the words that no other dares utter, the femme fatale did as she pleased and got whatever she wanted. However, her influence extends beyond psychological manipulation and hypnotic beauty. Unafraid of employing physical violence conventionally associated with male authority to satiate her desires, the femme fatale unsettles deeply entrenched gender roles. As Janice Haaken comments,

> the discovery of hidden female aggression served to fortify an original split between female purity and female malevolence. It was difficult for patriarchal authority to hold multiple representations of women in mind without suffering an existential crisis of its own, particularly in that virile manhood rested so heavily on its counterweight in female passivity and virtue. (Haaken 2002: 205)

The insidiousness of these femmes resided not just in the shock factor of their actions. Catherine Trammell's (Sharon Stone) infamous crotch shot, Alex Forrest (Glenn Close) boiling the Gallagher family's pet rabbit, and Rebecca Carlson's (Madonna) sadomasochistic sex rituals are beside the point. Their most unnerving trait is the ability to command the audience's gaze. The spectator becomes implicated in the distorted world of the femme fatale and compelled to watch. We become giddily lost in her labyrinthine maze of reworked rules and double entendre. Conjuring the image of the vagina dentata, the femme fatale is marked by unpredictability and ambiguity. She walks the tightrope between that which is desired and despised as we vacillate between attraction and repulsion.[1]

The problematic nature of the femme fatale is indicated by the film's resolution—the femme fatale's imminent punishment. The fact that audiences across America rallied together screaming "Kill the bitch" during screenings of *Fatal Attraction* is telling (Holmlund 1991: 25). Clearly, there is no safe flirtation, even in the darkened cinema, with the femme fatale. She is identified and blamed as the threat, thereby bypassing serious discussion of gender imbalance. Enclaves of "phallic women" supporters have claimed such figures as Lorena Bobbitt, Catherine Tramell, and Alex Forrest as feminist icons, arguing that dominant interpretations of the films reproduce misogynistic readings of domineering women (Keesey 2001: 47). This is demonstrated when Alex confronts Dan (Michael Douglas) in *Fatal Attraction* after their one-night stand.

> *Alex*: You thought you could just walk into my life and turn it upside-down without a thought for anyone but yourself … I won't allow you to treat me like some slut you can just bang a couple of times and throw in the garbage.

Alex's statement directly questions the integrity of Dan's masculine authority. When she informs him that she is pregnant with his child, he coldly dismisses her. It is insightful to witness how swiftly the audience acquits him of his personal offences and indicts Alex. By the film's end, the archetypes of the faithful wife, the reformed husband, and the wicked woman are reinstated after Alex is fatally shot by Dan's saintly wife, Beth (Anne Archer). The camera rests upon the family photograph as

---

1   Barbara Creed provides a comprehensive study of the monstrous female that populates cinema in *The Monstrous-Feminine: Film, Feminism, Psychoanalysis* (1993).

the final image. As Richard Corliss states, "*Fatal Attraction* transforms a theater full of strangers into a community: confidant to Dan, cheerleader to Beth, lynch mob for Alex" (1987: 74). Order is restored, the home is protected, and gender genres are once again shrink-wrapped and tightly sealed. The threatening femme has only two options—being buried six feet under (with her death a moment to celebrate), or remain in purgatory as the manipulative vamp the audience loves to hate. There is nowhere else for her to go.

This lack of options is nothing new. The killer babes of the 1980s and 1990s sexual thrillers hail from an established tradition of wayward women depicted in literature, art, and folklore that can be traced back to the closing decades of the 19th century. While mythological and biblical references to figures such as Medusa and Salome predate this period, it was the design style of Art Nouveau that popularized a distinctive iconography of the femme fatale, which shifted away from the idea of the fallen woman who commits sin to the wicked woman who is pure evil (Allen 1983: 1, 11–12). In *The Femme Fatale: Erotic Icon*, Virginia Allen (1983) closely studies the altering representations of this figure over the last three centuries in paintings. Although she notes the subtle changes—the shape of the mouth, the direction of the gaze, the posturing of the body, the surrounding scenery—Allen's interest resides in the defining features of the femme fatale that continue to be echoed in present day popular culture. As an enigmatic beauty who seduces and ruins men, the femme fatale's capacity for destruction is matched only by her inability to create because she is the antithesis to the nurturing "good woman" of the domestic sphere. Her blessing and curse is her less than human quality (Allen 1983: 1, 4). As Allen states, "there is a dimension to the meaning of the femme fatale suggesting that even though she might die, she will not be obliterated. She will rise to claim another victim, perhaps as one of the living dead, a vampire" (1983:2).

Although the good woman may go to her grave with her husband shedding tears and flowers on her tombstone, it is the vamp who lingers like a haunting apparition in his mind. To borrow from Allen's analogy, the femme fatale as vampire is profanity incarnate. This dangerous woman is "both Siren and Circe, Lilith and Delilah, seductress and devourer; as Shiva-like dissolver of identity; the woman as eternal enigma, baffler of Freud, destabilizing mystifier, one-way ticket to madness and self-destruction" (Rosenbaum 1996: 105). Her existence can only produce sexual, spiritual, and physical pollution that necessitates her termination.

The iconic status of the femme fatale gained further cultural currency in the 1940s and 1950s *film noir* in the United States. Bookended by the aftermath of the First World War and the beginnings of the Cold War, *noir* embodied an historical period associated with violence, rampant greed, cynicism, and suspicion (Kaplan 1998: 1). The need to reassert order and (masculine) authority in the nation-state manifested itself in the heart of home and government. Where Rosie the Riveter had once served her country in steel mills, the end of the Second World War required her reinstatement in the kitchen. The good woman was no longer the patriotic feminist fighting for her nation, but the doting wife to husband and family whose rightful place was the homestead. The return to conservatism became even more imperative in the McCarthy years when anything seen as contrary to the status quo attracted accusations of un-American activities and values.

Film noir reified the lived experiences and preoccupations of American citizens by transposing cultural fears upon the already familiar archetypes of the paternal figurehead, the virtuous woman, and the vamp. Residing in an unstable position, the male protagonist is at once obligated to the wifely character and drawn towards the femme fatale. He is an anti-hero who lacks the moral base and reference points that the classic Hollywood hero is equipped with. The urban landscape functions as a quagmire of seedy temptation associated with contemporary society and the metropolis. As public space is seen as an external projection of the private, control of the environment is tantamount to control of the self. The secretive dark alleys, the amoral smoky bars, and boudoirs of the modern metropolis are personified by the ultimate seductress—the Spider Woman (Place 1998: 53). As Janey Place comments,

> the visual movement which indicates unacceptable activity in film noir women represents the man's own sexuality, which must be repressed and controlled if it is not to destroy him … only in a controlled, impotent, powerless form, powerless to move or act, is the sexual woman no threat to the film noir man. (Place 1998: 57, 60)

The femme fatale's opposite is the asexual, nurturing woman who offers redemption and the "possibility of integration for the alienated, lost man into the stable world of secure values, roles and identities" (Place 1998: 60). Embodying the idealized, pastoral "remembered past"—she is the hero's link to tradition and conservatism— the nurturing woman is both removed in space (from the immediacy of the sordid city) and time (Place 1998: 51). She signifies the past that the hero must return to if he is to find salvation.

Unlike the good woman who is bound to the sphere and service of the home, the femme fatale is mobile and drifts between spaces. The paradox is that the only place she can never occupy is the sanctuary of the past, for she is a construction of modernity. Her certain demise is not redemptive, but like the surgical removal of a tumor. Conveyed as an agent of corruption whose modus operandi is premised on fierce independence and guiltless self-obsession, the femme fatale's power is the source and justification of her suppression. However, this figure is not a simple product of *film noir* but the fulcrum through which the narrative of social disorder and instability hinges. Although she is consigned to the shady corridors and backrooms, dwelling on the edge of insanity, she usurps the center.

Fast forwarding from the 1940s and 1950s of *film noir* to the sexual thriller of the 1980s and 1990s, adverse representations of threatening women have not been quelled as a result of feminist progress. According to Kate Stables, they have arguably worsened,

> Commentators writing in the 70s, when the *fatale* figure seemed safely historical, made the assumption that western cultural movements such as feminism and 'sexual revolution' would render the idea of the *femme fatale* obsolete, reducing her to a quaint fantastical figure produced by repressed, male-dominated societies. In fact, the reverse has happened—in a movie-producing culture which abounds with mediated images of sex and proliferating sexual discourses, the sexually threatening woman comes to take centre stage. (Stables 1998: 167)

Although the postmodern version poaches from 1940s *noir*, upon closer observation the former bears only a modest semblance. Aesthetic and narrative meaning is now filtered through the singular mesh of sexual performance in which the soft-porn inclinations of current sexual thrillers dislodge the femme fatale from the immediate historical context. In short, her function in the narrative is boiled down to titillation and perverse pleasures. While her 1940s counterpart was symptomatic of a diseased decade, the modern seductress of the 1980s and 1990s can generally claim no purpose other than embodying feminine evil for its own gratuitous sake. When Kathie (Jane Greer) is killed during a rain of police gunfire in *Out of the Past* (dir. Jacques Tourneur, 1947), law and order in the home and nation-state is re-established—the foreign enemy has been conquered. When Rebecca in *Body of Evidence* is fatally shot and plummets through a window, cheers in the audience reveal the consensus that she deserves a gruesome death because she is a wicked woman. For this fatal female, there is no public facet to her persona. She has become the doomed villainess so absorbed in narcissism—the body and foul mouth that always returns attention to the self—that her death is vital lest we too are drawn into her private obsession. Although this femme may have been beaten, raped, and ridiculed, her excessiveness far outweighs the wrongdoings in her past for which there is no sympathy. While the 1940s femmes may have been transgressive, the vamps of the 1980s and 1990s were arguably regressive.

Carrying the Banner: Killer Babes

The teenage bitch in youth cinema reconceptualizes the threatening female popularized in *film noir* and the erotic thriller. Typically, this lethal Lolita is the most envied girl in the school. Raised on a pedestal, the teen bitch is revered and loathed for her desirability. This is signaled from the onset by her unfailingly dramatic entrance. Flattering lighting, a lingering pan shot over her sculpted body to register her every movement—the turn of the head, the flick of her hair, the pout of her lip-glossed mouth, the fluttered eyelashes—are all part of her arsenal. It is encapsulated in the opening scene of *Bring It On* in which a team of cheerleaders is performing a choreographed routine. Each is athletic, nubile, sassy, and seductive. Although it soon becomes evident that it is a dream sequence, the lines of their cheer/jeer are intentionally candid. Not only are they hot and everything

Figure 5.1 **The bitchy, bold, and beautiful: Veronica Sawyer (Winona Ryder) and "the Heathers" (Kim Walker, Lisanne Falk, and Shannen Doherty) in *Heathers* (1989)**

Source: The Kobal Collection, The Picture Desk

the ordinary girl is not, as they declare in the opening quote, they also ruthlessly dominate the school. This is a theme that also runs through the film *Heathers*.

Heathers is an acerbic satire of the teenage experience that drips with rancor and fifth-gear bitchiness. The narrative centers on Westerburg High School's most powerful clique of female vamps. They are a quartet comprising Heather Chandler (Kim Walker), Heather Duke (Shannen Doherty), Heather McNamara (Lisanne Falk), and the protagonist Veronica Sawyer (Winona Ryder). The group indiscriminately inflicts humiliation upon students, including members within the circle, with insidious intent and success. In the film's opening sequence, the three Heathers are engaged in a game of croquet. They flit gracefully through a picturesque garden to the tune of Doris Day's "Que Sera, Sera." The image of civility and female decorum is swiftly eroded as the trio trample through a bed of flowers and malevolently smirk as they take turns swinging their mallets.[2] The scene concludes with a medium close-up shot of Veronica's head protruding from the ground and surrounded by croquet balls. Behold the begrudging human wicket. As the narrative progresses, it becomes apparent that only Veronica has any genuine guilt and sense of grave consequence.

After a heated argument, Heather Chandler threatens to expel Veronica from the clique. Veronica's reprisal—accompanied by her new lover Jason "J.D." Dean (Christian Slater)—is to concoct a bogus, morning-after remedy that will make Heather vomit wretchedly. Unbeknown to Veronica, J.D.'s psychopathic tendencies lead him to switch the drink with liquid drainer. Heather's impression of cold beauty and control is shattered when her poisoned, convulsing body plunges face first into a glass coffee table. Upon J.D.'s prompting, Veronica agrees to stage the mishap as a suicide, which results in a chain effect of phoney claims of amity among the student body, and Heather Duke swooping in like a vulture to claim the coveted position as the group's leader. After Veronica once again inadvertently assists J.D. in murdering two of Westerburg's star football players and making it appear a homosexual suicide pact, suicide is transformed into a trendsetting statement.

The femme fatale of 1940s *noir* is reappropriated through the bitch in *Heathers*, with female sexuality equated with danger and death. As with the femme fatale, the body beautiful of the bitch is a carefully manicured construction that is preened and primed to hold the gaze, connoting what Laura Mulvey refers to as its "*to-be-looked-at-ness*" quality (1992 [1975]: 750). Fashion and beauty become as lethal as scathing remarks and maniacal tricks. However, strict censorship guidelines require the sexual exploits of the bitch be less explicit than in the erotic thriller. The bitch of youth cinema is "a teened down version of the *femme fatale*, fit for the high school corridor" (Murphy 2002: 78). The steamy boudoir is transplanted with the teenager's bedroom and the back alleys with the winding high school corridors, while the eroticism of the femme fatale is displaced with sexy, bad attitude. Visual codes are loaded with meaning to the point of excess. The heightened aesthetics are discernible in the surrealism of the *mise-en-scène*, specifically costume and setting in *Heathers*.

---

2   There is an historical trajectory of powerful and dangerous women, whether beautiful or grotesque, who operate as a trio in art and folklore. Some of the most well-known examples are the three witches in William Shakespeare's *Macbeth* and in Greek mythology—the Siren sisters (Parthenope, Leukosia, and Ligeia), the Harpies (Aello, Okypete, and Kelaino), the Gorgon sisters (Medusa, Stheno, and Euryale), and the Graiai (Pemphredo, Enyo, and Deino) who were the sentries of the Gorgons. Although the number of Sirens varies according to source material, depictions in art generally show three women or winged creatures (see Rose 1964 [1928]).

In *film noir*, the femme fatale's body is represented as polluting and dangerous, and her less-than-human quality, that is, her unnaturalness, is naturalized. *Heathers* exposes this gendering of female identity—a conflation of culture with nature—as artificial and engineered. Attention is drawn to the body and to how it is accessorized. For example, obvious color motifs are signifiers of power whereby characters are associated with a particular primary hue. Heather Chandler's trademark is red as displayed through her scarlet attire, the furnishings in her home, and the lighting in which she is bathed at times. Veronica is distinguished by her penchant for blue, Heather Duke with green, and Heather McNamara with yellow. As the status symbol of superiority, the color red defines Heather "Number One" Chandler as the Machiavellian socialite early in the narrative. She is, after all, the one who makes the winning swing at Veronica's head in the opening scene, and rebukes her for fraternizing with those outside of their elite circle.

Heather Chandler: If you're going to openly be a bitch.

Veronica: It's just Heather, why can't we talk to different kinds of people?

Heather Chandler: Fuck me gently with a chainsaw. Do I look like Mother Theresa? If I did, I probably wouldn't mind talking to the Geek Squad.

After Heather Chandler's death, Heather Duke assumes the color red. The significance of this gesture is that relations of power are not closed, but subject to change. Power is not fixed but transferable, and social hierarchies are able to be rewritten. For instance, when Veronica eventually dethrones Heather Duke she does so by taking Heather's red rosette scrunchee and tying her own hair with it while proclaiming that there is a "new sheriff in town."

The three Heathers more closely resemble the femme fatale with their masochistic ideals of femininity, social exclusion, and repression—Heather Chandler's self-destructiveness manifests itself in meaningless, degrading trysts, Heather Duke's in her bulimia, and Heather McNamara's in an unsuccessful suicide attempt by swallowing sleeping pills. The emphasis on sex, diet, and a soft-suicide option firmly ensconces these females within a rigid patriarchal rendering of the female body and identity. On the other hand, Veronica offers a polemic movement away from this self-deterministic nihilism (Woodward 2002: 314, 316). Although popularity, feminine wiles, and prettiness initially provide Veronica with the tools to assert authority, they are unable to instigate real social change. Her frustrated tirades can only be vented onto the pages of her private journal, "Dear diary, I want to kill and you have to believe it's for more than just selfish reasons, more than just a spoke in my menstrual cycle." It takes J.D.'s persuasion to convert Veronica's fury into physical action by enacting "what Veronica can only feel and express inwardly … Her violent emotions must not be seen" (Woodward 2002: 315). Her eventual commandeering of the dominant position requires the subversion of dualistic structures of feminine/masculine, victim/victimized, and object/subject.

The cinematic gaze as a locus of power provides a useful point of entry for understanding the punishment complex that plagues the threatening woman. While discussions surrounding the cinematic gaze have conceded that the spectatorial act does not simply splinter male/active from female/passive, Mulvey's retraction from earlier writings—that there can be no female gaze—comes with the clause that it is only possible through the enacting of the active masculine. The female subject "shifts restlessly in its borrowed transvestite clothes" (Mulvey 1989: 33). While this assertion is not without flaws, what is importantly gleaned from Mulvey's work is the general unease surrounding the woman who dares to return the gaze. Mary Ann Doane articulates this paradox by arguing that the "woman's exercise of an active investigating gaze can only be simultaneous with her own victimization," in which the female gaze is no trump card but a liability (1984: 72). This borrowed power is never willingly relinquished and must be taken away by force, either by violently punishing the female or justifying a return to familial bliss and a "natural" social order. In short, it is the proverbial spoon of sugar to make the medicine go down.

In *Heathers*, however, the social order is intolerable. It is a repulsive tableau of middle-class mediocrity and conservatism, where the sanctuary of the well-adjusted nuclear family is missing, and there is no nostalgic community to return or regress to. Veronica's family personifies this absent origin, reiterated in perfunctory conversations carried out almost verbatim over the ubiquitous platter of pâté.

Father: So what was the first day after Heather's suicide like?

Veronica: I don't know, it was okay, I guess.

Mother: Terrible thing. So will we get to meet this dark horse prom contender?

Veronica: Maybe.

Father (looking at his cigarette): Goddamn. Will somebody tell me why I smoke these damn things?

Veronica: Because you're an idiot.

Father: Oh yeah, that's it.

Mother: You two.

Veronica: Great pâté, but I'm going to have to motor if I want to be ready for that funeral.

Similarly, the high school is depicted as a caricatured community of date-rape jocks, awkward geeks, detached stoners, deceitful do-gooders, and dimwitted faculty members no less vulgar than the parentals. There is great irony in the fact that Veronica's only admirable ally is a psychopath with a penchant for detonating things (buildings and people). If the textual eradication of *noir*'s femme fatale "involves a desperate reassertion of control on the part of the threatened male subject," the bitch in youth cinema often signifies an obvious lack of ideal masculinity (Doane 1991: 2). This is certainly the case in *Heathers* where paternal figures are clueless or demented. For instance, Veronica's father is emotionally vacant, and J.D.'s father is mentally unbalanced. Equally uninspiring are boyfriends and male colleagues who are all boorish, boring, or pathetic. There are no heroes to be found in this hellish vision of teendom. Veronica must rely on her own wits and initiative to save the school and reinstate order her way. While Veronica's death wishes provide the impetus for ousting toxic personalities from the school body—she is initially the foil for J.D.'s personal vendettas—she reappropriates the mantle of violence for creative purposes as opposed to anarchy, but this requires her to play the part of the bitch (Woodward 2002: 316).

Herein lies the fundamental difference between the bitch and the femme fatale. While the transgressive femininity of the latter establishes her as a social saboteur struggling against patriarchal codes of conduct, the bitch works within these confines to unsettle the (dis)equilibrium around her. The bitch's forthrightness and brutal honesty are able to unmask ideologies, and serve as a shock and warning that extend beyond her own selfish wants. While these moments may be rare, they provide an alternative to the punishment complex that inflicts the doomed femme fatale. The bitch wields both artifice and truth-telling like weapons. Transcending glamazon cattiness, the bitch is able to boldly go where no man has gone before.

Extracting herself from J.D.'s scheme to destroy the school in a misguided act of altruism—it is to appear a mass suicide pact by the students protesting against a society that degrades them—Veronica must exploit the same ruthless violence. By the film's finale, she has twisted the dichotomy of the female as the punished into the punisher and transformed her gaze into dramatic action. It is evident in the final conflict between J.D. and Veronica, which takes place in the school's boiler room where he has strategically planted explosives to blow up the school and the student body. After J.D. beats her to a pulp, Veronica responds by opening fire on him. It is important to note that her transgressive agency does not privilege masculine ideals of strength and toughness. After all, she requires a gun to mobilize J.D. rather than her own brute force. In fact, even Veronica's attempt to shoot him dead proves unsuccessful. When she staggers through the front doors of the school entrance after their violent altercation, her exit bears none of the fanfare, bravado, or stylings of the hardbody heroine evident in films such as *Terminator 2: Judgment Day* (dir. James Cameron, 1991), *The Long Kiss Goodnight* (dir. Renny Harlin, 1996), or *Girlfight* (dir. Karyn Kusama, 2000). The film's resolution, however, is no less significant or subversive.

J.D.: Color me impressed. You really fucked me up pretty bad, Veronica. You've got power. Power I didn't think you had. The slate is clean. Pretend I did blow up the school. All the schools. Now that you're dead, what are you gonna do with your life?

Veronica pulls out a cigarette from her blazer pocket, puts it into her mouth, then folds her arms, waiting for the inevitable. J.D. sets off an explosive that he has strapped to his waist as Veronica watches on. She does not recoil. Instead, she puffs on her cigarette with cool detachment, despite the fact that she is disheveled, singed, and smoking. J.D.'s final act of suicide is a resignation that she—not he— has the power. Claiming this defining victory, Veronica's competency and agency expand the limits of the bitch and angry femme archetype. It is her rationality and reason, coupled with a no-holds-barred retaliation against physical and psychological abuse, which forces J.D. to turn his irrational violence and gaze upon his own self. Veronica exercises the ability for self-restraint and reaction, negotiating that awkward terrain between nicety and nastiness, and being bold and bitchy.[3] Such empowering fantasies of dangerous and commanding women "carve out new possibilities for female subjectivity" (Lentz 1993: 398). Veronica has earned what no femme fatale could ever aspire to, or be given—respect. She willingly enters the boxing ring and gives as good as she gets. While her right hook is no match for J.D.'s attacks, she responds with an equally effective counter. When he flips her the bird, she unflinchingly shoots off his middle finger.

Heathers resolves any lingering discomfort of the dominating bitch in cinema, with Veronica and Westerburg's mascot for losers, Martha "Dumptruck" Dunnstock (Carrie Lynn), engaged in girly chat as a sultry jazz version of "Que Sera, Sera" plays sentimentally over the final scene. Opting to forgo her prom for an evening of movies and popcorn with Martha, the closing shot is of Veronica ambling down the darkened high school hallway with Martha circling around her in a motorized wheelchair in, as the screenplay terms it, a Bogart/Rains grand exit. While the bitch allows the performance of the difficult femme who disrupts the social structure, the film's resolution suggests that it cannot be maintained permanently. It needs a release valve for closure. This luxury is not so readily available to the heroine in *Freeway*, who is a more problematic rendering of the teen bitch.

A warped reworking of Little Red Riding Hood updated for the 1990s, *Freeway*—with its "refreshing dose of bad attitude and potboiler freakishness" (Smith 1996: 52)—replaces the fairytale's innocent heroine with an illiterate, shrill-voiced teenager hailing from a trailer trash caste. When her mother, Ramona (Amanda Plummer), is arrested for solicitation and possession of narcotics, and her

---

3   This is made clear through the film's characterization of female extremes. The "nice girls" always finish last. They are the outcasts and always downtrodden. At the other end of the scale are the unrelenting, cold bitches who slip into the punishment cycle that befalls the femme fatale. They are killed off, like Heather Chandler, or remain despised with no means for redemption.

stepfather, Larry (Michael T. Weiss), for multiple parole violations, Vanessa Lutz (Reese Witherspoon) embarks on a journey to Grandma's (Kitty Fox) house to begin a new life. She encounters the big, bad wolf—the aptly named Bob Wolverton (Kiefer Sutherland)—a therapist who turns out to be the I–5 (freeway) serial killer notorious for his signature rape, mutilation, and murder of young "wayward" girls. When Wolverton reveals his identity to Vanessa, she fights back and shoots him several times, believing she has dispatched him. After being captured by the police, Vanessa is detained in a juvenile detention center from which she escapes so that she can continue her jaunt to Grandma's. Ultimately though, there is to be no happy ending. Grandma has met a grisly fate after being raped and garroted by a severely deformed Wolverton whose body has been riddled with multiple gunshot wounds. In a final clash, Vanessa's rage reaches its apex in response to Wolverton's vicious beatings. The police arrive shortly after she has overpowered and strangled her attacker to death. Gavin Smith describes *Freeway* as "a mirror image of *Clueless*, except that its vision of blonde SoCal girl agency is backed up by a .45 instead of a credit card. Definite Guilty Pleasure" (1996: 52). Whereas *Heathers* posits the angry femme as privileged, wealthy, and with her rage seething beneath a pretty exterior and feminine politesse, Vanessa Lutz is more the screaming harpy. With her aesthetically abrasive appearance and personality, her bitch tendencies erupt with every corrosive diatribe and corporeal assault.

Premiering during the same period as the international Spice Girl phenomenon, *Freeway* is more aligned with the vehement protestations of the Riot Grrrl Movement. The film is a grating representation of the angry teenage female that starkly contrasts the more consumer-friendly Girl Power. Vanessa's body is coded to be looked at with her tight-fitting, skimpy outfits and her sexually suggestive statements. It is, however, a battered and bruised body that is an assault upon the visual senses. The eroticism of the spectacle is turned into an intentional demonstration and defiance of pleasure. After killing Wolverton, Vanessa emerges from Grandma's house a mess. Blood, sweat, tears, and mascara run down her face. It is turned into a disturbing portrait when Vanessa is caught, midway through laughter, in a freeze-frame as the eerie soundtrack reverberates in the background.

Freeway is no celebratory instance of perverse pleasure and punishment, nor does it pander to gratuitous fantasies of female empowerment and rage. Vanessa's outbursts are indicative of her lowly ranking at the bottom of the social food chain. Violence is neither a last resort nor approached ambivalently, but a necessary and normal survival tactic, which distinguishes Vanessa from Veronica Sawyer. While Veronica's "teenage angst bullshit has a body count," to borrow her words, death and injury done unto others is initially unpremeditated. By the end, her actions are geared towards correcting her wrongdoings. Vanessa, on the other hand, must employ violence to ensure her survival within regimes of systemic coercion. Even though there is no dark forest for this Red Riding Hood, there is a corresponding concrete jungle of freeways, Compton-like urban ghettos, and institutions of incarceration where Wolverton is not the only threat. For instance, Vanessa reveals that she is a victim of child sex abuse, having been repeatedly molested by her stepfather from an early age. Furthermore, law enforcement agencies continually disregard her testimony of Wolverton's true identity. As Kimberley Roberts writes, "Vanessa does not stand a chance when pitted against a criminal justice system that is inherently biased, a system that would convict rather than defend her" (2002: 225). Even when Detectives Mike Breer (Wolfgang Bodison) and Garnet Wallace (Dan Hedaya) realize that Vanessa has been wrongly accused, they arrive after she has saved her own skin. She is literally on her own, a point emphasized from the very start. Vanessa's fiancé, Chopper (Bokeen Woodbine), is fatally gunned down by rival gang members soon after she has bid him farewell as she embarks on the trip to Grandma's house. He is the only person she truly loves and can depend upon.

By grafting a well-known children's fairytale over the story, *Freeway* subverts and critiques meta-narratives that support dominant gender roles. As Anne Cranny-Francis writes, "Red Riding Hood is a particularly powerful image, the transgressive woman who acts on her own desires, and must be punished by being saved by some good male character" (1992: 125). As with the fairytale's numerous incarnations over time, Matthew Bright's *Freeway* similarly functions as a cautionary tale for young girls. While the Grimm Brothers may have emphasized the dangerous woods full of predatory men, Bright extends the threat to society itself. There is no safe path to tread upon, no heroic patriarchs, and no safe destination. Just as Vanessa is dislodged from familiar scenarios of girlhood in cinema, such as the high school, end-of-year prom, shopping mall, or cozy bedroom, so the fairytale's mooring is severed from an outdated ideal and expectation of the female subject as victim and/or object. The protagonist traverses through foreign landscapes where the only common denominator is her continued oppression in an adult world of drugs, sex, assault, and condescension. Vanessa's Red Riding Hood is inescapably part of a disempowered minority until the bitter end. She depicts a tough femininity that cannot be easily slotted into the role of the impassive female fighter, the bewitching femme fatale, or the hard-done-by victim driven to revenge; tropes that Sherrie Inness (1999) argues can mitigate female agency and violence as political intervention. As offensive quips and impressive couture alone have little currency, the embodied bitch is her armor.

Freeway sketches a degenerative society that is an endless gauntlet of obstacles for the teenage girl. Vanessa lacks the education and financial resources for upward social mobility. With no home, belongings, or support network, Vanessa can only claim ownership over her own body, which requires her voice and fists to deliver even greater clout. Her hyper-aggression is vengeance with a reason, and her actions commensurate with her anger. This is underscored in the first altercation between Vanessa and Wolverton. After he has beaten and berated Vanessa as white trash, cut off her ponytail, and promised to perform sexual acts upon her corpse, she retrieves a handgun from her basket and holds him hostage. She proceeds to earnestly lecture him on his repugnant inclinations and, after questioning his faith in God, she puts a bullet into his neck. When it becomes apparent that he is still alive, Vanessa fires several more rounds until she believes he has died. Her

Figure 5.2   Violent femme: Vanessa Lutz (Reese Witherspoon) on her way to Grandma's trailer park in *Freeway* (1996)

Source: The Kobal Collection, The Picture Desk

actions are decisive—to rid society of the threat that he poses. Following this gory shooting, Vanessa drives to a roadhouse and nonchalantly orders a "double He-man breakfast and a large size cherry cola." There is no room for remorse, hesitation, or sentimental vulnerability, rendering this breakfast scene simultaneously comical and frightening. After having committed an act of savage violence, Vanessa's casual demeanor is one of a teenager who has spent an exhausting day at the mall. When she realizes that her clothes and face are smeared with Wolverton's blood, she excuses herself to the bathroom to wash up. Vanessa exhibits a callousness that is rarely accorded to women, especially young girls. Her indifference is registered differently from that of the male hardbody of the action genre. Although the steely expressions of Keanu Reeves and Vin Diesel are seen as signs of self-control and coolness, Vanessa's detachment is regarded as a psychological defect. This default illuminates more on acceptable gender roles than of Vanessa's personality. In her article on tough women in cinema, Stephanie Mencimer comments that,

> Women are still only allowed to be violent within certain parameters largely proscribed by what men are willing to tolerate … in the old action films, at the end, the male hero always walks away from a burning building looking dirty, bleeding sweaty yet vindicated (Remember Bruce Willis' bloody feet after walking through broken glass barefoot in *Die Hard*?).

> None of today's action chicks come near that level of messiness. The violence is
> sterilized. (Mencimer 2001: 18)

In *Freeway*, the violence is ugly and messy, and a source of cultural anxiety. The conventional association of violence with males and the masculine is reiterated in Roberts' statement that, "The long history of the angry youth in film, canonized by James Dean, has by and large been a male story—one where the individual is valorized and set in conflict with the traditional mores of his parents and the larger society" (2002: 222). While the male may have been valorized, the teenage girl is pathologized. Vanessa is diagnosed by the authorities as having an antisocial personality disorder, described by a staff member at the juvenile jail as, "a sophisticated criminal and extreme danger to society." Whereas Wolverton's homicidal tendencies are masked by the façade of white, bourgeois citizenship, Vanessa is paradoxically penalized for her justified rage. Institutional and social discourse has no modality for imagining the violent teenage girl beyond the juvenile delinquent. As vigilante as they may be, Vanessa's actions attempt to fulfill civic duties of social responsibility by purging the streets of predators where the law has failed. At one stage, Vanessa holds a John Doe (Michael Kaufman) at gunpoint and castigates him when he solicits her for sexual tricks. Confused and terrified, he pleads to her as to why she is terrorizing him. She shrieks in response, "Because I'm pissed off and the whole world owes me!" Vanessa then empties the contents of his wallet and locks him up in the trunk of his car. While her reasons may appear individualistic rhetoric, her resolutions are for the greater good of the community. Unfortunately, this is recognized by only a handful of characters. Take, for example, the exchange of final words between Vanessa and Mesquita (Alanna Ubach), a fellow inmate, after they have absconded from the juvenile detention center,

> *Mesquita*: So, uh, you won't think I sound all feminist and shit. It's like, the
> one thing that I learned in jail is that girls gotta help out other girls, you know?
> Especially convicts girls, cuz if they don't they'd oughta be fucking dead. You
> know what I mean?
>
> *Vanessa*: I hear what you're saying.
>
> *Mesquita*: Okay.

With Vanessa headed for Grandma's (without a happy ending) and Mesquita back to the rough L.A. barrio, they articulate girl guerrilla warfare and a politics of desperation. The girls have no choice other than to form an alliance against oppressive institutions that punish a growing underclass of disadvantaged youth. Roberts writes,

As part of a Latino gang and a convicted murderer, Mesquita represents yet
another facet of the underclass of Los Angeles. Similar to Vanessa's relationship
with Chopper, her relationship with Mesquita serves to highlight the allegiance
she feels to other teenagers who have 'been in the system'—others who are
considered beyond the pale of middle-class respectability and law-abiding
behavior. Vanessa's relationship to Mesquita, however, is also deeply connected
to their position as women. (Roberts 2002: 229)

Racism, sexism, age discrimination, and class divisions are rife in *Freeway*'s
nightmarish vision of a contemporary America where democracy is power owned
and wielded by an elite minority. Henry Giroux delineates this dire predicament,
stating that the "welfare system's most vulnerable citizens—the young and the
poor—[are] no longer a focus of social investment but a matter of social containment
... viewed as depraved rather than deprived, troubling rather than troubled" (2003:
107). Whereas Giroux singles out the young and the poor, *Freeway* affixes female
identity to this catalog of condemning traits. When Vanessa shrieks that she is
pissed off and that the whole world owes her, it is not bratty bitchiness or the
voicing of a personal agenda, but a public protestation of society's failures. The
violence enacted is not hubristic, but a desperate clawing for justice and political
citizenship. As a disaffected, inner city teenager, Vanessa's resorting to actual
violence exercises the only power at her disposal, "the power to discomfit. The
power, that is, to pose—to pose a threat" (Hebdige 1988: 18). She must challenge
the symbolic order that would see her as merely a "kid," "a pathological girl," as
a condition of entry "into the adult domain, the field of public debate, the place
where real things really happen" (Hebdige 1988: 18). Despite her struggles, she is
ultimately denied entry.

While the femme fatale of *noir* and the sexual thriller must meet a macabre
demise or face a lonely, depraved future, the bitch expands the possibilities for the
angry femme. *Heathers* and *Freeway* suggest two trajectories of how female rage
can instigate social change, or at the very least provide a critique of stifling notions
of girlhood. Although both films present radical bitch politics, their divergent
endings are revealing. Veronica's vented violence achieves real change. The high
school is a better place because of her actions, and order is restored when she
assumes the role as the benevolent defender of the meek. While she still retains
an air of (tolerated) toughness, Veronica is no longer deadly. The same cannot be
said for Vanessa.

She may have defeated the demon that was Bob, but the real demons of
poverty, illiteracy, and a criminal record still exist. In fact, it is her very outlaw
mentality—and her raging need to take things into her own hands in order
literally to survive—that offers a critique of the ways in which girl power's
tendency toward a 'Just Do It!' ideology leaves those in the grip of systemic
oppression completely outside the fold and, indeed, often further subjects them
to it. Despite the bluster of her angry outbursts, we cannot help wondering at

the film's conclusion, what exactly can this particular girl 'just do'? (Roberts 2002: 230–1)

Vanessa's militant bitch mentality finds no outlet for satisfactory resolve. Even after she has been exonerated of her outlaw status by Detectives Breer and Wallace, she is still resigned to the margins. While Veronica Sawyer's bitch politics can be reappropriated with a new application of makeup and a chic outfit, Vanessa Lutz's transgressive bitch politics (read as grotesque) is too wieldy and excessive to contain. Matthew Bright's film may have given us one of the most shocking, memorable, and brazen cinematic depictions of teenage female rage and reprisal to date, but the fact that Vanessa is hardly better off from where she began is telling. The femme fatale's grave may have merely been traded in for a barred cell or a ticket to ride to nowhere.

While feminism has made women the siren call for social change after the Second World War, the bitch's politics of desperation indicate constant resistance to these advances. The bitch is at her best when she practices a raw, fierce femininity that is not afraid to get down and dirty. However, this only bubbles to the surface under extreme circumstances. The tension created by the bitch cannot be sustained, and her rage must exhaust itself. The prominent body of the bitch amplifies her protests, but also magnifies the open wounds and faded scars of an ongoing conflict. The 20th century *fin de siècle* and multiple waves of feminist activism have still yielded no end in sight for the bitch. This is a conundrum repeated in *Hard Candy* (dir. David Slade, 2005), yet another reworking of the Little Red Riding Hood fairytale. After a rendezvous with a 32-year-old man she has met online, 14-year-old "Hayley Stark" (Ellen Page) drugs, tortures, and performs a mock castration on Jeff (Patrick Wilson) before forcing him to hang himself. Hayley seeks retribution for every underage girl Jeff has ever sexually assaulted and killed. When prompted, she raises the rhetorical question to her victim, "Was I born a cute, vindictive little bitch or did society make me this way?" for which there is never an answer. Her victory is less triumphant than it is unnerving and ominous. The film ends with the image of Hayley, her signature red hood over her head, disappearing down the long and winding road again, and once more the anonymous specter (for her real identity is never uncovered). For this bitch, *what*, and *where* to, now?

Chapter 6
Club Casualties: Go-Go(ing) Girls of Rave

The weekend has landed. All that exists now is clubs, drugs, pubs and parties.
I've got forty-eight hours off from the world, man. I'm gonna blow steam out of
my head like a steaming kettle. I'm gonna talk codshit to strangers all night. I'm
gonna lose the plot on the dancefloor; the free radicals inside me are freaking,
man! ... Anything could happen tonight, you know? This could be the best night
of my life! I've got seventy-three quid in my backburner ... Calling all crusaders
of the dancefloor in green-light mode. Disco queens, club casualties, c'mon!
Let's join forces. Let's hoof it—aah!
(Jip in *Human Traffic* [dir. Justin Kerrigan, 1999])

As with generations of youth before them, the youth of the 1980s and 1990s will
be remembered for their invention/desecration of culture, more specifically, the
rave subculture. The narrative of rave is one of ephemerality, where the present
is ambivalently conflated with the past and future—wistful recollections of last
week's phenomenal party, and the intense anticipation of next week's event. In
recent years, there has been a nostalgic revival with reunion nights, the release of
popular 1980s acid house compilations, and DJs returning to the older technologies
to mix the warmer analog with digital (see Lynskey 2002; Rosen 2000). This
look-back is an idealization of halcyon days and rave's supposed culture of
egalitarianism and freedom from the pressures of the everyday. The character of
Jip (John Simm) espouses this freedom in the epigraph. As Jip states, rave was a
space where "anything could happen."

This chapter focuses on the unpopular politics of club casualties, specifically
the invisible woman who implicates inequalities of power based on gender, age,
and class. These biases can be traced back to the beginnings of clubculture. Take,
for example, Dave Haslam's *Adventures on the Wheels of Steel: The Rise of the
Superstar DJs* (2001). In Chapter 6 of his book, Haslam pays homage to the soul
disc jockeys of the 1960s and 1970s in northern England, weaving together a
narrative through the experiences of Brian Rae who was one of the first DJs to
enter the business. Of particular interest and amusement was Rae's recollection
of the two go-go girls who were an integral part of his early acts. With their
choreographed routines and "short skirts on and tassels in all the right places,"
Rae acknowledged, "I got some good gigs, and I was making a name for myself
for having these girls" (quoted in Haslam 2001: 114). One of the dancers worked
in the printing department of Lockers, a metal fabricators in Warrington that Rae
was also employed at, and the other dancer was her friend (Haslam 2001: 112,
114). The females remain nameless, referred to only as "the go-go girls." In 1967,
Rae successfully auditioned for a job at the Twisted Wheel Club in Manchester,

with the session presided over by the reputed Ray Teret. As an establishment that prided itself on its serious Northern Soul music, "The Wheel was no place for commercial fripperies; the go-go girls stayed in Warrington" (Haslam 2001: 116). Whatever happened to the go-go girls is never broached, and we can only assume it was back to the daily grind of work and domestic duties for both of them.

Rae's anecdote brings to the surface a whole history and tradition of the (in)significance of females, especially young women, in public spaces of music and dance. Familiar images of the wallflower at the cotillion, the bikini-clad hip-swingers of an Elvis Presley Sunday matinee, the twirling skirts and sparkling high heels of a disco diva, the faceless housewives obscured by rockstar husbands—these abound not only in cinema and television, but also in the recorded annals of biographies, photographic exhibitions, and historical compendiums of eras of popular music. Typically, the female has been objectified under the assumed male gaze, made absent, or is regarded the type of trivial nonsense that ensured Rae's go-go girls stayed at home while he attended to the more important job of spinning records.

The absence of women can be seen in Michael Winterbottom's self-referential *24 Hour Party People* (2002) that layers elements of fiction over actual events. The film explores the evolving music and dance scene in Manchester, from The Sex Pistols through to the age of Joy Division, and ending with the headiness of rave culture and its eventual demise. The protagonist and narrator is Tony Wilson (Steve Coogan), the television personality and founder of Factory Records and the infamous Hacienda. Speaking direct to camera, Tony declares, "this is not a film about me … I'm a minor character in my own story. This is a film about the music and the people who made the music." Interestingly, but not surprisingly, women are marginalized in this rendition of musical history as wives, prostitutes, girlfriends, or groupies. When Joy Division's lead singer, Ian Curtis, commits suicide on the eve of the group's rise to stardom in America, there is no sign of his wife at the funeral proceedings. In one scene, Tony is caught by his wife, Lindsay (Shirley Henderson), receiving oral sex from a hooker in the back of a van in a parking lot. His response is largely nonchalant, and he only goes to find her after he has been sexually satisfied. Tony finds Lindsay in the washroom having sex with frontman for the Buzzcocks, Howard Devoto (Martin Hancock). This act of spite, however, never actually took place. As Tony leaves the bathroom after the confrontation, he passes a cleaner who is being played by the real Howard Devoto. Devoto turns to the camera and states, "I definitely don't remember this happening." With Devoto's face in a freeze-frame, in a voice-over Tony responds, "He and Lindsay insisted we make clear that this never happened, but I agree with John Ford. When you have to choose between the truth and the legend, print the legend." It is an example of the serviceability of women to a masculine narrative. The saucy and sordid story of a scorned lover's revenge has outweighed the truth. Tony and his male cohorts remain the center of the text.[1]

---

1   Ian Curtis' widow, Deborah Curtis, has attempted to write women and their experiences back into a primarily male-dominated music history with her biography

Aside from the Day-Glo girl on the dancefloor, the female is conspicuously nowhere to be found in the rave culture. Arguably, the most recognized female associated with the early rave scene was Claire Leighton. The 16-year-old from Cannock was the first person to die from ingesting Ecstasy in 1989 at the Hacienda, and it is important to note that Leighton's *victimhood* was the reason for her newsworthiness across the United Kingdom. Women are rarely seen to fit the image of the raving "folk devil" generated by early press reports of the scene, and as such they are often sidelined or made out to be "the innocent" (Pini 1997b: 153). As Maria Pini writes, "women's invisibility can be seen as twofold; their marginality doubled by a perspective which attends solely to the more visible— and traditionally more 'meaningful'—levels of involvement and so constructs male experience as the 'significant' object of its story" (Pini 1997b: 153). The prioritizing of male narratives and experiences becomes evident when we closely study the cogs of the rave subculture, that is, the economics that allow it to operate. I first look at the right(s) to party in rave, the altered rules of engagement for participants, and the assumptions made about its egalitarianism. In upholding rave as a halcyon youth movement, gross inequalities have been overlooked. While it is indisputable that rave's innovations opened up a space for new subjectivities and experiences, it was not without contradictions and complexities, which I explore through the presence/absence of women in rave. The chapter concludes with Doug Liman's *Go* (1999) to put the woman—the metaphoric spanner thrown in the works—back in the picture.

Behind the Strobes and Smoke: The Politics of Partying

The origins of rave in the United Kingdom were not to be found in the style capital of London, but hundreds of miles away in the Mediterranean, and born "at the zero degree of popular culture: the package holiday" (Melechi 1993: 30). With its alluring cocktail of sun, sea, and modern comforts at an affordable rate, the Balearic islands became a fashionable destination for British holidaymakers escaping not only the chilling winters, but also a dire socioeconomic situation at home. As Sheryl Garratt writes,

> By the mid-eighties, unemployment in Britain had reached a record high. Prime Minister Thatcher was fond of telling us we'd never had it so good, but despite the stories of champagne-swilling yuppies in the City and loadsamoney lads in the property and building trades, for many young Britons the reality was the dole or pointless job schemes. (Garratt 1998: 94–5)

Thatcherism decreed a clean break from the old ways in favor of libertarian capitalism and meritocratic ideals. However, it soon became apparent that the

---

documenting the career of Joy Division and its lead singer. See Curtis (1995).

scheme was deeply flawed, privileging a select minority while the situation for a growing unemployed and minimum-wage populace continued to deteriorate. To make matters worse, "Thatcherite assaults on collectivism, pursued through a whole range of policies, intentionally created a society that was fragmented and individualised" which contributed to a shared mentality of futility and cynicism (Collin 1997: 6–7). The promise of a dream had become the fulfillment of a nightmare for the working class, and youth in particular. Change was imminent.

While the town of San Antonio in the Mediterranean was the initial port of call for British tourists, it would be the beyond-the-brochure Ibiza on the other side of the island that would mark the beginnings of a worldwide club and subculture (Melechi 1993: 30–1). Descriptions of Ibiza's premiere dance venues, Pacha and Amnesia, painted images of fantasy playgrounds that starkly contrasted with the industrial nightspots in the United Kingdom. Matthew Collin recounts,

> they weren't discos as the British knew them, typified by tinny sound systems, tacky flashing lights and carpets sticky with stale beer. Ibiza's clubs had alfresco dancefloors illuminated by the moon and the stars, bubbling fountains, palm trees, plush cushioned alcoves, and extravagant, ever-changing décor. And the clientele! Transvestite floorshows, flash young blades from Barcelona with sculpted torsos and immaculate hairstyles, fiftysomething millionaires prancing in their suits, pop stars sipping champagne, flamboyant gays, people of all ages and nationalities. (Collin 1997: 49)

Here, the student backpacker could mingle amongst celebrities. This flew in the face of the British class system. A combination of ambience, housebeats, and happy pills promised an unending party, and fostered a collective sense of unlimited possibilities and bodies unhindered by social conventions. This, of course, could not be sustained. Shadowing the cycle of an MDMA trip, youth returning to Britain after their annual pilgrimage to the Balearic Islands experienced the ultimate comedown. The optimism would find no avenue for its expression, especially during the four consecutive terms of Thatcher's Conservative government.[2] Collin captures the sentiments of dejected travelers arriving back home,

> Back at Gatwick, they stepped off the plane into a country they'd almost forgotten. *Fuck London for its dullness* ... Where to now? Back to their parents' homes to plaster Amnesia posters over the walls of their bedrooms, sit back and drift away in reminiscence. Grey mood closing in. They'd changed, but Britain hadn't. (Collin 1997: 54)

From the mid-1980s, elements of the Ibizan clubculture could be seen making their way into the UK. House music began to trickle into music venues after being

---

2   Andrew Hill argues that Acid House was an affront to the Thatcherite project and compromised the government's "'grid' of control over the national space" (2003: 230).

imported by DJs and avid devotees of the genre, and Euro-fashion dance wear that was a "weird mix of Mediterranean beach bum, hippy, and soccer hooligan—baggy trousers and T-shirts, paisley bandannas, dungarees, ponchos, Converse All-Stars sneakers—loose-fitting" found its way into clubs (Reynolds 1999: 58–9). All were ways of trying to bring the holiday back into urbanity and the working week, and to restage memories of pulsating Mediterranean nights. This restaging was also an attempt to build a type of community partly organized around the idea of sameness. For instance, the unisex clothing and dress-to-sweat emphasis of the scene was crucial to the "perceived erosion of sexual differences" (Pini 1997b: 161).

The transcontinental drift of the Balearic experience would become acid house. It was initially an exclusive scene with only a handful of promoters operating the low-key events. The manic energy and music, however, could not be kept a secret for long. The success of evenings at clubs such as London's Shoom and Future saw more venues opening up, and one-off dance parties being staged around the country. It would herald the birth of rave as a new youth-associated subculture that would see a virtual explosion of rave parties between 1987 and 1989 in the UK (and globally). As a sociocultural phenomenon, it captured a significant moment in the history of popular youth culture. The rave ethos was not just about good times, but a better way of existing. It was evident in the PLUR (peace, love, unity, and respect) manifesto and the obvious hippie references, such as the Second Summer of Love and the smiley face logo (Bennett 2000: 101). The PLUR mantra opposed the more masculine traits of aggression and machismo perpetuated in rock subculture. As Angela McRobbie notes, laddishness was replaced with friendship, which saw men undergoing a "conversion to the soft, the malleable and the sociable rather than the anti-social" (1994: 168). The supposed demasculinization of identity and behavior was literalized not only through a reversion to infantilism and usurping stereotypically feminine traits, such as open affection, but also in the symbolism of bodies unshackled from dominant, patriarchal discourses. For instance, in the documentary *Better Living Through Circuity* (dir. Jon Reiss, 1999), British musician and artist, Genesis P-Orridge, states, "If you take something like a corporate logo, or you take a piece of commercial art or television, and then you cut it up and reassemble it, in a very real way you're also emasculating its power over you." Sampling, whether it was in the artwork or music of rave, revealed the malleability of culture, and therefore the malleability of identity and (gender) roles. Almost all interviewees in the documentary recounted, with verve, the inspired transcendental and egalitarian aspects of rave.

While it was able to fly under the radar as a subcultural formation, it would only be a matter of time before rave attracted public scrutiny. Initial media reaction was a mix of curiosity and eagerness to jump on the cultural wagon to cash in on the new fad. *The Sun* even marketed its own version of the smiley face logo t-shirt (Critcher 2000: 148). Predictably, the backlash followed once reports of drug overdoses and unruly behavior surfaced. The moral panic that surrounded the Mods, Rockers, Punks, and Skinheads in previous decades reappeared with a revised lexicon. The folk devil for the 1980s could now be identified by glowsticks and a slavish following of the Pied Piper on the turntables. Stoking the wrath of the justice system, a series of laws and sanctions were passed by the British government in an attempt to curtail "any event featuring amplified repetitive beats" (Rietveld 2000: 29). For instance, the Licensing Act (1988) granted police greater power to conduct inspections on licensed premises. The Entertainments (Increased Penalties) Act (1990) was a direct attack upon unlicensed rave events. Penalties included jail sentences of up to six months and hefty fines of up to £20,000 for operators. The severity of the Criminal Justice and Public Order Act (1994) treated both event organizers and participants as potential criminals. In reference to the Criminal Justice and Public Order Act, Steve Redhead states,

> Aimed at a particular dimension of dance music culture, and its coming together with the anti-materialism of new age travellers in the early 90s, this draconian Act, on the statute book since 1994, symbolically outlawed a new generation which had since the 80s fought the law—and nearly won—in establishing a new underground culture of music, drugs and lifestyle which eventually became mainstream as corporate 'clubculture' by the mid to late 90s. (Redhead 2000: xvi)

The stifling regulations saw ravers and organizers burrow deeper to evade prosecution. According to conservative estimates, the weekly number of ravers in Britain alone in 1994 was in the hundreds of thousands, which was no minor feat considering the panoptic gaze of the legal system and its agents (Merchant and MacDonald 1994: 18). Ravers saw their civil liberties as being violated. Their right to party had become political. Dissatisfaction with the state of the nation was acted out by ravers who extracted themselves from the home, school, or workplace to enter a space that defied the sensibilities of the everyday. Outlandish fashions and accoutrements, such as pacifiers, dolls, stuffed toys, and suckers—"knickknacks from childhood"—injected playfulness that refused the drabness of wintry dystopias in Britain (Farley 2000). Offering an existence comprised of the nonlinear cumulus of the past (memories, infantilism, and childhood), the present (living for the moment), and the future (the optimism of a renewed nation-state), rave was regarded a site for bodies in motion, spaces in transition, and fluid identities. Social divisions based on class, race, gender, and sexuality were ideally checked at the door. Morgan Gerard argues that the central paradigm of rave was its liminality (2004: 174). Its transgressive and transformative qualities were its greatest appeal. Even the decentering of the solo performer by an often faceless DJ (before the rise of the celebrity DJ) was significant as it rewrote the relationship between the artist and audience. As Philip Tagg argues, "techno-rave puts an end to nearly four hundred years of the great European bourgeois individual in music" (1994: 219). The individual on the floor became as important as the individual on the stage, elevating the status of the teeming masses of (mostly) young people. This would contribute to an overarching metanarrative/myth of rave as a utopian space, which shall be expanded upon shortly (this historical prelude is necessary to foreground how the heady optimism surrounding rave's revolutionary potential has clouded its instrinsically hierarchical structure).

The drug culture further reconstituted the rules of conduct in public spaces. Methylenedioxymethamphetamine (MDMA), otherwise known as Ecstasy, had two major effects upon ravers. Its chemical-altering and stimulant properties simultaneously created an overwhelming sense of emotional empathy with other ravers, and saw participants, hopped up on adrenaline, dancing for hours on end. Simon Reynolds describes how the new drug culture dissipated territorial rivalry in parts of London, as was seen between different soccer team supporters. It replaced the "box cutter-wielding troublemaker" with the "love thug" and "emotional hooligan" (Reynolds 1999: 63–4). The changing rules of engagement were captured by DJ Paul Oakenfold's remark about the Project Club, "The idea was 'if you're not into dancing, then don't come down'" (quoted in Reynolds 1999: 58–9). Rave community aspired to, and achieved in certain respects, a degree of egalitarianism with many bodies under one roof who were bound by a common agenda. Within this shared space, Ecstasy had the added effect of de-emphasizing sexual relations and conventional narratives of heterosexual romance (Hutson 1999: 69). As Reynolds writes,

> Both ecstasy and amphetamine tend to have an anti-aphrodisiac effect. E may be the 'love drug,' but this refers more to *agap ē* than to *eros*, cuddles rather than copulation, sentimentality rather than sticky secretions. E is notorious for making erection difficult and male orgasm virtually impossible. A real dick-shriveller, it also gets rid of the thinks-with-his-dick mentality, turning rave into space where girls can feel free to be friendly with strange men, even snog them, without fear of sexual consequences. (Reynolds 1998: 88)

Rave's altered dancefloor dynamics, seen as a shift in sexual politics, contrasted with the more traditional meatmarket of the club and pub scene. This had significant implications for female ravers. The rave scene represented, "an undoing of the traditional cultural associations between dancing, drugged, 'dressed-up' woman and sexual invitation, and as such opens up a new space for the exploration of new forms of identity and pleasure" (Pini 1997b: 154). Despite this fact, few studies have looked at how women fit into the scene. If anything, the missing woman still remains a recurring theme.

Work by Maria Pini has shown that the various clubcultural levels that critical attention gravitates towards is still predominantly male-centered. Women tend to be marginally represented in event organization, music production, drug distribution, and profit-making. As Pini states, "were we to chart an objectivist history of rave culture, focusing upon its more outwardly visible signs, women would make a very fleeting appearance" (2001: 30). When they are acknowledged, there is still an entrenched gender bias. This is evident when respected female disc jockeys are marketed as sexual icons in music magazines, which downplays their musical skills. Hillegonda Rietveld's own personal account is telling, "When I mention my experience in an electronic dance music group (as a programmer and keyboard player), the first question I often hear is: 'Were you the singer?'" (2000: 30).

While various theorists have attempted to reinsert women back into the subcultural landscape, much of the earlier subcultural literature has tended to locate females in the realms of teeny bopper pop or the domestic sphere. The focus has been upon how (young) women's cultural production and engagement with the outside world takes place largely within the private space of the home; for example, discussions with other girlfriends, reading romantic fiction, fantasizing over male idols pinned on their walls. By concentrating on bedroom/household culture, this problematically neglects the stasis in the personal circumstances of young women and girls, and their lack of power and opportunity in the political spectrum. As Bill Osgerby notes, while these discussions highlighted unique aspects of patterns of consumption by young women, it also underestimated their roles as an active (media) audience (2004: 121).

Studies of "bedroom culture" rely heavily upon what Paul Willis (1990) terms "symbolic creativity"—those activities and pursuits that arise from, and are integral to, the work performed to sustain human existence on a daily basis—which seek out the extraordinary in the ordinary. As a result, common culture is imbued with a relevance that is generally conferred to high art and aesthetics of fine taste. Willis' contention, that within the play of youth there is work, unravels the clear divisions between labor and leisure, politics and pleasure. Symbolic creativity becomes a "kind of humanly necessary work," in which new meanings are invented by applying human effort and capacities to "symbolic resources and raw materials (collections of signs and symbols for instance, the language as we inherit it as well as texts, songs, films, images and artifacts of all kinds)" (Willis 1990: 9, 10). It is a democratic mode of informal production that is no less valuable than material commodities of commerce. As signs are readily available to be reappropriated, resistance can be found in the most mundane of duties and in the most uninspiring of settings. In other words, social change takes place at a gestural and symbolic micro-level. However, these private acts rarely translate into public intervention. This becomes obvious from Willis' observations of the function of symbolic play for young women,

> these women make some space for rest and relaxation to be themselves for themselves—and symbolic materials play a part in this. The television gives them the minimum means of escape. Many have the television on all day. Like most viewers, they combine watching television with other activities. They glance at and listen to it throughout the day. Only when programmes that they like are on, do they try to sit down and watch them. (Willis 1990: 121)

In romanticizing the "twilight domestic world of the imagination"—where fantasy resists the demoralization of being housebound and being bored—the unequal distribution of cultural resources and means for social mobility are overlooked

(Willis 1990: 126). While the interludes of daytime soap operas watched over a cup of tea provide moments of relief and creativity, discontentment has merely been displaced with distraction as a short-term panacea.

Going My Way: Beyond the (G)rave

In Doug Liman's second film, *Go*, Ronna (Sarah Polley) is employed as a checkout clerk at a supermarket somewhere in suburban Los Angeles. She has no money, detests her dead-end job, and is facing eviction from her apartment on Christmas Day. It is Christmas Eve. On top of that, she has just been dumped with a double shift. Her youth sucks.

The day takes a turn when Ronna is accosted by two customers seeking Ecstasy. Unbeknown to our unlikely heroine, Adam (Scott Wolf) and Zack (Jay Mohr) are television soap actors collaborating with the LAPD in a narcotics sting. As the resident drug supplier, Simon (Desmond Askew), is in Las Vegas for a weekend jaunt of all-you-can-eat buffets, gambling, and strip joints, Ronna resolves to go directly to Simon's dealer. Over the course of the night, she manages to acquire the 20 hits of Ecstasy, evade drug trafficking charges, make a sizeable profit selling Paracetamol to unsuspecting youths at a warehouse rave party, have her life threatened (several times), and become a victim in a hit-and-run car accident. Ronna survives the ordeal *and* manages to make it to work the following day, albeit bruised and battered. It is just another day. And Ronna's life still sucks.

When it was first released in 1999, *Go* was described as a contemporary update of the narratives of the young and restless. But unlike James Dean, the characters were slated as having no sense of responsibility or legitimate excuse for protest. They were rebels without a cause. In an arts review for *The West Australian* newspaper, Mark Naglazas commented,

> No matter how hard you try you won't find too much significance in *Go*, not even a commentary on notions of fate, chance and redemption. So if *Go* has any meaning it's about capturing that moment of abandonment in people's lives when decisions are made without a thought for the consequences, when sheer intensity is the life-blood of one's existence. (Naglazas 1999: 97)

Naglazas' piece tellingly balks at the film's apparent depthlessness—a criticism that was also hurled at the rave scene itself. References to the film's "hip hyperkinetic pleasures at ground level," the "energy level," and "racing pulses" betray a preoccupation with the hypnotic, scintillating surface of *Go*.

Taking place over two days, *Go* moves erratically to the rhythm of a techno beat, and pulsates visually through its rapid editing and mobile cinematography. While Ronna's story constitutes one of three interlocking tales, the film starts and ends with the apathetic counter girl. The conclusion is almost analogous to its

Figure 6.1   Going nowhere fast: Claire (Katie Holmes) and Ronna (Sarah Polley) in *Go* (1999)

Source: The Kobal Collection, The Picture Desk

beginning. Ronna is hardly better off by the time the closing credits have begun rolling. There is no lightbulb moment, no promise of an Ivy League scholarship, and no prospect of a knight in shining armor coming to her rescue. Ronna goes back to her tedious job without any aspirations to be anything more than a disgruntled sales clerk. End of story, or so it would seem.

Go navigates the precarious terrain of the traditionally male-oriented domain of rave culture, and in doing so reveals it to be a highly problematic landscape. The film itself may seem an incongruous choice for a critique of rave and requires some qualification. It is, after all, 1999 America and not 1988 Britain.[3] While synonymous with the UK, it is important to remember that the subculture also had roots across the Atlantic with disco, house, and techno music as the precursors. Secondly, although *Go* is set nearly a decade after the heyday of rave, the unfulfilled promises of prosperity in an ailing 1980s Britain would find its counterpart in a great American Dream that had already reached its use-by-date for youths of the 1980s and 1990s. Ruminating on the relationship between youth, sex, drugs, and music (including the rave scene), Andrew Ross wryly remarks, "America's great social experiment, arguably, has not been democracy but the pursuit of happiness—

---

3   Rave did not start to feature prominently in films on either side of the Atlantic until the subculture had been appropriated by the mainstream and become commercialized.

that distinctively modern idea, ordained by the Fathers as an inalienable right and wielded ever since like some vibrating megadildo, available at the right price, though with no long-term effects" (1994). The tongue-in-cheek irony of the quote points to an inherent sarcastic streak of a Generation X disenchanted with their circumstances.

With no money or prospects, Ronna becomes the loaded signifier of disaffected youth. Her second-class citizenship—she is discriminated against on the grounds of being young, working-class, and female—becomes even more apparent in relation to the male characters around her. While Simon and his posse of friends are able to take off to Vegas for a weekend of debauchery, and Zack and Adam are urban yuppies (a financially-free, gay couple) who cruise the cityscape in their stylish Miata, Ronna has no means of escape and lacks the resources for upward social mobility. For this character, there is no Ibiza. Only the possibility of a Christmas Eve where anything could happen, including her own death.

Ronna trades in her pumps for the heavy Doc Marten boots of industry and production to become a small-time drug dealer. Shunning the shimmering fac(ad)e of rave, *Go* skirts around the sordid back alleys and secret rooms of the scene. It exchanges the hippie trippie vibe for the gritty underbelly of the capitalist creature that lurks beneath the surface of the funhouses of youth. The film is a reminder that the "production and consumption of 'fun' is as much about industrial production, distribution and exchange as traditional manufacture" (Redhead 1997: 93–4). Although Ronna's age (she is only 17 years old) and inexperience are partly to blame for her blunders and mishaps, her gender is the defining factor that shapes the course of events. By extracting this character from the customary mould of the Day-Glo girl, drug addict, chanteuse, or the accessorizing girlfriend, Ronna becomes difficult to monitor. In a business recognized as a male-dominated genre—from the organizers of events, to the DJs and the dealers—she wedges herself like a splinter in the finger (Tomlinson 1998: 198). This is underscored in a conversation between Ronna and her two hesitant sidekicks, Mannie (Nathan Bexton) and Claire (Katie Holmes). They are making their way to the apartment of Simon's dealer, Todd (Timothy Olyphant), so that Ronna can acquire Ecstasy.

> *Mannie*: But it's an evolutionary leap … You're moving up the drug food chain without permission.
>
> *Claire*: You shouldn't do this Ronna.
>
> *Ronna*: Why can't you chill the fuck out, okay? It's just once. When Simon gets back, we can still overpay for quarters if it makes you feel all warm and happy, alright? But this is my deal. Just sit back and relax.

Within a drug trade that is highly gendered, Ronna resides at the lowest rungs of rave culture's pecking order. As Fiona Measham points out, female drug suppliers are subjected to institutionalized sexism and are "more likely to be involved in the high-risk, low-reward aspects of drug cultures, with resulting health, financial and legal implications" (2002: 343, 346). The Dionysian dreamworld of rave reads more like Dante's inferno for Ronna as her movements are scrutinized within misogynistic spheres at every point.[4] Refusing to play the invisible, anonymous subject within rave, and unable to lose herself under the influence of Ecstasy or in the throes of abandoned dancing, Ronna's awkward position results in numerous attempts by the antagonistic male characters to literally erase her via imprisonment or death, or objectify her. For instance, after Ronna agrees to fill in for Simon's shift, he casually ends the conversation by offering her 20 dollars for a blowjob. When she meets with Todd, he condescendingly makes her strip down to her underwear to check if she is wired as a police informant, and he later tries to kill her. She is seen as dispensable. After enlisting Ronna to supply drugs, Adam and Zack accidentally run her down in their Miata later that night. They absolve responsibility for their actions by conveniently dumping her unconscious body into a ditch, thinking she is dead. When they realize she is still alive, they dump Ronna onto the hood of a nearby car like a soiled rag doll. Even those whose duty it is to serve and protect are out to get her. Police officer Burke (William Fichtner) automatically labels Ronna a "crack-whore" and attempts to arrest her for possession of drugs. He employs the bullying tactics that his position of authority grants, both as an officer of the law and an older man. Ronna's body is continually seen as a source of vexation, instigating and justifying the violence that is inflicted on her. Not only is she a minor, but she is also a female trespassing and breaking all the rules … and getting away with it. Ronna has, in Mannie's words, made an "evolutionary leap" but it is a precarious jump without guarantee of a working parachute.

With the backdrop of the rave as the site of struggle, Ronna's unpopular politics make use of hard economics to claim identity and autonomy. In a reversal of the utopian rave ethos, the ideal of community gives way to the importance of the individual. Wrenching the opportunities and resources from the hands of the socially and economically privileged, it is meritocracy Ronna's way. As Matthew Collin writes, "The dance-drug scene, as it did with technology, reappropriated libertarian capitalism and puts it to uses for which it wasn't intended" (1997: 7). Ronna's real achievement is that she has inserted a young, white, working-class female into this picture. Refusing to ride pillion, she pushes the driver out of his seat and commandeers the capitalist vehicle that would exploit her.

Ronna's exploitation is obvious from the onset of *Go*. When we first see her, she is listlessly working the cash register at her dead-end job for minimum wage. It is endured out of financial necessity. Like the checkout conveyor belt, she is on the human hamster wheel and going nowhere with her life. She is begrudgingly

---

4   In her study of women in club cultures, Fiona Hutton states how being a female drug dealer is a particularly risky business (2006: 108). Women need to avoid the law, and are also faced with potential suspicion, aggression, and intimidation from male dealers.

bagging groceries for a trailer trash, middle-aged housewife (Suzanne Krull) who has a toddler on her hip. When the customer snidely remarks, "Don't think you're something you're not. I used to have your job," Ronna snidely replies, "Look how far it got you." In a way, we are given a glimpse of one possible future for Ronna being played out. Her discontentment and bitterness is reminiscent of Jip's complaints about work to his colleague in *Human Traffic*.

> *Jip*: We spend nine hours a day, five days a week incarcerated in this wanky, fucking store, having to act like C3PO to any twat that wants to condescend to us, do you know what I mean? We have to brown-nose the customers, then we get abused by some mini-fucking Hitler who just gives us stick all day ... I take the corporate cock-shafting like the next person because I need to pay the rent. But if you ask me, the anti-Christ has been with us for a long time and he means business. Big business.

Unlike Jip, however, Ronna does not have the luxury of "forty-eight hours off from the world," or "seventy-three quid in [the] backburner." Soon to be thrown out of her apartment for not meeting her rent, even the lukewarm space of a squalid apartment and television set robs her of the twilight world of housebound daydreaming. Fueled by her own impromptu plan to avoid homelessness, Ronna's response is urgent and it must effect real change. Symbolic creativity is no option. While the insolent pout of dissatisfaction, the vitriol directed towards customers, or the cigarette shared during a five-minute work break with workmates may provide temporary respite, it is not enough.

In order to instigate change beyond the symbolic and gestural, Ronna must eschew the household/bedroom culture by literally moving beyond these spaces. Floating between the spaces of the supermarket, the dealer's den, the site of a narcotics sting, the dancefloor, and the ditch, Ronna's mobility is seen as disruptive because she transgresses demarcated, ordered spaces (Cresswell 1996: 87). As Daniel Martin states, a "disciplinary map cannot be constructed over an object which refuses to remain static" (1999: 84). This requires Ronna to use those attributes that brand her as the marked sign to her advantage, that is, she must manipulate the rules of the game. After realizing she has been set up by the police, she flushes the Ecstasy pills down the toilet before making a hasty exit from the premises. When Burke badgers her to make a deal and refuses to let her out of the house, she subverts the situation by threatening *him*. With malice and awareness, she sneers, "Do you know I'm only seventeen? I probably shouldn't be drinking this beer, should I? Seeing as I'm so underage and all." Swigging the Cerveza he offered upon her arrival, she keeps her watchful eye over him, implicating the police officer in the supply of alcohol to a minor. The tools of his trade—the law— are wielded against him. Ronna's transgressions are necessary tactics that allow her to slip between the cracks of systems of power, only to resurface later out of their reach. Ronna exemplifies how, as Fiona Hutton argues, "Female dealers can 'play the game' or negotiate in the hegemonic masculine world of dealing despite being excluded as the female 'other' lacking in subcultural capital" (2006: 52). She refuses to be fucked over by others.

Clearly, the myth of the anonymous (and androgynous) body in the space of rave is exposed in *Go*. The film calls into question postmodernist readings of rave that erase, at one extreme, authenticating narratives of selves. This assumes that identity politics becomes more difficult to justify, assemble, or codify, and inequalities of sexuality, gender, class, and ethnicity become atrophied in a pool of purposeful anonymity (Baudrillard 1994: 83). Identity and communal formation are reduced to blissful nothingness that, according to Ted Polhemus, captures, "Who is real? Who is a replicant? Who cares? Enjoy" (1997: 151). Antonio Melechi goes so far as to argue that subjectivity in rave is relinquished in "a seductive absence and enticing void where one can partake in the ecstasy of disappearance" (1993: 32). This idealistic, spiritual state imagines the transcendence of the body and consciousness, where markers of difference are temporarily erased, or rather forgotten. However, as we have already seen, gender is never neutralized, even in the fun factories of rave culture. Maria Pini captures this in the following statement, "the experiences of rave cannot be detached from the sexually-specific body ... a woman's perception that rave affords her an 'ungendered' sense of self clearly implies an escape from a body which is always already specifically coded, and such a claim would carry different implications and speak of different issues were it uttered by a man" (1997a: 117–18).

As Ronna's problematic positioning within the film shows, the notion of dissolved identity in rave is quixotic. This is also exemplified by the male characters whose masculinities are not only emphasized, but also problematized. Traditional sites of male roosting—economics and the justice system—become the domains of power struggles. The men are initially like strutting peacocks. However, their aggressive and flamboyant exhibitions of machismo are swiftly unveiled as all show and no substance. Adam and Zack turn out to be a squealing, cowardly couple. Burke never succeeds at capturing the criminal. His manliness is further compromised by his sexually suggestive remarks and gestures to Zack and Adam. For instance, he keeps commenting on their impressive pectorals at inappropriate moments. When they retire to Burke's home for Christmas Eve dinner, Zack is confronted by a naked Burke at one point. Instead of recoiling, Burke insists the two try out how comfortable his bed is. On top of that, Burke (as with his oddball wife) has a passion for selling Confederated Products, which he vehemently insists is "not Amway." When Simon and his three companions go to Las Vegas, their boys' weekend quickly goes awry. First, Tiny (Breckin Meyer) and Singh (James Duval) become incapacitated and confined to their hotel room with chronic diarrhea from buffet-induced food poisoning. Meanwhile, Simon and Marcus' (Taye Diggs) visit to the Crazy Horse strip club for an evening of manly indulgence ends up with the former shooting one of the bouncers before making a clumsy getaway. Upon returning to Los Angeles, Simon is tracked down by the wounded thug, Victor Jr. (Jimmy Shubert) and his boss, Victor Sr. (J.E. Freeman), who is also his nagging father. Both are seeking bloodlust revenge. But instead of a violent brawl, the opposing parties end up squabbling over which part of Simon's arm should take a bullet as payback. By this point, the adversarial standoff has become a ridiculous afternoon nattering session held in Todd's apartment. Todd himself has transformed from a psychopathic drug dealer into an obliging, happy host. His about-turn is comically captured as he gives the Vegas ruffians directions to Simon's apartment. With gentlemanly politesse, he obligingly sketches a map describing the most efficient route, pointing out the finer details, such as possible delays from road constructions. When Claire, who has been held hostage, sarcastically remarks, "Why don't you just drive him yourself? You could help him pull the trigger," the irony is lost on Todd. His masculine bravado is an act.

In *Go*, masculinity as an unstable formation is exemplified by Marcus who is by far the film's most competent male. Articulate, athletic, dressed in the uniform of authority—the suit—and oozing with confidence, he is a perfect specimen of dominant masculinity. However, as the only African-American character in the narrative, his authority is continually undermined by others. In Vegas, Marcus is mistaken on two occasions for being a low-level laborer—first as a washroom attendant and then a parking attendant. His blackness overrides his masculinity. Even when his blackness is not an issue, his position of power is questioned and attacked from other angles. After telling his friends that he practices tantric sex, the others are in disbelief that a protracted orgasm need not culminate in ejaculation. When Marcus admits that he has not done so in six months, this display of discipline and self-control is read as perversity and an opportunity to humiliate his manliness.

The inadequacies and defective façades of maleness in *Go* are not isolated. In *Human Traffic*, Jip is hounded by the fear of impotence. While his insecurities stem from a lack of control over his own body, Koop's (Shaun Parkes) results from an imagined loss of control over an external one. Paranoia leads him to believe his girlfriend, Nina (Nicola Reynolds), is cheating on him. Koop's male ego renders him irrational and infantile. Their drug dealing friend, Moff (Danny Dyer), is similarly lacking in the masculine department. Aside from being unemployed and still living at home with his parents, Moff experiences several embarrassing turns. His father (Terence Beesley) finds out that Moff has racked up a £145 bill for phone sex, and his mother (Carol Harrison) later catches him masturbating in his bedroom. The female leads are undoubtedly the most self-assured characters in the film. Nina is the only character brave enough to quit her miserable job at a fast food restaurant, shouting "Fuck this" at her sexually harassing boss, Martin (Giles Thomas), before ceremoniously throwing down her cap and storming off the premises. She has, in Lulu's (Lorraine Pilkington) words, given "her Mc-Job the finger." Lulu herself refuses submission. When she finds out her boyfriend has cheated on her, she promptly tells him where to go. There are no tears or tantrums.

In *Groove* (dir. Greg Harrison, 2000), a plurality of masculinities are also displayed and problematized. Colin (Denny Kirkwood) proposes to his girlfriend, Harmony (Mackenzie Firgens), at a rave party. After taking Ecstasy, Colin's inhibitions are loosened and he makes out with another man, only to be caught in the act by Harmony. She later initiates sexual intercourse out of fury, exasperation, and a need to reinstate his heterosexuality. The following day, she is crying in her bed while a remorseful Colin is alone in the bathroom. The hedonism of rave has consequences, and utopia comes at a price. The acts of free love and freedom have ramifications long after the warehouse has been emptied and the sun has risen. As the films discussed in this chapter have shown, no one, and no problem, magically disappears in the delirium of drugs and dance. *Go* poses a particularly interesting case study because its primary narrative revolves around a young, female character, and through a series of comic mishaps, the film upsets common perceptions of rave as a utopian, egalitarian space where identities dissolve into the beat, the lights, the dance, and the drugs.

Rave occupies that ambiguous area of overlap between pop and politics, resistance and appropriation. It is "riddled with Zen-like paradoxes. It's music of resistance and acquiescence, utopian idealism and nihilistic hedonism. It's both escape route and dead-end, orgasmotron and panopticon, space and cage" (Reynolds 1998: 92). It would be the perfect subcultural manifestation for a generation stuck between a rock and a hard place, but desperate for something better. Ronna represents this desperation for real change (not only for youth but also young women). When Mannie casually asks, "What are we doing New Year's?" the day after the rave party, Ronna grins. She knows there is always next weekend, and that she will be there, "going for broke, going for more, or, maybe, just going" (Olsen 1999: 7). Unlike Rae's dancing girls, this Go (Go) girl is not staying at home.

Chapter 7

Boys to Men and Back Again: The Historian and the Time Traveler

Mysterious thing, time. Powerful, and when meddled with, dangerous.
(Dumbledore in *Harry Potter and the Prisoner of Azkaban* [dir. Alfonso Cuarón, 2004])

As the line above suggests, to control time is to control how bodies move through space, thereby influencing how history unfolds. The ability to alter its speed and direction reveals not only a fascination with the unbounded potential of scientific theory, but also unveils our deepest desires, dreams, and demons. Even the most basic fantasy of turning back the clock is an exercise in nostalgic longing and regret. The time traveler—be it the historian or fictional character in a novel—commands an unparalleled power to rewrite the course of events (Lee 2008: 1–2). It is of no surprise then that the time traveler's domains of science, science fiction, and history have been, and continue to be, dominated by men, from the likes of Herodotus and H.G. Wells to Stephen Hawking. As such, time travel is also invariably a display of masculine power that is rarely questioned.

In this chapter, attention is directed to representations of masculinity in relation to the rites of passage narrative where the boy becomes a man. With a focus upon the teenage time traveler, these portrayals of boyhood allow an exploration of the strained relationship between power, time, history, and (crises of) identity. The chapter is anchored to a concluding analysis of *Back to the Future* (dir. Robert Zemeckis, 1985) and *Donnie Darko* (dir. Richard Kelly, 2001). These two films present a rare moment in cinema history where coincidence becomes poetic synchronicity. With the benefit of hindsight, the films travel back to the past to cover half a century of American history, with the 1980s overlap a site of divergence. Robert Zemeckis' *Back to the Future* is a commentary of the 1980s and 1950s from the perspective of 1985, whilst Richard Kelly's *Donnie Darko* is a retrospective of the year 1988 that was produced in 2001. Through the discourse of a masculine crisis and a homeland under attack, I look at how these time travel films capture the zeitgeist of two eras that were ideologically chasms apart.

Time Travelers: Masters of the Universe

In his seminal essay entitled "Time, work-discipline, and industrial capitalism," E.P. Thompson discusses the impact of "time-sense" in modern society (1967: 56–97). Tracking the structural changes in the workforce from the 13th century onwards, Thompson identifies the intimate relation between notions of time, labor, and hegemonic order. He argues that the movement from pre-industrial to (post)industrial society witnessed a transition from a *task*-oriented to *time*-oriented economy where the timekeeper became omnipotent (Thompson 1967: 60–61). The former, most common in domestic and village industries, was characterized by an individual's investment in the completion of daily tasks and a natural work rhythm, "sheep must be attended at lambing time and guarded from predators; cows must be milked; the charcoal fire must be attended and not burn away through the turf … once iron is in the making, the furnaces must not be allowed to fail" (Thompson 1967: 60). With the advent of industrial time and widespread implementation of the timekeeper—both the mechanical apparatus and the wardens in charge of employee timesheets—came a new way of regulating people's movements (Thompson 1967: 82). The onus of productivity had been transferred from the individual to external agents that were beyond the control of the laborers. This is exemplified in the following excerpts from a mill and factory worker respectively in the 1800s,

> There we worked as long as we could see in summer time, and I could not say at what hour it was that we stopped. There was nobody but the master and the master's son who had a watch, and we did not know the time. There was one man who had a watch, I believe it was a friend who gave it him. It was taken from him and given into the master's custody because he had told the men the time of the day. (Samuel Kydd quoted in Mantoux 1961 [1928]: 417)

> … in reality there were no regular hours, masters and managers did with us as they liked. The clocks at the factories were often put forward in the morning and back at night, and instead of being instruments for the measurement of time, they were used as *cloaks* for cheatery and oppression. Though this was known amongst the hands, all were afraid to speak, and a workman then was afraid to carry a watch, as it was no uncommon event to dismiss any one who presumed to know too much about the science of horology. (Myles 1850: 12–13)

The effects of manipulating and withholding time underscore the potential debilitation of being bound to the clock. There is a lucid delineation between those who wield time and those who do not. The latter are either shackled so tightly to its constraints or are pushed outside of it as to become ghosts of the past that are destined to be forgotten. Time carries with it a host of ideologies of power and progress coded not only by class but also gender. Thompson captures this in the following observation,

> A clock or watch was not only useful; it conferred prestige upon its owner, and a man might be willing to stretch his resources to obtain one … despite school times and television times, the rhythms of women's work in the home are not wholly attuned to the measurement of the clock. The mother of young children

has an imperfect sense of time and attends to other human tides. She has not yet altogether moved out of the conventions of 'pre-industrial' society. (Thompson 1967: 69, 79)

So tied to the wristwatch and the calendar are we that it is commonsense to "keep time." In fact, it has become naturalized to the point that our biorhythms now coincide with the mechanical clock. As a result, we forget that the modern concept of time is not natural but culturally constructed. In other words, the precision of a timepiece that segments events into measurable units does not create a universal and egalitarian sense of global time, where business hours in Tokyo correspond to an exact equivalent in London simply shifted nine hours ahead. By accepting that absolute, linear time is a myth, this presents a plethora of possibilities as events need not be recorded according to seconds, minutes, hours, and days. Willingly abandoning her wristwatch, a foreigner's visit to some rustic, hillside town may be experienced and measured according to the pungent aroma of freshly brewed coffee when the cock crows, the warmth of the skin at the hottest point of the day, the fatigue in the legs after walking, and the setting of the sun. In this example, the urgency and immediacy of (keeping) time is loosened and a more personal concept of it emerges where, as Stephen Hawking proposes, "clocks carried by different observers would not necessarily agree" (1988: 151). A close examination shows us that time dredges up, but also masks, inequalities of power. This becomes even more evident when history is mixed into the fold.

History is often regarded as shorthand for truth and reality—the "official" past and even common knowledge—with artifacts and documentation providing the evidence of a chain of events. Reliance upon history to provide a faithful, unbiased recollection overlooks that it is an ideological construct, a selective process of reconstruction and recovery of the past. Keith Jenkins draws attention to the importance of distinguishing between the past as "all that has gone on before everywhere," and historiography as the "writings of historians" (1991: 6). Writing history is not an exact (human) science. It produces an incomplete jigsaw puzzle with missing sections, parts that are forced together, and pieces that are buried beneath others. This problematically ignores marginalized, unpopular narratives. Jenkins states,

> One cannot recount more than a fraction of what has occurred and no historian's account ever corresponds precisely with the past: the sheer bulk of the past precludes total history ... As the past has gone, no account can ever be checked against it but only against other accounts ... there is no fundamentally correct 'text' of which other interpretations are just variations; variations are all there are. (Jenkins 1991: 11)

Historiography cannot claim an objective distance between the subject of interest and the historian's vantage point. As E.H. Carr points out, "The historian belongs not to the past but to the present" (1987 [1961]: 25). Narrative accounts of yesterday are saturated with the ideologies of today. We can therefore argue that "doing" and writing history functions as a type of time travel, permitting a visit to a past with an assured return ticket back to the present. The excursion, however, is never without an agenda. The historian and time traveler are like the tourist who frames events and people, and has "the power to reshape culture and nature to its own needs" (MacCannell 1992: 1). Their long hands reach back to a bygone era and, by taking what they want, they permanently alter the landscape. Historiography allows the present to write (over) the past. It is temporal and spatial neocolonization at its most efficient.

Time travel in cinema has featured as a viable way of correcting space, society, and self. As tales of heroic conquests, the dominance of men is evident. The Time Traveler (Rod Taylor) in the film *The Time Machine* (dir. George Pal, 1960), Superman (Christopher Reeve) who reverses time by making the Earth spin in the opposite direction to save Lois Lane (*Superman*, dir. Richard Donner, 1978), the cyborg (Arnold Schwarzenegger) and human renegade, Kyle (Michael Biehn), in *The Terminator* (dir. James Cameron, 1984), and the treasure-hunting dwarves in *The Time Bandits* (dir. Terry Gilliam, 1980) are but a few examples. The outcomes are predictable. Humanity is saved, order is restored, and the protagonist is triumphant. Time travel enables a masculine reassertion of control over the past, present, and future. On the rare occasion that the Other is granted this privilege, it becomes clear that the reasons for, and effects of, time tampering are markedly different. One of the few films to showcase a female time traveler is *Peggy Sue Got Married* (dir. Francis Ford Coppola, 1986) in which Peggy Sue (Kathleen Turner) is transported back to 1960 after she suffers a heart attack at her high school reunion. Time travel in this case is not intentional. Peggy Sue's ticket to ride enables her to resolve personal issues of depression, associated with middle-agedness and a failed marriage, by reinvigorating her youthfulness. She does not rewrite public history, but rather influences her own private experience. Even in the slapstick teen film, the concept of time travel as an extension of masculine authority is not lost. For example, in *Bill and Ted's Excellent Adventure* (dir. Stephen Herek, 1989), two high school students embark on an odyssey to pillage the past in a time travel contraption disguised as a telephone booth. In danger of failing History, Bill (Alex Winter) and Ted (Keanu Reeves) go back in time to collect historical figures for their class presentation. Their list includes Socrates (Tony Steedman), Joan of Arc (Jane Wiedlin), Abraham Lincoln (Robert V. Barron), and Sigmund Freud (Rod Loomis).

> In an amusing series of extended gags, historical figures are let loose on modern society—Joan of Arc ends up leading a Jazzercise class, Napoleon pigs out at an ice cream parlor, Beethoven admits Bon Jovi's *Slippery When Wet* among his favorite pieces of music, and there is that ever so delightful moment when a cop asks Sigmund Freud 'Why do you think you're Freud?' to which the natural rejoinder is 'Why are you so certain I'm not Freud?' (Scheib 1992)

Bill and Ted are modern-day historians who literally take from the past for their own purposes. As intellectually vacant as they are, the pair improve social conditions by inventing a radical philosophy that unites all life forms in the not-too-distant future. Their masculine competence—they are responsible for universal peace and score two bodacious princess babes in the process—is asserted.

Exit Wounds: Making the Man

Coming-of-age films serve a pedagogic function by showing young boys what the model male *is* by what it *is not*, with the comedy genre an exaggerated representation. David Greven describes the contemporary teen comedy as a veritable pageantry of "boys in men's drag, donning and discarding codes of manhood that have dominated our culture for so long that they seem 'natural'" (2002: 15). While boyhood offers temporary relief from adult responsibilities, the baggage of gendered identity is never left behind. Greven writes, "Crammed with disorientating, occasionally bracing and shocking forays into socially perverse sexual and gendered territories, [the films] nevertheless squarely situate these forays in the primeval forest of teendom, from which boys emerge as men" (2002: 21). The teen film enacts an equivalent of the construction of the self-made man. The teenage boy gains autonomy through experience and the passing of time. His wayward tendencies and impulses are groomed into acceptable forms of adult masculinity and mastery. Suspect masculinities are either expelled, rendered harmless, or erased. For example, in *40 Days and 40 Nights* (dir. Michael Lehmann, 2002), Matt's (Josh Hartnett) vow of celibacy for 40 days *must* reach an end. His bout of abstinence is firstly seen as abnormally unhealthy by his male friends (even his brother, a priest-in-training, cannot resist his manly urges and admits to trysts with nuns), but Matt regains their faith after having sex with the girl of his dreams for 38 hours straight. Obviously impressed by his performance, the admiration of Matt's compadres re-establishes his credibility. Yet another example is the *American Pie* trilogy in which Jim's (Jason Biggs) various conquests bring him one step closer to accomplished manhood. In *American Pie* (dir. Paul Weiz, 1999), he succeeds in losing his virginity in high school. In *American Pie 2* (dir. J.B. Rogers, 2001), he reaches emotional maturity in college when he is able to admit his feelings of love to his girlfriend, Michelle (Alyson Hannigan). In the final film, *American Wedding* (dir. Jesse Dylan, 2003), Jim marries his high school sweetheart and assumes the role of the family man. These young men demonstrate the tightly policed borders of gendered identity by actualizing the rifts and rigors of dominant masculinity.

For teenage boys in cinema, problems of male identity are often milestones en route to manhood, whether it is a farcical comedy or a staid drama. Exemplary of the former is *Dude, Where's My Car?* (dir. Danny Leiner, 2000). While it panders to a certain toilet humor, nevertheless it relays conventional gender roles where dominant masculinity prevails. Jesse (Ashton Kutcher) and Chester (Seann William

Scott) spend the entire movie trying to track down their missing car, which has their girlfriends' anniversary gifts in the trunk. Inspired by the promise of what they believe will be sexual treats, the two dimwitted dudes become embroiled in an intergalactic mission that sees them pursued by "hot alien chicks," a sect of science fiction fanatics, a transsexual, and Barbarella-esque Martian men, amongst others. Although Jesse and Chester are hardly mature, serious men by the film's conclusion, they do succeed in saving the universe and redeeming themselves before their girlfriends (which is their crowning glory). This reinstates their heteronormativity against the abnormal sexual types that surround them, and cancels out any trace of a homosexual bond.[1]

At the opposing end of the genre spectrum is a film such as *Dead Poets Society* (dir. Peter Weir, 1989). A drama set in 1950s Vermont, it follows a group of senior students at a private boys school called Welton Academy and their journey towards autonomy and manhood. Encouraged by their unconventional English teacher, John Keating (Robin Williams), each overcomes personal obstacles that pave the way to manhood. Knox Overstreet (Josh Charles) transcends his fear of rejection to pursue a seemingly unattainable girl who later falls in love with him, Neil Perry (Sean Robert Leonard) opposes his domineering, right-wing father to follow his acting passion, and Todd Anderson (Ethan Hawke) goes from being a self-deprecating, meek pupil into a confident individual and admirable leader, which is showcased in the final rousing scene. After the English teacher has been unreasonably blamed for Neil's suicide and dismissed from his post, Todd stands atop his desk in defiance of the academy's draconian headmaster to show his support of Keating's teachings. Although *Dead Poets Society* offers a strong critique of an uncomplicated, wondrous 1950s, it still models an ideal masculinity that revels in primal impulses.

The group's journey is sparked by their formation of a secret club, called the Dead Poets Society, spurred on by Mr Keating. Meetings are convened in an old Indian cave deep in the woods where, as Keating describes, "spirits soared, women were wooed, and gods were created." It is a literal translation of Greven's primeval forest of teendom, complete with rituals, bongo drums, and chants. Heightened masculinity is imagined and then practiced. In one instance, the rebel of the collective, Charles Dalton (Gale Hansen), draws a lightning bolt on his chest with red lipstick, which he claims is an ancient Indian warrior symbol for male virility. As an inspiring narrative of the trials and tribulations of male adolescence, *Dead Poets Society* is also a cautionary tale. The stirring finale does not smokescreen

---

1   In a brief scene, Jesse and Chester's car pulls up alongside that of über-man, Fabio (played by himself), at a set of traffic lights. In a public display of his machismo, Fabio revs up his car engine, wraps his arm around the woman in the passenger seat, and then passionately kisses her to parade his sexual prowess. Unwilling to be shown up, the Dudes mimic and respond to each of Fabio's challenges. The scene culminates in Jesse and Chester locking lips, in deep embrace, and completely oblivious of the homosexual nature of their act.

the fact that Keating has been fired for his unconventional teaching methods, that Neil's suicide arose from desperation (he is about to be sent to military school after disobeying his father's order to cease acting classes), and Charles has been expelled for his retaliation against the school board. As Jonathon Rayner comments, "Keating's return to Welton to replay his adolescent revolt only reinforces the gap between youth and age, and the compromises the former vilifies only to accept them at a later stage" (2003: 202). The safety of the cave and forest cannot last forever. Punishment and discipline await those who emerge from the wilderness. The severity of their exit wounds is proportional to the deviation from acceptable gender roles. The difficulty in offering alternatives to masculine ideologies has witnessed the harking back to the mythic past or nostalgic times. The Dead Poets' attempt to return to a bygone era of deceased bards and primordial man to find their true identities is symptomatic of an ongoing sociocultural trend.

Rites of passage films rarely question crises of masculinity because there is the tacit assumption that any abnormalities will naturally be sorted out over time and boys will become men. However, it was precisely the threat of the masculine destabilized that saw the discipline of Men's Studies develop in the 1970s. By the time of second-wave feminism, there was already a deeply set anxiety over men's legitimacy as the default sign of power. This had begun percolating in the 1950s (Urschel 2000: 408). Anne McLeer argues that postwar cultural texts established and popularized narratives of domestic bliss and the new nuclear family, while "Race, youth, and gender revolt foment[ed] under the surface of the American dream in the 1950s" before exploding in the 1960s (2002: 82, 83). This prompted a feverish cultural investment in the family as the symbol of the nation's stability and order where Father always knew best. With their neatly manicured front lawns and sit-down Sunday roasts, the Cleavers and the Andersons *were* middle-America. The 1950s was captured and contained as Pleasantville. But it was a myth that would not last long.

By the 1960s, and certainly in the 1970s, the dominant patriarchal institution was deemed in dire straits. From the housewife returning to the workforce, to the Communist Charlies hundreds of miles away who were winning *their* war, such events were regarded as proof that the nation-state and American sovereignty were being assailed from foreign agents and those within the homeland (Walzer 2002: 210). The apprehension became discernible in cultural representations that sought to re-erect a patriarchal structure to restore the social balance. Nowhere was this more apparent than in the über-masculine action films of the late 1970s and 1980s.

The lingering aftershocks of the Cold War and Vietnam paved the way for a generation of hulking heroes whose bodies seemed as indestructible as their spirits. Sylvester Stallone's characters of Rocky and John Rambo, Jean-Claude Van Damme's renditions of a life-size G.I. Joe in his numerous roles, and Arnold Schwarzenegger's personalities in *Commando* (dir. Mark L. Lester, 1985), *Predator* (dir. John McTiernan, 1987), and the *Terminator* oeuvre seared into the national psyche an image of infallible American patriotism and resilience. The mutilation of the masculine, for example, the gunshot wound or bodies beaten to a pulp, was read as a direct assault on the United States. The nation was redeemed only by a rebuilding of the body that would see Schwarzenegger's alter egos overcoming exhaustion and injury to avenge the wrongdoings done unto him and the country, and Rocky rise time and again from a blood and sweat-drenched floor from a near ten-count humiliation. The perfect body was iconic of brute strength, discipline, endurance, industrialization, and the successful colonization of public space (Lee 2005: 560). These films re-injected into the public imagination the legendary heroes of the past that existed in history books, folklore, and popular memory—the early frontiersmen, Wild Bill Hickok, and the lone cowboy. Violence was justified on the grounds of restitution, with Father rightfully the head of the home, the righteous President at the helm of the nation-state, and America commanding the free world.

By the 1990s, the picture would be very different. Cynthia Heimel went so far as to call for a masculine revolution because contemporary men had, according to Heimel, been buffeted from all manner of conflicts and lost control (1993: 119, 122). In short, they had been pussy-whipped. The catchcry of a full-fledged masculine crisis spawned a culture of activism to reclaim men's entitlements. The decade was declared as "the time of the men's movement, a time for American males (primarily straight, white, and affluent) to bond together and affirm themselves as males" (Ruether 1992: 13). A salient body of literature flooded bookshelves in the style of self-help manuals with such telling titles as *Absent Fathers, Lost Sons: The Search for Masculine Identity* (Corneau 1991), *Fire in the Belly: On Being A Man* (Keen 1991), *In A Time of Fallen Heroes: The Re-creation of Masculinity* (Betcher and Pollack 1993), and *Masculinity in Crisis: Myths, Fantasies, and Realities* (Horrocks 1994). Robert Bly's *Iron John: A Book About Men* (1990) was typical of this new genre in its support for a nostalgic masculinity. The author advocated a "deep masculine" of ancient and exotic, tribal rituals and mythology to counter the effects of (post)industrial, capitalist, and consumer society (Pearce 2001: 51–2). Bly's veneration of the "Wild Man" and "interior warrior" reflected a growing concern of the emasculation of America's fathers and sons, and the urgency for an almost primal state of manhood unhindered by the trappings of contemporary society (1990: 6, 146). It could also be seen in the explosive popularity of the Promise Keepers. This non-profit Christian organization paralleled Bly's Wild Man with the righteous man of biblical times. In both cases, the past represents an idyllic place where an essentialist model masculinity is to be rediscovered, and where home—the domain of the patriarch—is to be found.

Public shows of male solidarity—hundreds of men descending upon a city to preach and praise a fraternal brotherhood—and backlash against feminism in the 1980s were bolstered by the military machismo of American forces in the 1993 Gulf War that "exultantly declar[ed] that it had 'kicked' the last remnants of the 'Vietnam syndrome'" (Ruether 1992: 14–15). Cinema, as a potential ruse for conveying dominant discourses of gender identity, was at the same time being undercut by a new breed of films that problematized the roles of men. The "office movie" genre became emblematic of a "'disempowered' middle-class white male: the drone of the new corporatized, managerial late capitalist culture ... caught in the mid-rungs of an increasingly corporate culture" that Bly had warned about (Hunter 2003: 72). With the shift to digitalization, the worker's worth had an early expiry date. This had severe repercussions. With self-control and self-making no longer within their power, the loss of employment had "deep identity consequences even more powerful in the rhetoric of masculinity than anti-institutionalism" (Catano 2000: 4). The indignation of unemployment denied a large population of men from earning a living, thus compromising their ability to fulfill the traditional role of provider for, and authoritarian of, the family.[2] Two films that illustrate this corporate emasculation are *Falling Down* (dir. Joel Schumacher, 1993) and *American Beauty* (dir. Sam Mendes, 1999).

In *Falling Down*, William Foster (Michael Douglas), also known as D-FENS, embarks on a mission to "return home" after a day at work. In the exposition, he is caught in gridlocked traffic. Trapped in his car and tormented by the sweltering heat, a pestering fly, the cries of children in a nearby vehicle, and the sensory overload of blinking road signs, William's sanity snaps. After abandoning his vehicle, he enacts his own warped justice upon those whom he encounters en route to his ex-wife's house. William causes grievous bodily harm, destroys public property, and commits murder along the way. In his cubicle-class uniform of horn-rimmed spectacles, short-sleeved shirt, and tie, he is a frightening vision of the suppressed office drone. Teetering on the razor's edge of rationality, restraint, and manic fury, this image of a man more computer geek than commando brandishing a shotgun in gangland suburbia is a disturbing portrait of American masculinity attempting to reclaim the homeland. As the tagline for *Falling Down* states, it is the "adventure of an ordinary man at war with the everyday world." However, the character's quest is doomed from the onset. Not only is he estranged from his ex-wife, Beth (Barbara Hershey), and young daughter, Adele (Joey Hope Singer), but a restraining order further prevents him from even seeing them. At the film's conclusion, William's only means of redemption is death. In a final confrontation with the police, he is fatally shot when he reaches for his firearm that turns out to be a plastic water pistol.

---

2   A similar trend could be seen in the United Kingdom after heavy industry was severely curtailed in the 1980s and 1990s. For instance, the coal mining industry had all but disappeared by the mid-1980s as a result of labor laws, and Britain went from being one of the leading automotive exporters to falling under foreign ownership by the mid-1990s. As Andrew Marr remarked in the documentary *History of Modern Britain* (dir. Francis Whately, 2007), "The world of heavy industry, heavy men and heavy unions was no longer, it seemed, wanted. This was a defeat for the industrialised Britain of brick terraces, grit, soot and smoke and clank, making way now for a new economy—un-unionised, privatised, white-collar, the service economy, the blander, virtual economy."

American Beauty continues the theme of the suburban nightmare in the corporate age. Lester Burnham (Kevin Spacey) is a middle-aged, apathetic writer at an advertising magazine company who lives a dull existence without determination or fulfillment. Lester joins the ranks of a growing, expendable workforce. His family life is miserable. He despises his wife, Carolyn (Annette Bening), as much as she does him, and his only child, Jane (Thora Birch), thinks he is an embarrassment. Lester is, in his own words, "a gigantic loser." But his failures are not an isolated case. We see the first sign of a man taking back the power that middle-management has stripped from him when Lester blackmails his supervisor, Brad Dupree (Barry Del Sherman), for an impressive severance package after being unfairly fired. When Brad accuses him of being "one twisted fuck," Lester smugly retorts that he is "just an ordinary guy, with nothing to lose." In that instant, he becomes the all American (anti)hero. Latham Hunter writes, "Cue the music. Lester strides past the cubicles and out of the office, pumping a fist triumphantly in the air. Every time I hear this 'ordinary guy' line, I think about *American Beauty*'s color scheme: the frame is frequently washed in reds, whites and blues" (2003: 79). Lester's reinvention involves shedding his timid office demeanor, working out with weights in the garage (surrounded by the male accoutrements of tools and a workbench), reasserting his presence in the home, pursuing his daughter's teenage friend as an object of lust, and smoking pot with the neighbor's son. The making of the self-made man (through a regression to youth) is evident in a scene midway through the film. Carolyn returns home from work to find a new vehicle parked in the driveway. Entering the house, she sees Lester toying with a remote control car in the living room. The ensuing icy conversation contrasts Carolyn's frustration and petty nagging with Lester's simultaneous cool (teenage) defiance, and husbandly arrogance and assertiveness.

> *Carolyn*: Uh, whose car is that out front?

> *Lester*: Mine. 1970 Pontiac Firebird, the car I've always wanted, and now I have it. I rule!

> *Carolyn*: Uh-huh. Where's the Camry?

> *Lester*: I traded it in.

> *Carolyn*: Shouldn't you have consulted me first?

> *Lester*: Hm. Let me think. No.

Lester's recovered manhood is juxtaposed alongside a lineup of "aberrant" masculinities that live next door—an openly gay couple, a closet homosexual ex-marine, and an artistic loner who is more interested in philosophy than frat parties and football. Ironically, it is Lester who meets a gruesome demise at the film's conclusion. Colonel Frank Fitts (Chris Cooper) makes a move on Lester thinking he is gay, only to have his advances rejected. Frank later shoots dead his neighbor. *American Beauty* offers no convenient manifesto for an ideal masculinity, and no easy resolution for the characters' individual journeys. Lester's rite of passage ends with a bullet through the back of his head.

Both *Falling Down* and *American Beauty* present masculine identities that shift uneasily in their boots. Whereas the 1970s and 1980s action films asserted a calculated violence that was integral to a system of domination, the disorganized violence of the 1990s office films was a sign of its entropy (Connell 1995: 84). Aggression and forcefulness had gone from being displays of control to signs of desperate struggle. With masculinities no longer "individual possessions, but … institutional practices located in structures of power," dominant masculinity becomes a point of friction that elucidates the slippages, cracks, and contradictions of the center (Hearn 1996: 206). When the William Fosters and Lester Burnhams of the world—white, middle-class, heterosexual, married men—have lost control, it is a serious undermining of traditional gender genres. The so-called 1990s masculine crisis is, as Hunter writes, "symptomatic of an ongoing process through which the patriarchy broadcasts a fragility that has never really come to fruition" (2003: 74). The following section focuses on two films to explore further this idea of masculine power in trouble, within the context of the time travel narrative. When linear time is corrupted, this has implications for those who control history, opening up the potential for chaos and creation.

I've Got A Tikka To Ride: Teen Time Travelers

The plot of *Back to the Future* begins in small-town USA in the community of Hill Valley. It is the year 1985. Our hero, Marty McFly (Michael J. Fox), is a typical high schooler who dreams of being a rockstar, the weekend, and a new set of wheels. Marty's journey back in time is set in motion when enlisted by his nutty professor friend, Doctor Emmett Brown (Christopher Lloyd), to assist with a science experiment. During the test trial of a time travel contraption—a souped-up DeLorean—that Doc has invented, the pair are hunted down by Libyan terrorists from whom Doc has stolen plutonium to fuel the machine. After witnessing the fatal shooting of his friend, Marty flees in the DeLorean and is dispatched 30 years to the past. He must seek out a young Doc to help him return to 1985. The mission is complicated when Marty accidentally comes into contact with his mother, Lorraine Baines (Lea Thompson), who disastrously develops a crush on him instead of her future husband, George McFly (Crispin Glover). With Marty's very existence in jeopardy, he must manipulate events so that they are able to run their natural course. Equilibrium is only restored when his parents are brought together at the Enchantment Under the Sea Dance where they kiss for the first time, fall in love, and seal the future as Marty knows it.

Figure 7.1   Masters of the temporal universe: Doc Brown (Christopher Lloyd) and Marty McFly (Michael J. Fox) in *Back to the Future* (1985)

Source: The Kobal Collection, The Picture Desk

In the year 1985, the situation is less than ideal. Marty's father, George, is a spineless geek terrorized by local bully Biff (Thomas F. Wilson), and his mother is a dispirited alcoholic. In fact, Biff has even infiltrated the McFly home—sexually harassing Lorraine and terrorizing George. Marty's older siblings, Linda (Wendie Jo Sperber) and Dave (Marc McClure), are dowdy, stuck in dead-end jobs, and hardly role models for him. They are certainly not the faces of a new generation. Even Marty's own sense of worth is continually battered. When his band, The Pinheads, audition to play at the annual dance, they are dismissed as devoid of talent and being too loud. Chastising by a tyrant of a teacher adds further insult to injury. Mr Strickland (James Tolkan) sees Marty as an extension of his loser father. When Strickland cruelly taunts that, "No McFly ever amounted to anything in the history of Hill Valley," Marty's defensive reply is, "Yeah, well history is gonna change." But in order to realize this, Marty must travel back in time for this to occur. Riding the tail end of the Baby Boomer era, *Back to the Future* looks to 1950s idealism to seek solutions to an ailing 1980s of rising divorce rates and unemployment.

Upon arriving in 1955, Marty is faced with the same condition of defective masculinities that plagued him in 1985. Biff is ever the detestable lout and George the village idiot, both representing the extremities of destructive machismo and cowardliness. Marty's function as time traveler allows him leverage to intercept history by reforming certain individuals to alter the social hierarchy. After befriending George, Marty cajoles him into believing that Lorraine has affections for him. A plan is devised by which George will, upon cue, rescue her from Marty's advances to flaunt his manly competence on the night of the dance. The plan is botched when Biff reaches the couple first and tries to take advantage of Lorraine, thus forcing George to overcome his fear of the thug and deal with the situation for real with his right hook. In that moment, George reclaims his manhood and takes back what is rightfully his. Romance is kindled between George and Lorraine, leading to that critical kiss on the dancefloor.

Marty's intervention ratifies a quintessential 1950s America to reinstate the boundless potential of the future. This era has featured as a mainstay in collective memory as a safe and splendid time. Popular culture and public celebrations then and today continue the illusion of a model decade that boasted its innocence, glamor, and white-bread values. The zeitgeist of the era was encapsulated by the likes of Lucille Ball, Marilyn Monroe, John Wayne, and Gene Kelly. Slapped with a fashionable vintage tag, the imperfections of the 1950s have been largely ignored. This is hinted at in the political nuances that run throughout *Back to the Future*. The mayor of 1985 Hill Valley is an African-American, Goldie Wilson, who is running for re-election. His motto proudly reads, "Progress is his middle name." In an almost identical fashion in 1955, we witness the current mayor's election van doing rounds in the town square. While the slogan is the same, this time the face that stares back at us is that of Red Thomas, a middle-aged WASP. The intertextual political reference comes to the fore when a teenage Goldie Wilson (Donald Fullilove) is sweeping the floor of the local diner and lecturing George on taking a stand against Biff's coercive tactics. When Marty accidentally divulges Goldie's future, the ensuing conversation that takes place between them and Goldie's boss, Lou Caruthers (Norman Alden), underscores the centrality of Baby Boomer success and optimism.

> *Goldie*: No sir, I'm gonna make something out of myself. I'm going to night school and one day I'm gonna be somebody.
>
> *Marty*: That's right! He's gonna be mayor!
>
> *Goldie*: Yeah, I'm—mayor. Now that's a good idea. I could run for mayor.
>
> *Lou*: A colored mayor, that'll be the day.
>
> *Goldie*: You wait and see, Mr Caruthers, I will be mayor and I'll be the most powerful mayor in the history of Hill Valley, and I'm gonna clean up this town.
>
> *Lou*: Good. You can start by sweeping the floor.
>
> *Goldie*: Mayor Goldie Wilson. Like the sound of that.

The comic effect of the scene relies upon our knowledge that Goldie will in fact become a successful political figure in less than 30 years time. It is comforting to know that an even better future is approaching, where justice and liberty will ensure the deserving are rewarded. In short, progress is imminent. We know because we have already seen it.

Marty's impact upon the future is no less than miraculous. By the end, he has unwittingly improved it altogether. Doc's death has been prevented. Lorraine and George have morphed into an attractive couple and highly respected members of the community—Lorraine is no longer a frumpy, dissatisfied housewife, and George is an acclaimed science fiction novelist. Biff has also been reduced to an emasculated sycophant doing odd jobs for the family. In this switch, conventional gender roles are put back in place with Father the head of the home and the outsider (Biff) victoriously kicked out. Marty's elder brother and sister have also transformed from social outcasts into hip, young adults with enviable jobs and clout. This scenario is testament to Reaganite meritocracy and Boomer opportunity. The template of the 1950s has been grafted onto the 1980s. At the conclusion of *Back to the Future*, Marty and his girlfriend are whisked off to the future by Doc on another mission. It is history in the making, once again. In the DeLorean, Marty is the living hand of history. To borrow from E.H. Carr, he is the scribe and chronicler of tomorrow, today, and yesterday (1987 [1961]: 14).

Familiar depictions of (teenage) time travelers as masters of the temporal universe are twisted in Richard Kelly's *Donnie Darko*. While *Back to the Future* basks in the potential of the 1980s and the glories of a golden past with its burnished nostalgia, *Donnie Darko* sketches a darker, more cynical portrait of the decade. Whereas Marty McFly's travels take him eventually back to contentment in the present, Donnie Darko's journey is locked in the past (of 1988) where the future is uncertain and celebration has been replaced with a wake. Set in October 1988 amidst a looming presidential election, *Donnie Darko* tells the story of a disaffected teenager who must save the universe from collapsing in on itself when the events of one parallel universe collide with another. Donnie (Jake Gyllenhaal) escapes death when a plane engine mysteriously plummets from the sky and crashes into his bedroom. When he should have been asleep, he was sleepwalking at a country club golf course. This short-circuits the natural course of events. Guided by a six-foot rabbit named Frank (James Duval), a macabre traveler from the future, Donnie is instructed to carry out a series of increasingly violent acts while sleepwalking to realign the space–time continuum. If he fails, Frank informs Donnie that the world will end in "28 days, 06 hours, 42 minutes, and 12 seconds." Donnie's acts of vandalism—he puts an axe into the head of the bronze "Middlesex Mongrel" (the school's mascot), graffities "They made me do it" on the pavement, and floods the school premises—escalate to arson and eventually murder. Catastrophe is averted only through the protagonist's gruesome death which reverses time. This replaces one reality where Donnie lives but loved ones die, with another in which Donnie's life is sacrificed instead, rendering it "a distorted version of *It's A Wonderful Life*" (Felperin 2002: 34).

The ending is déjà vu of the film's beginning, but this time Donnie is killed (he is laughing hysterically to himself moments before). In the extended DVD version of the film, we see that he has been impaled through the chest by a wooden beam from the ceiling.

Described by Lucius Shepard as an "effective period piece," *Donnie Darko* represents 1980s conservative America as a time of pseudo psychobabble and profitable sloganeering, relentlessly driven by an apocalyptic paranoia (2002: 113). Donnie's mystifying somnambulistic episodes point to a psychosomatic manifestation of wider ailments plaguing a society already rotting at its core. As Mark Olsen so aptly describes, beneath the "dreamily, idyllic neighborhood, full of leaf blowers, power-walkers and double-sided refrigerators" there is a "creeping sense that something is amiss, as if the skewed, off-kilter sensibility of David Lynch had moved in across the street from John Hughes' well-adjusted sensitivity" (2001: 16). *Donnie Darko* foreshadows the social and political unease that would pockmark the nation throughout the 1990s, and is a scathing commentary of the greed and hypocrisy of a post-Second World War generation that enjoyed the spoils of their success, but left behind the debris of an American dream. James Walters argues that,

> a central conflict exists between [Richard Kelly's] nostalgia for a decade in American history and his desire to reevaluate and problematize its Reaganite cultural ethos, which effectively promoted capitalist greed and social responsibility … [*Donnie Darko*] depicts a dystopian fantasy world in which dark, uncomfortable possibilities are played out and explored, rather than a type of utopian fantasy in which an individual's dreams and desires can be indulged. (Walters 2008: 191, 199)

Walters outlines how the use of iconic 1980s references, from fashion to music, are employed in *Donnie Darko* to render that historical period as strange and unsettling, instead of encouraging feelings of belonging and familiarity for the audience. This engages us in a self-conscious critique and enquiry of the decade (Walters 2008: 191, 198). Comparing *Back to the Future* with *Donnie Darko*, there is a palpable movement away from blind faith in the virtues of the nation and a promising future, towards the jaded cynicism and suspicion seen as characteristic of Generation X (a child of the 1980s, Kelly was 26 years old when he directed *Donnie Darko*). This generational divide is manifested in the numerous crises of identity and moral conflicts experienced by the characters in *Donnie Darko*. The characters' confidence in capitalist civil society, which Carole Pateman argues is structured by patriarchy and patriarchal institutions, now falters (1988: 25).

The dramatic ideological shift between the Baby Boomers and Generation X can best be explained with Francis Fukuyama's 1992 monograph *The End of History and the Last Man*. In an impressive but misguided display of empirical facticity, the author cites the rise and fall of regimes—from monarchies and aristocracies, to fascism and socialism, and with specific reference to the collapse of communism in the Soviet bloc in 1989—that have left liberal democracy as the only "competitor standing in the ring as an ideology of potentially universal validity" (Fukuyama 1992: 42). This signaled the final stage in the ideological evolution of mankind in which primitive governments would naturally be superseded by the superior paradigm of uniform liberalism and equality (Fukuyama 1989: 3–18). However, as Mark Poster explains, "Fukuyama's celebration of the end punctuates more than anything else the era of unselfconscious patriarchy" (1997: 64). Indulging in the afterglow of America's supremacy in the Gulf, the book is a homage to this superpower as the virile, virtuous protector of not only the sovereign state, but also the entire world. It is reminiscent of, even nostalgic for, an American-centric 1950s confidence before it was tainted by the rise of anti-Americanism and the protest movement in the 1960s and 1970s. Boasting technological advancement, economic prosperity, moral integrity, unity, and power, Fukuyama's "end of history" serves to preserve the image (and myth) of strength and superiority. Ultimately, this deluded end of history is a resplendent structure made of glass and ersatz metal that is beautiful and dazzling to gaze at. But when the foundations are shaken, this utopic creation begins to slide and topple to reveal its flimsy scaffolding. Liberal democracy and the American way are left vulnerable and naked, with their weaknesses unveiled as the dust rises and eventually engulfs them. This analogy not only refers to the destabilizing of the nation-state, but also the masculine authority that underpins it.

Unlike the Watergate scandal which damaged public trust and demanded severe reparations, high-profile court cases in the 1990s, such as the impeachment of then-President Bill Clinton in 1998 and the marathon murder trial of OJ Simpson in 1995, demonstrated that two decades later, perjury and homicide would become a source of entertainment. It would make a mockery of the justice system. America's golden era was rapidly becoming a distant memory. With polls indicating greater support for Clinton after his affair was made public and Simpson's acquittal despite damning evidence against him, it seemed moral bankruptcy was no longer a symbolic skeleton in the closet to be ousted. Rather, it was to be expected. The distinction between right and wrong had become relative, easily swayed by the convincing words of a high-priced team of attorneys. The failure of the system is clearly evident in the injustices that remain unpunished in *Donnie Darko*. The futility is emphasized in the defining track in the film, a cover of the 1982 Tears For Fears song "Mad World," which describes "familiar faces, worn-out places, worn-out faces" that go nowhere because there is "no tomorrow" (Jules 2001).

Following in the wake of the so-called crisis of masculinity, *Donnie Darko* resumes the theme of (masculine) control lost using the time travel journey. The film is a parable for troubled times seen through the eyes of a teenager coming of age. As Olsen comments, "If last year's *Ginger Snaps* mapped the trials of female adolescence through the bloody bodyshock and revulsion of the horror film, then *Donnie Darko* applies the mind-warping possibilities of science fiction to teenage male development, exploring alternate worlds hidden within the fabric of everyday adolescent reality" (2001: 16).[3]

Within the alternate worlds, Kelly eschews a purely romantic reminiscence of the 1980s. This is conveyed through the treatment of the male characters. There are few models of adult masculinity to be admired and aspired to. For instance, the most popular man in the community is a self-help guru, Jim Cunningham (Patrick Swayze), who bears all the external signs of masculine success—wealth, charisma, confidence, and power (recurring images of his stately home are a constant reminder of Jim's status). However, this paragon of power is hollow on the inside. Like the traveling medicine man of old with his suitcase of bogus serums, Jim's mottos and steps towards self-empowerment have no real effect and become the butt of Donnie's jokes. In one scene, Jim visits the local high school to host a motivational seminar for the students, teachers, and parents. One by one, he delivers advice to cure a host of problems such as high school bullying and low self-esteem (one of the participants is actually a paid child actor we have seen earlier in Jim's "Cunning Visions" infomercial). Frustrated with the empty rhetoric, Donnie takes to the microphone, calls Jim out on his useless counsel, and begins to administer his own advice.

> *Donnie*: Are you telling us this stuff so that we can buy your book? Because I gotta tell you, if you are that was some of the worst advice I ever heard.

> *Jim (to audience)*: You see how sad this is?

> *Donnie (to the various people onstage)*: You want your sister to lose weight? Tell her to get off the couch, stop eating Twinkies, and maybe go out for field hockey. You know what, no one ever knows what they want to be when they grow up. You know it takes a little, a little while to find that out. Right Jim? And you. Yeah you. Sick of some jerk shoving your head down the toilet. Well, you know what? Maybe you should lift some weights or, ah, take a karate lesson, and the next time he tries to do it you kick him in the balls.

> *Jim*: Son. Do you see this? … This is an anger prisoner, a textbook example. You see the fear, people? This boy is scared to death of the truth. Son, it breaks my heart to say this but I believe you are a very troubled and confused young man. I believe you are searching for the answers in all the wrong places.

> *Donnie*: You're right actually. I am. I'm pretty troubled. And I'm pretty confused … and I'm afraid, really afraid … I think you're the fucking Anti-Christ.

---

3   *Ginger Snaps* (dir. John Fawcett, 2000) is a coming-of-age horror story. A teenage girl, Brigitte (Emily Perkins), must choose between becoming a werewolf and joining her sister in a murderous pact, or relinquishing the tight bond with her sibling.

**Figure 7.2   Dystopian vision of the 1980s: Donnie (Jake Gyllenhaal),
                  Gretchen (Jena Malone), and Frank the Rabbit (James Duval) in
                  Donnie Darko (2001)**

Source: The Kobal Collection, The Picture Desk

While Donnie is cheered on by the students at the end of his diatribe—equal
parts admiration and mockery—he is escorted out of the auditorium by the
teachers for being a menace to society. Later on, Jim is exposed as being part of
a child pornography publishing ring. The most influential and revered man in the
community turns out to be a sham, and Donnie's jibe that Jim is the Anti-Christ
turns out to be shockingly closer to the truth than anyone could have imagined.

   As for Donnie's father, Eddie (Holmes Osborne), there is something strange
about his authority. He is the archetypal WASP who stands for the Great American
Dream. He has the impressive home, a white picket fence with double garage, a
doting wife, and three children. Kelly explained that the visual aesthetics of *Donnie
Darko* attempted to evoke "a Norman Rockwell feeling to Middlesex" (2003:
xxxviii). However, the façade of white-bread America is swiftly dismantled at the
start of the film when the pleasantries of a "sitcom family mealtime discussion"
go askew (Kerr 2002: 45). Talks of the upcoming presidential election between
George Bush Sr. and Michael Dukakis, and the eldest daughter's aspirations to
enter Harvard escalate into caustic name-calling between Donnie and Elizabeth
(Maggie Gyllenhaal), Accusations of Donnie's mental illness and inane debates
on how to correctly use the F-word fly in the face of civility. Sordid secrets behind
the smiling faces in suburbia erupt on the surface like an abscess. Eddie's reaction

is a muffled laugh at the ridiculous nature of the discussion. Similarly, when Eddie and his wife are called in to see Principal Cole (David Moreland) after Donnie has verbally abused one of his teachers by telling her to forcibly insert a Lifeline exercise card into her anus, Eddie chokes back his laughter as Rose (Mary McDonnell) looks on in consternation.[4] Eddie's is not a publicly paraded masculinity. It exhibits few of the hallmarks of power that Jim exhibits. Instead, Eddie's command and knowledge only surfaces in private moments and those knowing glances shared between a select few. This is most telling in a deleted scene from *Donnie Darko*. In a father-to-son conversation in which he tries to convince Donnie that he (Donnie) is not clinically insane, Eddie unloads a stream of hackneyed sayings. Realizing that they are placebos for an otherwise complex situation, Eddie then strips his paternal advice of its nonsense to reveal the root of Donnie's predicament.

> *Eddie*: Be honest. Tell the truth. Even if they do look at you funny. They will. They'll call you fool. Tell you wrong. But there's something you gotta understand son, and that's almost all of those people are full of shit. They're all a part of this great big conspiracy of bullshit. And they're scared of people like you. Because those bullshitters know that you're smarter than all of them. You know what you say to people like that? Fuck you.

In this case, Father does know best. But no one gives a damn. The most honest people in the film are labeled as mentally unstable or as unsuitable figures of authority. Their truth-telling is continually undermined. It is a commentary of the state of the nation in no uncertain terms. In fact, Donnie's mental illness functions to detract from real social issues. Philip Kerr writes,

> Donnie's shrink, played by Katherine (*Butch Cassidy*) Ross is working on the assumption that her patient is borderline schizophrenic, rather than the witness to a phenomenon first described by Stephen Hawking. Wherein lies the true significance of the movie's initially puzzling time period, for September 1988 was when Hawking's book *A Brief History of Time* was published, and in which he described the possibility of time travel through worm holes. (Kerr 2002: 45)

Donnie's astute observations are reduced to the ramblings of a mad man, even though he appears to be the only stable center while everything around him plunges into confusion and chaos. The medical diagnosis of borderline schizophrenia has repositioned the parameters of deviation and depravity, shifting the blame from a dysfunctional society in denial onto the individual. The symptoms, not the cause, have become the focal point. A perfect example of this hypocrisy and misguided

---

4   The "Lifeline" exercises are part of Jim Cunningham's self-help program. Participants are given hypothetical character dilemmas on Lifeline cards which they must place on a spectrum split into the polar extremes of fear and love.

blame takes place during a school concert. While the pre-teen dance troupe, Sparkle Motion, perform to Duran Duran's "Notorious," Donnie is torching Jim's house. Intercutting between the two, there is irony in juxtaposing the young girls with their silvery Lycra dresses and adult pouts strutting onstage—a repulsive image of endorsed child exploitation and excess—as the home of a pedophile goes up in flames.

Arguably the most credible of male characters in *Donnie Darko* is Professor Kenneth Monnitoff (Noah Wyle), a physics teacher at the high school. As one of the few people able to understand time travel, Kenneth is able to validate Donnie's theories of pre-ordained destinies and alternate universes, thereby reinforcing that the teenager's visions may be a very real possibility rather than delusional rants. As with Eddie, revelations of the awful truth (that Donnie may not be crazy) are only to be uttered in an empty classroom as there is no place for its public acceptance. When the Professor later informs Donnie that by encouraging progressive thinking he may end up losing his job, it is a defining moment in the narrative. Scheming politics, conservatism, and the persuasiveness of spin doctoring have taken precedence over the pursuit of truth and knowledge. Through the depictions of its male leads—Donnie, Jim, Eddie, and Kenneth—it is obvious that the integrity of the institutions of civil society, that is, education, medicine, law, and family have been irrevocably damaged. The ideological apparatuses of the state have all but deteriorated.

Straddling the tripartite dimensions of time where he is literally at the crossroads of past, present, and future, Donnie's ability to reverse events allows him to become the self-made man and to assert control, but it also requires him to relinquish it. His visions offer two outcomes that trap him in a moral dilemma. If he lives, justice is served but those closest to him (such as his mother, youngest sister, and girlfriend) die and the universe is obliterated. If he dies, the universe remains intact and the others are spared. However, all knowledge of the heinous crimes committed, such as Jim's pedophilia, is erased. In fact, the destruction of the Tangent Universe is paralleled by a dystopic future of corruption and fears of the coming of the end (one could say we are living it right now—global environmental disaster, a worldwide financial crisis, the constant fear of terrorism and nuclear annihilation). Fukuyama's grand vision of a unified, liberal democracy will never arrive. For Donnie, there is no idyllic past or nostalgic masculinity to turn to for the answers. Unlike Bill, Ted, and Marty McFly, Donnie is unable to completely reimagine history as his ability to navigate the space–time continuum is restricted. Kelly's depiction of the once formidable time traveler as a frustrated teenager with limited powers reads like a barometer of our dark times. The frustration of being wedged between a dysfunctional past and an even more defective future manifests itself in Donnie's bouts of violence. As with D-FENS in *Falling Down*, the desperation of the characters' actions are guided by esoteric missions to return home to destinations that are sinister and somber. As the end approaches, Donnie watches dark clouds gathering in the distance, like an ominous black vortex, as his girlfriend's corpse lies in the passenger seat of his car. As he counts down, he says with a sense of relief, "I'm going home." The lyrics of

"Mad World"—"The dreams in which I'm dying / Are the best I've ever had"—are a fitting epitaph for Donnie's final moments before his death. It does not get any better, or worse, than this.

Although there is no fanfare to salute Donnie's heroic self-sacrifice, his act of time traveling is far from insignificant. Futility is replaced with hope as the actions, no matter how small, of a lonely teenager prove to have an impact on a cosmic level. Donnie's power derives from what he leaves behind—a conscience and sensory memory—which present possibilities for change, reinvention, and creation. This is actually articulated in two points during the narrative. During English class, Miss Pomeroy (Drew Barrymore) asks Donnie to give his opinion on Graham Greene's *The Destructors*, specifically the acts of vandalism carried out by a group of children who rip the inside of a house apart, flood it, and knowingly burn a pile of money hidden in a mattress.

> *Donnie*: … destruction is a form of creation. So the fact that they burn the money
> is ironic. They just want to see what happens when they tear the world apart.
> They want to change things.

Donnie's response is an omen of things to come. His acts of destruction, and his own destruction, leave a deep impression behind. In a later scene during a hypnotherapy session, his psychiatrist, Dr Thurman (Katherine Ross), similarly forecasts the consequences of his actions.

> *Dr Thurman*: If the sky were suddenly to open up there would be no law, there
> would be no rule. There would only be you and your memories, the choices
> you've made and the people you've touched.

After Donnie has reversed time, characters relive the same events with only a vague feeling that they have experienced it all before in the Tangent Universe. In the final montage sequence, for instance, Frank (Elizabeth's boyfriend, who is dressed as a giant bunny for Halloween) touches his eye because in another reality he was shot in the eye and died. Jim is sobbing uncontrollably because his crimes are exposed and knows he is a ruined man. Kenneth cannot sleep because he has that strange sensation that something terrible is going to happen—and it does. The characters remain troubled. This emotion lingers. It does not simply disappear.

In the final scene, Gretchen (Jena Malone)—who in this universe has never even met Donnie—joins a crowd that has gathered outside the Darko home the day after he has been killed. She and Rose Darko stare at each other for an unusually long amount of time. Gretchen waves to Rose who then returns the wave. In the script, Gretchen is described as if "trying to locate a memory that is slipping away," while Rose "seems to recognize Gretchen … from somewhere in the vast reservoir of her memory" (Kelly 2003: 105). There is recognition that their existences are interlocked, even though they have never crossed paths in this world. The weight of Donnie's actions become lucid at this point, as do his last words, "I hope that when the world comes to an end, I can breathe a sigh of relief because there will be so much to look forward to." His legacy is to ensure that the "hours of pain and darkness" will not be forgotten, and that history will not repeat itself *exactly*. Events will no longer simply be seen as random coincidence, absolving us of all responsibility. Considering the current socioeconomic and environmental climate, Kelly's film was a prophetic warning. The blind acceptance of the state of the world gives way to the curiosity of *why* it is so. Through Donnie's acts of destruction comes the creation of a tactile trace, that is, a residue feeling, a mood, that will remain long after he has gone. An energy is invested into those transient moments, such as the smile of a stranger and a shared feeling of grief and loss. All is not doomed after all.

When thinking about the ideological disparity between *Back to the Future* and *Donnie Darko*, I am reminded of Alan Lightman's poetic imagining of a world where,

> time is like a flow of water, occasionally displaced by a bit of debris, a passing breeze. Now and then, some cosmic disturbance will cause a rivulet of time to turn away from the mainstream, to make connection backstream. When this happens, birds, soil, people caught in the branching tributary find themselves suddenly carried to the past.
>
> Persons who have been transported back in time are easy to identify. They wear dark, indistinct clothing and walk on their toes, trying not to make a single sound, trying not to bend a single blade of grass. For they fear that any change they make in the past could have drastic consequences for the future. (Lightman 1993: 13–14)

While Marty McFly fears destroying the future as he knows it, he nevertheless struts through the 1950s with a confidence and cockiness because, in a way, he already knows how things will end. His only surprise is that the future proves to be so much better than what he could have envisioned. Donnie Darko is more like the time traveler in Lightman's book who wears "dark, indistinct clothing," and seems to float through his surroundings as if the whole world has been anaesthetized. Ironically, he is also the one given an axe to hack away at the present and past so that the future will arrive. His reclamation of power is not without great struggle and comes with a heavy price. When his bloody end arrives, Donnie's final laughter is a haunting reminder that the tragedies of contemporary society and crises of identity are inevitable—a case of history repeating itself—but, more importantly, that they will be learned from. That is the future he hopes for. It might not be enough, but it's a start.

Chapter 8

Another Sunrise, Another Sunset: Beyond Generation X

Memory is a wonderful thing if you don't have to deal with the past.
(Celine in *Before Sunset* [dir. Richard Linklater, 2004])

This final chapter tracks the movement of Generation X, from youth to post-youth, through the cinematic vision of Richard Linklater.[1] The director of critically acclaimed films such as *Slacker* (1991), *Dazed and Confused* (1993), *Before Sunrise* (1995), *Before Sunset* (2004), *Waking Life* (2001), *Fast Food Nation* (2006), and *A Scanner Darkly* (2006), Linklater's movies offer a critique of contemporary American society explored predominantly through the eyes of adolescents and young adults. Although middle-aged and elderly characters play a significant role in several of the films, they act more as interlocutors who intervene briefly in the narratives. Linklater's less commercial ventures paint portraits of suburban existence that are painfully poetic in their philosophical ramblings, confessions, and admonitions, and which appear seductively arcane and random. While Quentin Tarantino, Steven Soderbergh, and Kevin Smith are regarded as the most influential and progressive filmmakers to have emerged from the 1990s with a distinctive Generation X sensibility, Linklater's incessant experimentation with style and densely layered narratives give uncanny expression to the postmodern experience of Generation X youth. The auteur creates a living history, or rather an historical rendition, which is as invested in "hard politics" as it is in memories, dreams, and emotions.

Linklater's oeuvre, specifically between the early 1990s and mid-2000s, functions as a type of unofficial history of post-1970s youth. The films balance between the extremities of the violent, bitter, and cynical world of Larry Clark and the romantic idealism of John Hughes. The plots progress at a languid pace, often without any definite goal or destination. The narratives privilege continuity over the more orthodox conclusiveness of a Hollywood production—evident in the

---

1   While Richard Linklater is recognized as the originator of the 1990s slacker iconography in cinema and the vanguard of a generation, his background is not strictly classified as typical Generation X. As John Pierson writes,

> As the multibrats, like his doppelganger Kevin Smith, were massing at the gates, Rick was the last of the Mohicans. His inspiration came from Ophuls' *La Ronde* and Buñuel's *The Discreet Charm of the Bourgeoisie*. You'll find Antonioni and Fassbinder one-sheets on his walls, and he'd much rather talk about Bresson's *Lancelot du Lac* than either *Jaws* or *The Brady Bunch*. (Pierson 1995: 186)

way characters and actors are woven through several of Linklater's films to serve as recognizable reference points. For instance, Ethan Hawke and Julie Delpy star in *Before Sunrise*, the sequel *Before Sunset*, and *Waking Life*. In the former two, they play the parts of Jesse and Celine. Although it is never made obvious if they resume these fictitious personas in *Waking Life* (they are nameless), it is the tacit assumption and hopeful fantasy of the audience that they have. The narrative's meaning relies on the spectator's deeper engagement in building backstories for the characters and their transient situations. This is suggested in *Before Sunrise* when Celine theorizes the profound moments shared between people onscreen and offscreen.

> *Celine*: You know, I believe if there's any kind of God it wouldn't be in any of us, not you or me but just this little space in between. If there's any kind of magic in this world it must be in the attempt of understanding someone, sharing something. I know it's almost impossible to succeed but who cares, really. The answer must be in the attempt.

The narratives in Linklater's films are carried through the affinities made, maintained, and broken, and those unseen experiences where connections and causal relations are imagined. In a time of momentous change, this mentality would define a generation of youth coming to terms with its own identity. There is always the feeling that every dialog remains unfinished and that we have left a conversation midway. To illustrate this, I present two parallel analyses that juxtapose *Slacker* with *Waking Life*, and *Before Sunrise* with *Before Sunset*. The films capture a collective consciousness and historical identity of a generation through unconventional narrative structures and stylistic elements.

Slacker and *Waking Life*

Richard Linklater's *Slacker* was the auteur's acclaimed debut into the independent film circuit in 1991. The narrative commences with a young traveler (Linklater) on a Greyhound bus. He disembarks at a station in Austin, Texas and then catches a taxi back to his residence. During the ride, he engages in a lengthy one-way conversation with the taxi driver as to the nature of his dreams, contemplating the idea that the choices not taken in life splinter into alternate realities. Soon after, he encounters a hit-and-run victim (Jean Caffeine) who is sprawled on the road with her groceries strewn around her. This event marks the end of Episode 1 and the traveler's involvement in the narrative.

The camera tracks backwards down the road away from the accident scene. A car enters the frame and parks on the side of the street. A man (Mark James) exits the vehicle and enters a house. We discover he is the victim's son and also the one who has committed the crime. He begins to cut out pictures from a glossy book and burn them on a makeshift altar adorned with religious iconography. Using a television screen as his canvas, he projects looped footage of a little boy on a child's toy car being pushed along by a woman. From the poor quality of the film stock, we assume it is a home movie of the young man and his mother. There is an unhurried tempo to the scene, even when the police arrive to arrest him. As he is escorted to the squad car, a pedestrian (Samuel Dietert) and street musician (Keith McCormack) pass by, signaling the end of Episode 2.

The narrative turns its attention to the street musician who is carrying a guitar. The next scene shows him busking on the street. The camera lingers momentarily on him before focusing upon a young woman (Jennifer Schaudies) who drops some change into his guitar case. Like the busker, she functions as a vehicle—a link in a chain—to proceed from one situation to the next. *Slacker* resumes this pattern throughout the entire film, in which there are almost three dozen separate stories. It concludes with a group of youths romping around a hilltop, one of whom tosses a camera off a cliff. The final shot is a dizzying image, from the perspective of the camera, of shapes and eddies of light swirling together before the final black screen.

At a surface level, *Slacker* appears as a linear progression of arbitrary encounters with no climax. Events do not culminate in a single defining moment, nor are characters developed. They are, as Linklater writes in his production notes on *Slacker*, "People without a history or dramatic evolution" (2004b: 32).[2] Characters and their unique circumstances are never revisited and are rarely named. For instance, they are identified in the end credits with descriptions such as "Should Have Stayed At The Bus Station" (Linklater), "Giant Cappucino" (Maris Strautmanis), "Sidewalk Psychic" (Gina Lalli), "Conspiracy A-Go-Go Author" (John Slate), and "Old Anarchist" (Louis Mackey). While certain episodes are accorded more screen time and emphasis, such as during an exchange of detached monologues, the relative anonymity and brief appearances of the characters prevent the audience from building emotional attachments to individuals.

The episodic structure of *Slacker* and the blasé demeanor of its characters attracted criticism of the "affected and dull" narrative (Hanson 2002: 63). In a letter of complaint, one irate viewer wrote, "Why are the lives of these unproductive, pretentious, and boring people documented on film? The movie does not mean anything" (Anon. quoted in Pierson 1995: 189). For instance, in one scene, "To Be Buried In History" (Nolan Morrison), "Masonic Malcontent" (Dan Kratochvil), and "Going To Catch A Show" (Kyle Rosenblad) criticize the "Masonic pyramid bullshit" that has skewed social history and perpetuated a hierarchy determined by a male-dominated, privileged elite. They proclaim, "the slate of American history needs to be wiped clean," and propose putting "Larry Feyman in the history books" and "Squeaky Fromme on the one-dollar bill." The topic of their vehement

---

2   The *Slacker* booklet is a 64-page accompaniment to the Special Edition DVD release of the movie. It is a compendium including production notes and stills, review extracts, and essays from several authors, including Linklater. As it is untitled, I have credited this source as the *Slacker* booklet.

disgust quickly switches when one of the men suggests they buy more beer. The new pursuit of pleasure ends their lecture in politics without further thought. In another scene, "Pap Smear Pusher" (Teresa Taylor) relays to bystanders the antics of a suicidal gunman on the freeway. She then tries to peddle a Madonna pap smear sample that was retrieved from a gynecology laboratory in Hollywood. This absence of forward momentum and satisfying resolution was sufficient reason for critics to slate the film as a series of trite, arbitrary suburban tales without (conventional) form.

Vilifications of *Slacker*'s aimlessness missed the point that the deliberate structure of the film *was* the point. While the narrative moved at a lethargic pace, this rendered the separate scenes all the more intense. The audience is asked to tune in and turn up the volume. Theories of existence, grand ideas, and astute observations of the mundane are placed on the proverbial table where "vignettes in Linklater's picture accumulate into a statement from which viewers can choose to extract meaning if they so desire" (Hanson 2002: 64). *Slacker* is, to quote Linklater, a "film of posing problems, even in a confused state (possibly to be solved or addressed differently elsewhere)" (2004b: 31). Conversations pivot around notions of reality, personal and ideological fantasies, and the very core of existence. They broach a cornucopia of subjects that at times verge on the inane, delusional, and the paranoid. One of the most memorable scenes in *Slacker* involves "Video Backpacker" (Kalman Spelletich). The chair-bound recluse has a monitor strapped to his back, and works in a claustrophobic room overcrowded with television sets playing looped footage of disasters and scenes of violence. When he is visited by "Cadillac Crook" (Clark Walker), Video Backpacker expounds his fascination with the televisual medium.

> *Video Backpacker*: Well, we all know the psychic powers of the televised image. But we need to capitalize on it and make it work for us instead of us working for it ... Well, like, to me, my thing is a video image is much more powerful and useful than an actual event. Like back when I used to go out, when I was last out I was walking down the street and this guy like came barreling out of a bar, fell right in front of me and he had a knife in his back. Landed right on the ground. And I have no reference to it now. I can't refer back to it. I can't press rewind. I can't put it on pause. I can't put it on slo-mo and see all the little details. And the blood, it was all wrong. It didn't look like real blood and the hue was off and I couldn't adjust the hue. I was seeing it for real, but it just wasn't right. And I didn't even see the knife impact on the body. I missed that part.

In this isolated and strange sequence, this odd character becomes the street philosopher. Melding televisual literacy with personal observations, Video Backpacker articulates the crossover of fact and fiction within a postmodern context. Experiences of the everyday bind the characters where, "the coffee houses and beer gardens of Austin are stand-ins for the agora of Athens" (Rosenbaum 2004: 17). Their musings eschew the derogatory stereotype of the lazy, unproductive slacker shirking duties and responsibilities. Far from the losers that the term connotes, and which Linklater plays upon, the individuals are modern-day theorists and activists. They find reason for, and meaning in, their existence, despite their derelict condition. For this cohort, upward mobility is virtually nonexistent, unemployment is rife, and the American Dream has long soured. The characters in *Slacker* do not dwell in the present because they fear the future, but because there is no future. It is fitting that the film's final image is taken from a camera hurtling down a precipice. All recordings of today—tomorrow's past—are destroyed. This moment is all they/we have.

Despite the often anaesthetized demeanor of its characters and the dejected urban landscape of rundown apartment blocks, littered streets, seedy clubs, and dingy coffee houses, *Slacker* is not a dystopic narrative. While the episodes remain incomplete, the film's structure points to the journey, as opposed to the destination, as the most significant aspect of life. As Paula Geyh points out, there is a deliberate attempt to avoid the modernist predicament that T.S. Eliot captured in "Four Quartets," a poem notable for its reflection on individual struggle and the search for meaning in a time of dramatic social change (2003: 2).

> We had the experience but missed the meaning,
> And approach to the meaning restores the experience
> In a different form, beyond any meaning
> We can assign to happiness. (Eliot 1969 [1941]: 186)

The youth of the 1990s in *Slacker* do not, however, "miss the meaning" searching for sublime happiness. The purpose of existence resides in the questions asked, rather than the answers sought, which makes every discussion, point of contact, and situation an opportunity for higher understanding. Jesse Fox Mayshark articulates the importance of their work, "They're not making money, but they're making music, constructing art, concocting theories, writing, reading and—especially—talking. They are engaging with life on their own terms" (2007: 22). The grimy bars, sidewalks, and crowded diners have become the mobile classrooms for a generation that has lost faith in tradition and social truths. As Chris Walters states,

> Evidence that twentieth-century radicalism has long been at the end of its tether pervades the movie; the people who inhabit it are overwhelmed by a sense of waiting for the fullness of time to bring word of something—anything—new. Most of them are too young to remember a time before official culture devoured or colonized everything that once held out a promise of vitality; they've claimed inertia as their birthright. The all but total decay of public life has atomized others into subcultures of which they are the only member, free radicals randomly seeking an absent center as the clock beats out its senseless song.

> The movie buries its treasures here, in the crevasses of its drollery and craziness.
> Nothing in the current climate is more permissible than mocking or reducing
> such people; *Slacker* celebrates their futility as a sign of endurance and mourns
> the passing of time by marking it with emblems of affection and empathy: the
> only prizes worth having. (Walters 2004: 25)

While the established institutions of education, government, and economy have
failed these Texan citizens, their sardonic and offhanded quips are indicators of
fortitude in the face of futility. Lacking the necessary cultural capital to effect direct
change, words and simple actions are all the youths in *Slacker* have to structure
days that are reduced to fleeting moments. The detritus of an ailing society and
troubled history becomes the material for new debates, knowledge, and ideas. Geyh
notes that postmodernist irony is "about 'play,' both in the sense of enjoyment
and in the poststructuralist sense of a production of possibilities of interpretation
without end or definitive resolution," which stands in stark contrast to modernist
irony, that is "pervaded by a sense of nostalgia, of loss and longing beneath the
surface archness" (2003: 19). The endless possibilities for interpretation evident in
Slacker produce a multiplicity of narratives that are in constant flux.

A ten year period separates *Slacker* and Linklater's 2001 production *Waking Life*.
Although a completely different story set in an unspecified locale, the premise of
Waking Life is so similar to its predecessor that it is arguably the auteur's response
to his earlier project. Shot in New York, Austin, and San Antonio, *Waking Life*
shifts fluidly through this hybrid cityscape that is concurrently "everywhere and
nowhere." While *Waking Life* continues the episodic structure, it stresses the idea
of connectivity and progress narratively, thematically, and stylistically, which was
absent from *Slacker*. The film opens with two young children (Trevor Jack Brooks
and Lorelei Linklater) playing a game with a piece of paper folded up and inscribed
with words and messages—one of which is "Dream is destiny." Shortly after, the
boy watches a falling star and begins to float upwards. He must hold onto the door
handle of a nearby car to stop himself ascending into the sky. The following shot is of
Wiley Wiggins' character—the only recurring character in the entire film—waking
up on a train.[3] We assume he has dreamt the previous scene. His many encounters
are with nameless characters who enter the story briefly and are never revisited.[4]
They "pontificate, rather than converse" a wide array of subjects that initially seem
to have little cogency, from "the nature of consciousness, to theories of film, to grisly
fantasies of murder" (Abeel 2001: 26).

As with *Slacker*, *Waking Life* unfolds at a sedate pace. Wiggins' character floats
through time and space. Each new encounter seems to have no bearing on the
previous, or the following. The only constant is Wiggins' presence and his growing

---

3   Wiley Wiggins featured in *Dazed and Confused* as the character of Mitch.
4   Whereas characters are identified by obscure descriptives in *Slacker*, they are devoid
of names altogether in *Waking Life*. Images of the animated characters are paired with the
actors' real names in the end credits.

anxiety as to whether his waking life is actually a permanent state of dreaming or reality. Each time he rouses from sleep, he discovers he has not escaped the dream world. For example, light switches do not work and the numbers on his digital alarm clock keep morphing and swirling into incomprehensible patterns. The closing scene of *Waking Life* is déjà vu of its beginning. Wiggins' character levitates. He grasps onto the handle of a car door, but then releases it. The film ends ambiguously "with an image perfectly pitched between transcendence and terror" (Jones 2001: 39). Wiggins drifts into the stratosphere until he vanishes from view altogether.

Waking Life works as a type of ten-year reunion. It takes up the contemplative conjectures of *Slacker*, but with a more defined quest and mature acceptance of the final outcome. Kent Jones argues,

> *Waking Life* takes a deceptively simple path, segueing, like *Slacker*, from one idea, inspiration, and pronouncement to the next, each reckoned definitive by the person voicing it. On the surface, this procession may seem repetitive and hopelessly collegiate, a gaggle of earnest professorial types and eccentrics with big theories about the nature of existence blended with sociopathic malcontents and inner-journeying slackers. But it's the resounding certainty behind their statements more than their actual content that counts, the poignant folly of banking on ideas that promise to Explain It All. (Jones 2001: 39)

While *Waking Life* exhibits many of the trademarks of *Slacker*, its philosophical quandary is more overt and its style more refined. *Waking Life* is an experimental piece of art amalgamating animation and photography. Originally shot on location with consumer-level digital cameras, each individual frame was then illustrated over using specially designed interpolated rotoscoping software to create "paintings in motion" (Robertson 2002: 13–14). The visual images manipulate perception with their "shifting planes of space appear[ing] isolated, as if there were discrete strata between foreground and back" (Chang 2001: 22). With over 30 artists contributing to the animation component of the project, each scene has a distinctive texture and appearance that oscillates between a real-life likeness to the phantasmagoric (Chang 2001: 22). The hallucinatory wavering effect is an apt and deliberate metaphor for the film's overarching theme of the enigmatic spaces between the imagined and the actual. The "fundamental questions about reality, unreality, existence, free will" are explored and captured through a sophisticated visual mode where form becomes crucial to meaning (Linklater quoted in Arnold 2001: 28).

The hyper-reality of *Waking Life* draws attention to itself as pure artifice in the making. Linklater explained in an interview that the mantra of the film was "process, not product" (quoted in Abeel 2001: 28). This concept is crystallized in a scene in which a young woman (Kim Krizan) is conversing with Wiggins. She claims, "creation seems to come out of imperfection ... a striving and a frustration," arguing that words are symbols incapable of expressing the intangible. It is only

Figure 8.1   Art imitating life: Julie Delpy and Ethan Hawke as nameless characters in *Waking Life* (2001)

Source: The Kobal Collection, The Picture Desk

through conscious effort to interpret and construct meaning that they attain any significance. This parallels the process by which the audience reads the film. In one of the more life-like portrayals of characters in *Waking Life*, the illusion of realism is disrupted by "thought images" (similar to speech bubbles on a comic strip) which appear intermittently throughout the discussion. For instance, when the woman details the path of the spoken word from the speaker's mouth to the receiver's brain, a sketch of the auditory canal materializes to illustrate the trajectory. As with the inert nature of language, the visuals are incongruous planes of colors and shapes that only make sense in the attempt to assign them with some sort of alternate logic. We become implicated in the visual construct through the self-conscious processing of the image (Fuchs 2001).

If the characters in *Slacker* are on the cusp of posing critical questions of existentialism, those in *Waking Life* provide diverse responses that range from rational exegeses to obsessive diatribes, romantic musings to political rants. The film articulates "the way that life can seem to keep turning over another page, forever promising that it's bringing us one step closer to some ultimate reality," but without ever reaching that elusive end (Jones 2001: 39). The satisfaction of each new encounter in *Waking Life* is short-lived, with each riposte lasting long enough only to be superseded by the next. This is depicted in a scene in which Wiggins is watching a documentary entitled *The Holy Moment* in an empty theater. Actor and director, Caveh Zahedi (the only identified character in the film), discusses André Bazin's theory that reality and God are essentially the same. He explains that the power of cinema is its ability to capture versions of reality that are varying manifestations of God. Zahedi then suggests to his companion (David Jewell) that they have a "Holy moment." Chris Chang writes,

> Caveh stops speaking and locks eyes with his friend. His hair has been moving in wave-like patterns throughout his speech, but it now takes on supernatural pulsations. His pupils dilate wildly. It's as if they have indeed become one with the moment. They begin to speak, the moment is broken, and at the end of the scene the characters morph into clouds. (Chang 2001: 24)

The divine experience is brief but intense. There is the implicit proposition that the "meaning of Life" is not to be found in the search for certainty, but in those transitory moments of spiritual transcendence where bonds are made between individuals and their surrounds. The free-floating style of *Waking Life* is a literal translation of this basic principle. The quest for truth is the creation of meaning and progressive thought. It is an invitation for self-cultivation that can never be complete because idealism and truth are relative. It is significant that Zahedi and his friend transform into clouds at the end of the episode. The tangible evidence of their holy moment has vaporized, leaving behind only the shared memory of the experience between the characters and the audience—both Wiggins and our own selves as spectators. According to Linklater, this aspect of *Waking Life* is a slow evolutionary step up from the "disconnect between society and the individual, and between one another"—a movement away from self-imposed alienation—that defined *Slacker* (quoted in Keough 2002).

As with many of Linklater's works, motifs of movement and transition are important in *Waking Life*. The characters are the eternal travelers. As the "Boat Car Guy" (Bill Wise) describes it, they are "in a state of constant departure while always arriving." In *Waking Life*, we are introduced to Wiggins asleep on a train. *Slacker* opens with Linklater's character arriving at the bus station. In *It's Impossible to Learn to Plow by Reading Books* (dir. Richard Linklater, 1988), the main character (Linklater) is first shown aboard an Amtrak train. The narrative follows him as he roves from one place to the next carrying out mundane tasks. Early in *Waking Life*, Wiggins hitches a ride with the Boat Car Guy and a fellow passenger (played by Linklater) from the train station. In a short conversation between all three men, the ethos of this postmodern *Bildungsroman* comes to the forefront.

Wise: So, where do you want out?

Wiggins: Ah, who me? Am I first? Um, I dunno. Really anywhere is fine.

Wise: Well ... just give me an address or something, okay?

Wiggins: Ah.

Linklater: Tell you what. Go up three more streets, take a right, go two more blocks, drop this guy off at the next corner.

Wiggins: Where's that?

Wise: Well I don't know either, but it's somewhere and it's gonna determine the course of the rest of your life.

The importance of the journey—of going "somewhere"—is paramount to the text's interpretation. Characters are not static and the landscape is never permanent. Long tracking shots, smooth crane flyovers, and the tilting and panning of the camera continually transport us from one situation to the next in the cityscape. We unobtrusively traverse different spaces, from the intimate setting of a couple's bedroom to the jail cell of a violent inmate. Visitations are only long enough to pique our curiosity, fascination, or disgust before we are whisked away. This roaming underscores the film's ideology that human survival and sanity is incumbent upon the need to push ever onwards. While the characters in *Slacker* ponder their existence without ever really posing "those questions," there is a more willing acknowledgment of the mutual "struggle for meaning and purpose, for a destination or goal—or at least for a way of reconciling themselves to the absence of these things," and of endless possibilities in *Waking Life* (Metaphilm 2002–2003).

If *Slacker* is an exploration of the digressions of Generation X youth, *Waking Life* is the older, more self-aware version of itself one decade later, where the past meets, and directly converses with, the present. Wiggins, whose character is the alter ego of Linklater's persona in *Slacker*, encounters Linklater for a second time towards the tail end of *Waking Life*. Linklater's character cannot recall their first meeting. When Wiggins attempts to extract a coherent response from him as to his permanent dream state, he receives yet another abstract, tangential discussion on existentialism. While Wiggins is finally able to utter the questions that Linklater could not in *Slacker*, hindsight, experience, and time still cannot provide satisfying answers.

References to characters, scenarios, and locations featured in previous Linklater films lend *Waking Life* a certain uncanniness. Akin to a living photo album that is constantly being added to, the film captures private experiences that map out and record an incomplete, ongoing collective memory and a shared history. This creates its own popular meta-memory. As the narrative progresses, *Waking Life* gradually enters into a more troubling and mysterious realm where "the nature of time seems to be urgently imparting itself, *through* dreaming" to the protagonist (Jones 2002). The preoccupations with the present in *Slacker* give way to a fluid, moving timeline that brings together the past, present, and future in *Waking Life*. Without history or future projections, the Now is absolved of social responsibility. While the youths of *Slacker* have no dreams for the future, dreams become the very essence of existence, identity, and meaning in *Waking Life*.

Before Sunrise and *Before Sunset*

The narrative link of *Slacker* and *Waking Life* is revisited in *Before Sunrise* and its sequel, *Before Sunset*. The opening images of *Before Sunrise* are of railway tracks receding into the distance and the landscape rushing by. The story pivots around two characters, American traveler Jesse (Ethan Hawke) and French student Celine (Julie Delpy), who meet on the train. After an involved conversation, Jesse proposes that they spend the evening together in Vienna, Austria where he is to catch a flight back to the United States the next day. In their short time together, the couple wander through the foreign Viennese landscape engaged in an extended discussion in which they expound their beliefs, personal philosophies, and concerns about the future. Throughout the evening, they cross paths with several minor characters who resemble the transitory and enigmatic faces from *Slacker* and *Waking Life*. They include a palm reader (Erni Mangold) who tells Celine, "You need to resign yourself to the awkwardness of life. Only if you find peace within yourself will you find true connection with others," and a street poet (Dominik Castell) who composes poetry that will "add to your life" in exchange for money. By sunrise, Jesse and Celine have become lovers and vow to meet again in six months at the same train station platform. In the final scene of *Before Sunrise*, a montage sequence of places the pair visited is shown in the early light of day—a train overpass, a secluded alleyway, a gravesite, an empty café, a public park where the remnants of an empty bottle of wine and glasses mark where they spent the night. We cut to Jesse aboard a bus headed for the airport. He falls asleep with a gentle smile on his face. This is followed with Celine onboard the train bound for Paris. The framing of the image suggests a type of shot-reverse-shot dialog with Jesse, even though they exist in separate spaces. Celine too smiles before surrendering to sleep.

In *Before Sunset*, nine years have elapsed since the initial meeting between Celine and Jesse in screen time and in real time (between the release of the first and second film).[5] *Before Sunset* opens with shots of the Parisian landscape before coming to rest at the famous Shakespeare and Company bookshop in Paris' Left Bank where a press conference is in progress. Jesse is completing the last leg of a European tour to promote his new novel. As he fields questions from journalists as to the relative fictional or factual nature of the book, it becomes apparent that its subject is based on the romantic liaison in Vienna in 1995. The scene intercuts with footage from *Before Sunrise* to simulate his memories. As Eddie Cockrell points out, it is significant that, "In the midst of a complicated thought involving the idea that 'time is a lie,' Jesse glances over to see Celine herself … smiling

---

5   There is crossover between fictional and actual events in *Before Sunset*. As with his character of Jesse, Ethan Hawke is a published novelist—he is the author of *The Hottest State* (1996) and *Ash Wednesday* (2002)—and lived in New York City. Hawke's own marital breakdown with actor Uma Thurman further informed his heated diatribes in the film. Like Celine, Julie Delpy spent time studying at New York University in the years leading up to *Before Sunset*, and is an ardent activist. See Grigoriadis (2004) and Zuel (2004).

shyly at him" (2004: 36). With less than two hours before Jesse must leave for the airport, the film's 80-minute drama takes place mostly in real time.

The narrative structure of *Before Sunset* proceeds in a similar fashion to *Before Sunrise*. The two characters spend their time together navigating through the landscape of cafés, parks, and cloistered backstreets, and in a protracted dialog of their life events since 1995. Both project images of success. Celine is an environmental activist and in a steady relationship, and Jesse is the accomplished writer, blissfully married, and with a five-year-old son. The façade soon breaks down as each confesses the loneliness and despondency of their current situations, and the regret at not having fulfilled their promise of a reunion. Echoing the opening quote, the characters surrender to the simple fact that memories inevitably incur a working through of their past. Echoing the opening quote, the characters surrender to the simple fact that memories inevitably incur working through their past. Celine later admits that the death of her grandmother prevented her from reaching the rendezvous, to which Jesse confesses that he did in fact turn up. It becomes obvious that the chemistry between the two has not waned, and their conversation reprises the romantic idealism that characterized the first film. *Before Sunset* concludes at Celine's studio apartment. By the time Jesse must leave to catch his flight, neither is prepared to bid adieu. Midway during a playful impression of Nina Simone, Celine remarks to Jesse, "You are going to miss your plane," to which he grins and replies with content resignation, "I know." As Celine dances around the apartment, the screen fades to black. There is the suggestive promise of a future relationship as Simone's "Just in Time" plays in the background.

As with *Slacker* and *Waking Life*, *Before Sunrise* and *Before Sunset* underscore the idea of a perpetual journey. There are the recurring motifs of planes, trains, and automobiles, and meanderings through foreign cityscapes. The leisurely pace of earlier films is repeated in *Before Sunrise* and *Before Sunset*, but only slightly hurried by a deadline that expires in several hours—to catch that flight or train home. The most divergent feature of *Before Sunrise* and *Before Sunset* is that they follow a more conventional narrative form with their in-depth character studies of Celine and Jesse. While *Slacker* and *Waking Life* are abstractions of social experiences, *Before Sunrise* and *Before Sunset* provide a more grounded and tangible account of the postmodern experience of Generation X. The uniqueness of the two projects becomes all the more apparent when compared with a film such as Ben Stiller's *Reality Bites* (1994)—a story of a group of friends in their 20s who are struggling to preserve their identities in corporate culture and avoid turning into their parents. Tackling issues including AIDS, youth unemployment, the slacker mentality, and generational confusion, *Reality Bites* is distinctly Generation X with its MTV-flavor and popular culture retorts.[6] Despite its laudable attempts to capture the verve of Generation X in a fashion they could identify with, the

---

6   The reference to MTV takes form in the parodied *In Your Face TV* program featured in *Reality Bites*. One character, Lelaina (Winona Ryder), describes it as "MTV but with an edge."

moralistic keystone of the film undermines its effectiveness (Hanson 2002: 65). As Peter Hanson points out,

> *Reality Bites* was an attempt to document a generation that had yet to mature. In that light, it makes sense that some conjecture was required, and that some wishful thinking manifested onscreen. Just as Linklater walked on virgin terrain in 1991 when he made *Slacker*, Stiller and his collaborators had to think ahead of societal curves in order to give their story closure. And who knows? When *Reality Bites* celebrates its twentieth anniversary in 2014, perhaps the film's vision of a tentative solidarity among the divergent factions of Generation X will seem prescient. (Hanson 2002: 64)

Before Sunrise and *Before Sunset* offer a more accurate portrait. The films trace the progression of Generation X *as* it happens. The stories unravel in tandem to actual social changes as indicated in the sequel's *real*-time expression. *Before Sunrise* marks the beginning of Generation X youth in 1995, with Jesse and Celine in their early 20s. Situated in that uncomfortable zone between the innocence of childhood and the weighty responsibilities of adulthood, they struggle with their conflicting emotions of romantic idealism and sense of futility that becomes manifest in even the most trite subjects of discussion. When Jesse informs Celine that four years of learning French in high school has amounted to a less than impressive mastery of the language, there is the implicit suggestion that even the cornerstones of social progress—knowledge and information—can be rendered useless. Similarly, Celine's quixotic principles for female empowerment crumble as she confesses that her desperation for affection drives away male suitors. As with *Reality Bites*, *Before Sunrise* articulates the concerns of Generation X but it does not provide easy resolutions or closure. The film's final scenario is satisfying because there is no finality. Echoing the words of the Boat Car Guy in *Waking Life*, the state of constant departure and arrival is the promise of infinite possibilities for new beginnings.

In *Before Sunset*, Jesse and Celine are older and more mature. They are the image of Generation X post-youth. Their projections in the past have come to fruition. For both, the future has arrived. Jesse has become the type of author he revered in his youth, his memories of boyhood are now replaced by recent recollections of his own son, and the divorce of his parents is mirrored in Jesse's own miserable marriage. Celine has become the independent woman she admired and subtly referenced in *Before Sunrise*. The palm reader foretells, "You are interested in the power of the woman. In the woman's deep strength and creativity. You're becoming this woman." As an activist for several causes, Celine has put her creativity and political agendas into action, and balances a career and a long-term relationship. Both characters have, as Celine foreshadowed in *Before Sunrise*, converted their "fanciful ambition[s] into these practical moneymaking ventures." While the first installment is a more sanguine portrait of the aspirations of youth, an undercurrent of bitterness and anger flows beneath the darker, more somber sequel. As the duo's angry confessions escalate, it becomes clear that the end of

**Figure 8.2   Nostalgic interplay: The nine-year reunion between Celine
                 (Julie Delpy) and Jesse (Ethan Hawke) in *Before Sunset* (2004)**

Source: The Kobal Collection, The Picture Desk

Generation X has not resolved the existential quandaries that troubled them as
youth. If there were no answers to the meaning of life a decade ago, the solutions
now are equally obscure.

Herein lies the most profound parallel of *Before Sunrise* and *Before Sunset*
to *Waking Life*. In overlapping of past, present, and future, they construct an
ongoing, living history collated from personal memories, collective experiences,
and a generational conscience. Time, as with history, is threaded together by the
common denominator of a humanistic nexus. Grand narratives give way to more
important micro-narratives composed of revelatory and mundane moments shared
between people. This finds expression in the narrative development of both films
and in their distinctive style. *Before Sunrise* and *Before Sunset* utilize the Linklater
trademark of fluid camera movements. As Jesse and Celine amble through Vienna
and Paris, the camera similarly snakes its way through the landscape. Lengthy
tracking shots are complemented by uninterrupted long edits. The effect of this
unobtrusive style of filmmaking is that we feel we are pleasantly eavesdropping
on their conversation (Kermode 2004: 45). The constant movement of camera
and character through time and space is a metaphor of the life passage from youth
to young adulthood and post-youth. The dream-like cadence is counterbalanced
by the incessant need to resist inertia, while at the same time slowing down long
enough to gaze back at the past to contemplate the present. John Frow argues,

"Place is a marker and guarantee of the continuity of personal identity; memory is a way of identifying, and perhaps repairing, loss" (1997: 245). When place is in a state of perpetual change, the gravity of transient interactions becomes all the more cogent. This is seen in the spontaneity of Jesse's and Celine's actions, which are attempts to remain in the moment. At first, they reach a mutual decision to never meet again in *Before Sunrise*, thereby savoring the brief time they have together. This vow is eventually overturned in the realization that remaining in a presentist state is not liberating but stifling.

Memory and nostalgia play a significant role in anchoring the transitory experiences of these Generation X youth in time and space. In *Before Sunset*, the Parisian landscape is virtually identical to the Vienna topography. While nine years and 950 kilometers separate the films, by grafting the past on the present, memory takes on a concrete and uncanny form. A Viennese café finds its equivalent in Paris, and a boat cruise on the River Seine takes the place of the Blue Danube. Time itself become nonlinear, a theme reiterated in the films. When Jesse first suggests to Celine that they spend the evening together in Vienna in *Before Sunrise*, he forwards the proposition as an exercise in time travel.

> *Jesse*: Jump ahead ten, twenty years, okay? And you're married. Only your marriage doesn't have that same energy that it used to have. You know, you start to blame your husband. You start to think about all those guys you've met in your life and what might've happened if you'd picked up with one of them, right? Well, I'm one of those guys. That's me. You know, so think of this as time travel from then to now to find out what you're missing out on.

Celine later comments that she has the recurring sensation that she is an old woman on her deathbed whose life is made up only of memories. This confession is later replicated in *Waking Life* by Delpy's unnamed character. The borders between time, text, and memory have become porous. Nostalgia is no longer a yearning for what is lost, but hindsight to repair the future. While we (and the characters) revel in the subtle nuances and crossovers between the films—the way Jesse likes to move Celine's hair away from her face, his penchant for cartoonish hand gestures, her endearing, impassioned arguments—we long for more, and that the story go on. Jesse and Celine embody the transition from youth to post-youth, not an *end of youth*.

If Richard Linklater's films offer versions of the trajectory of Generation X to post-youth, the narrative arc is evolving, but still far from complete. The transitions from *Slacker* to *Waking Life*, and *Before Sunrise* to *Before Sunset* are significant movements from detachment to interpersonal reconnection beyond the immediate present, that is, they are positive steps forward. Identity and self cannot exist in a vacuum devoid of social interaction. The desire to question and understand others, as the films suggest, have come to rely upon divine, Godly moments to transcend our current state of despair. Jesse and Celine turn to love and the unknowable future to repair their lives. It is their second chance. By the end of *Before Sunset*, they have accepted that life will remain a mystery, but that there is integrity and purpose in striving for those elusive answers. The film offers an ideal scenario in which the future of Generation X does not conclude in the spectacular, apocalyptic fashion that Douglas Coupland had imagined in *Generation X: Tales for an Accelerated Culture*. It finishes with a sultry jazz track and two individuals on the brink of renewed romance. It is a quasi-utopian recourse that can only be achieved by focusing almost exclusively upon the self. Linklater comments,

> All we can do is live forward and you just do the best with everything around you. It's very much the way [*Before Sunrise*] was—just a moment in time. *Before Sunrise* was roughly 14 or 15 hours in these two people's lives at a random intersection in a town neither of them lived in. In that film, to me, they were sort of like ghosts in this city that they didn't really belong to, almost in their own world, this ethereal world of their own imagination. [*Before Sunset*] is very much about and takes place in the real world. It's Paris. [Celine] lives in Paris. It's her world, and it's very realistic. (Linklater 2004a)

The searing honesty of *Before Sunset* edges towards a remarkably poignant depiction of Generation X, only to withhold its pedagogical potential by displacing political and generational concerns into the privatized sphere of relationships and the plight of the individual. For instance, Celine's heated diatribes of the declining state of contemporary society and increasing environmental problems falter into complaints of her current love life. However, as Henry Giroux argues, there needs to be a "connection between private troubles and public discontents, between social transformation and democratic struggles, between political agency and public life" (2003: 120).

Coupland's vision of a thermonuclear cloud at the end of his novel was his conclusive, ironic still-life portrait of Generation X in 1991. The situation fast-forwarded to 2004 would be more unbelievable and dire than the work of fiction could conjure. Coupland's mushroom cloud would become the rising dust from the imploding World Trade Centers. The threat of terrorism has made every foreigner a dangerous suspect, sanctioning discrimination against certain ethnic groups. Civil wars have escalated into international firefights and new forms of colonization parading under the guise of protecting the free world. And the greed of unscrupulous bankers and brokers has thrown the global economy into one of its darkest times in contemporary history. While Linklater posits that "all we can do is live forward," there is perhaps more need than ever to turn our gaze from the far horizon back to the immediate present, without forgetting the past or denying the future. Social action must take place in the Now. While Celine's and Jesse's epiphanies of the value of human relationships are a marked advancement from the individuals in *Slacker*, the next step is to transfer this agency and purpose into the realm of the public. The individual alone is an ineffectual figure to instigate social change. Ultimately, it must occur at the level of the collective.

Representational politics in popular culture is only effective when it challenges the way we presently think. Reading Richard Linklater's films in relation to the sociohistorical context, dominant discourses, and histories of youth (in popular culture), it is discernible "that the struggle over meanings is, in part, defined as the struggle over culture, power, and politics" (Giroux 2002: 12). Private experiences cannot be separated from public affairs. As they travel through their post-youth phase, Generation X have been handed the keys to the house from their predecessors. With this comes the responsibility for the legacy they leave behind. While the party has officially ended, the cleanup is yet to begin.

Conclusion
Thanks for the Good Times, Where to Now?

There is a moment in *Grosse Pointe Blank* (dir. George Armitage, 1997) where Martin Q. Blank (John Cusack), a professional assassin, is asked by a former classmate at their high school reunion, "How's life?" to which he replies, "In progress." Set to a weekend soundtrack of 1980s numbers—Queen, Violent Femmes, The Clash, a-ha, and Echo & The Bunnymen are among the list of surefire memory triggers—the film works as a homecoming at many levels for a Generation X still figuring out who they were, and where they are going. As one of the icons in the 1980s wave of teen films, and one of the few actors to have made the successful transition to adult roles, Cusack's part in the film articulates the movement of Generation X from youth to post-youth. As a narrative convention, the reunion forces Martin's critical introspection of the past that, despite initial denials of its significance, really is important to him. For instance, when he discovers that the site of his old house is now a convenience store, he is overwhelmed with disbelief and confusion. Personal anxieties of absent links to one's own history are accentuated by the fact that Martin's mother Mary (Barbara Harris), a patient in a psychiatric institution, is unable to recognize her own son moments after she has had a lucid conversation with him. Furthermore, Martin is haunted by the same recurring dream of his high school sweetheart, Debi (Minnie Driver), whom he stood up on the night of prom, never to be seen or heard from again until his return to Grosse Pointe a decade later.

As with *Grosse Pointe Blank*, *Screening Generation X: The Politics and Popular Memory of Youth in Contemporary Cinema* performs a reflective nostalgia that simultaneously is a longing for, and a critical meditation on, the past. As with any cultural study of a particular era, filmic representations of Generation X are more easily observed from a temporal distance, that is, when removed from the immediate context and with the benefit of hindsight. After all, Generation X has now been superseded by the equally nebulous Generation Y. The former have outgrown MTV, are now raising children and accruing mortgages, and led the charge towards a dot-com empire. Defying their critics, Generation X did grow up eventually. Fears of a loser, slacker generation now seem like a foolish moral panic of the 1980s and 1990s.

As the successors of the 1970s neoclassical filmmakers, such as Steven Spielberg and George Lucas, Generation X filmmakers are now making the movies that dominate our theaters. The success of directors such as Richard Linklater, Kevin Smith, Darren Aronofsky, Quentin Tarantino, Steven Soderbergh, Spike

Jonze, Sofia Coppola, Paul Thomas Anderson, and Bryan Singer has made them a formidable presence in the film industry (see Hanson 2002). At the same time as entertaining us, the films also perform important cultural work. Just as the 1940s and 1950s saw the rise of *film noir* and the proliferation of the monster and alien-invasion genre, respectively, in response to the increasing concerns of a nation under attack, what can be gleaned from representations of Generation X youth in 1980s and 1990s cinema? How are our collective fears, anxieties, and aspirations conveyed in audiovisual culture? In an ever-accelerating (popular) culture, the gravity of cinema as an historical artifact is captured in Richard Dyer's statement that, "Images also have a *temporal dimension*. Structured polysemy does not imply stasis; images develop or change over time" (1998 [1979]: 64). In looking back, the altering meanings of images allow us to see how far we have come, and how far we have yet to go. A critical investment in popular culture, as bell hooks argues, is important because it creates a powerful site where intervention, challenge, and change can occur (1994: 6). Cultural critique encourages dialog on issues of class, gender, sexuality, race, and age-based discrimination. For instance, the broadening of roles for young women has cleaved a space beyond the stereotype of the beauty queen or the dowdy, spectacle-wearing wallflower. Films such as *Heavenly Creatures* (dir. Peter Jackson, 1994), *Girls Town* (dir. Jim McKay, 1996), *Girlfight* (dir. Karyn Kusama, 2000), *Bend It Like Beckham* (dir. Gurinder Chadha, 2002), *Juno* (dir. Jason Reitman, 2007), and *Towelhead* (dir. Alan Ball, 2007) counterpoint the submissive female, while at the same time expose the difficulties of transgression and resistance. Similarly, films such as *My Own Private Idaho* (dir. Gus Van Sant, 1991), *What's Eating Gilbert Grape?* (dir. Lasse Hallström, 1993), and *Finding Forrester* (dir. Gus Van Sant, 2000) presented a plurality of male subjectivities and experiences.

While the banners of "Generation X" and "youth" have been applied liberally to the texts discussed in the book, by no means does this codify a stable, unified aggregate. The quandary that ails historians, economists, and social scientists in their analyses of this group derives from a fundamental quest to write *the* definitive story of Generation X. The goal itself is premised on reductionism. I have opted to focus upon several icons in order to ride the ambiguities and absences in dominant historiography. A glance at the chapter topics shows a lineup of the usual suspects, such as the rebel, the bitch, the prom and pop princesses, the raver, and the slacker. However, a closer study reveals a multidimensionality that challenges and problematizes stereotypes of youth.

In youth culture, spaces of leisure become potential sites for protest and agency, and acts of consumption and production become invested with purpose. In arguing for the resistive potential of popular youth culture, however, it must be stressed that it is a negotiative process. The fundamental paradox of a politics of pleasure is that unless it instigates change in social conscience and responsibility, it is but a panacea, a symbolic resolution, with an early expiration date. Acts of resistance uncover hegemonic power relations at work, whether it is justifying punishment of aberrant sexualities or patronizing the working class and young people, as has been seen throughout the book. *Screening Generation X* explores the strained and complicated relationship between youth identity, power, and culture. By making visible bodies that are spectacular, transgressive, subversive, constrained, and/or battered, this has underscored social inequalities and given insight into the cultural milieu of the 1980s and 1990s. The book is not concerned just with cinema, but also with the politics, popular memory, and preoccupations of that era as conveyed through cultural constructions of youth.

The cultural currency of youth cinema, as with popular culture in general, lies not only in its pedagogic function, but also for the simple fact that such cinema and culture matter. I recall a vivid memory from my own youth when Kenny Loggins' hit single "Footloose," from the film of the same name, was played at the local disco shortly after the film's theatrical release. It became an instant anthem. The other children and I did not have the words to express the euphoric feeling of life, freedom, and being young, but we *felt* it. In that fleeting moment of abandoned dancing and optimism, celluloid, soundtrack, and (private and collective) experience converged. Kevin Bacon's character was no longer a fictional persona. He was on the dancefloor with us. That moment *meant* something. That became a part of *our* history. A history of ephemerality needs to include the workings of popular memory. As Greil Marcus writes,

> what is history anyway? Is history simply a matter of events that leave behind those things that can be weighed and measured—new institutions, new maps, new rulers, new winners and losers—or is it also the result of moments that seem to leave nothing behind, nothing but the mystery of spectral connections between people long separated by place and time, but somehow speaking the same language? ... If the language they are speaking, the impulse they are voicing, has its own history, might it not tell a very different story from the one we've been hearing all our lives? (Marcus 1989: 4)

Marcus acknowledges the significance of affective traces and the need for a plurality of subjectivities and more nuanced understandings of human experience. When the voices of the marginalized are drowned out by the dominant, alternative conduits can be found in popular culture, whether it be film, music, pulp literature, websites, and so on. Cinema is a particularly effective medium for such expression. It is able to capture, through sight and sound, the seminal moments that permeate our own lives, but are so transitory or intimate that they do not seem to merit public recognition.

The images of Generation X presented in the book are dynamic and evolving. Their meaning and importance changes over time and through space, creating a living history that is indicative of the resilience of youth amidst escalating local and global turmoil. Faced with seemingly insurmountable obstacles, Generation X nevertheless continues the struggle for social democracy and visibility. To reiterate the earlier words of Happy Harry Hardon, there is need for youth to "go crazy, get creative" to counteract the blindness and blandness of politically conservative and intolerant times. Social intervention must incorporate the ability to laugh in the face of hardship and formulate a politics that puts communal concerns into affirmative action. As our own histories are being written as we speak, that is, it is "in progress," it is imperative that we—as cultural critics and consumers—are wary of the narratives being recorded, recalled, and validated. With hindsight, the past is not Molly Ringwald. With foresight, the future is not Donnie Darko. What will we remember after (Generation X) youth? And who will remember?

Bibliography

Abeel, Erica (2001), "Dream project: Richard Linklater breaks new ground with *Waking Life*," *Film Journal International* vol. 104(11), November, 26, 28, 52.

Agamben, Giorgio (1993), *Infancy and History*. London: Verso.

Agger, Michael (2004), "Don't you forget about me," *New York Magazine*, December 6. <http://www.newyorkmetro.com/nymetro/arts/theater/10522/>

Ainslie, P. (1988), "Watching TV: a mobile audience," *Channels '89 Field Guide to the Electronic Environment*, December, 127.

Allen, Virginia M. (1983), *The Femme Fatale: Erotic Icon*. New York: The Whitston Publishing Co.

Annesley, James (1998), *Blank Fictions: Consumerism, Culture and the Contemporary American Novel*. New York: St. Martin's Press.

Aplin, Rebecca (1997), *Spice Girls: Giving You Everything*. London: UFO Music.

Ariès, Philippe (1962), *Centuries of Childhood*, Robert Baldick (Trans.). London: Jonathan Cape.

Arnold, Gary (2001), "Movies in the mind," *Insight* vol. 17(44), November 26, 28.

Badmington, Neil (2004), "*Roswell High*, alien chic and the in/human," in *Teen TV: Genre, Consumption and Identity*, Glyn Davis and Kay Dickinson (eds). London: British Film Institute, 166–75.

Bail, Kathy (1996), "Introduction," in *DIY Feminism*, Kathy Bail (ed.). St. Leonards, NSW: Allen and Unwin, 2–16.

Bakan, David (1971), "Adolescence in America: from idea to social fact," *Daedalus* vol. 100(4), 979–95.

Bakhtin, Mikhail (1994), *The Bakhtin Reader: Selected Writings of Bakhtin, Medvedev and Voloshinov*, Pam Morris (ed.). London: Arnold.

Baron, Stephen W. (1989), "Resistance and its consequences: the street culture of punks," *Youth and Society* vol. 21(2), December, 207–37.

Barthes, Roland (1972 [1957]), *Mythologies*, Annette Lavers (Trans.). London: Jonathan Cape.

Baudrillard, Jean (1994), *Simulacra and Simulation*, Sheila Faria Glaser (Trans.). Ann Arbor: The University of Michigan Press.

Bauman, Zygmunt (2001), "Space in the globalising world," *Theoria*, June, 1–22.

Bennett, Andy (2000), *Popular Music and Youth Culture: Music, Identity and Place*. Houndmills: Macmillan Press.

Bernstein, Jonathan (1997), *Pretty in Pink: The Golden Age of Teenage Movies*. New York: St. Martin's Griffin.

Best, Amy L. (2000), *Prom Night: Youth, Schools, and Popular Culture*. New York and London: Routledge.

Betcher, R. William and William S. Pollack (1993), *In A Time of Fallen Heroes: The Re-creation of Masculinity*. New York: Atheneum.

Bly, Robert (1990), *Iron John: A Book About Men*. Reading: Addison-Wesley.

Boym, Svetlana (2001), *The Future of Nostalgia*. New York: Basic Books.

Brabazon, Tara (2002), *Ladies Who Lunge: Celebrating Difficult Women*. Sydney: University of New South Wales Press.

Brand, Stewart (1999), *The Clock of the Long Now*. New York: Basic Books.

Broadcasting (1989), "By the numbers: summary of broadcasting and cable," *Broadcasting*, July 17, 14.

Cannon, Carl M. (2000), "The '80s vs. the '90s," *National Journal* vol. 32(16), April 15, 1186–94.

Carr, E.H. (1987 [1961]), *What is History?* 2nd edn. London: Penguin Books.

Catano, James V. (2000), "Entrepreneurial masculinity: re-tooling the self-made man," *Journal of American and Comparative Cultures* vol. 23(2), 1–8.

Chambers, Iain (1990), *Border Dialogues: Journeys in Postmodernity*. London and New York: Routledge.

Champion, Dean J. (1992), *The Juvenile Justice System: Delinquency, Processing, and the Law*. New York: Macmillan.

Chang, Chris (2001), "Cosmic babble," *Film Comment* vol. 37(5), September–October, 22–4.

Clark, Larry (n.d.), "*Kids*: synopsis." <http://www.larryclarkofficialwebsite.com/KidsSynopsis.html>

Clarke, John, Stuart Hall, Tony Jefferson, and Brian Roberts (1976), "Subcultures, culture and class," in *Resistance Through Rituals: Youth Subcultures in Post-War Britain*, Stuart Hall and Tony Jefferson (eds). London: Routledge, 9–74.

Clover, Carol J. (1987), "Her body, himself: gender in the slasher film," *Representations* (*Special Issue: Misogyny, Misandry, and Misanthropy*), issue 20, 187–228.

Cockrell, Eddie (2004), "Vienna daydreaming: 'sun' still hasn't set," *Variety* vol. 394(1), February 16–22, 36, 54.

Cohen, Phil (1972), "Subcultural conflict and working class community," *Working Papers in Cultural Studies*, issue 2, 4–51.

Cohen, Stanley (1987 [1972]). *Folk Devils and Moral Panics: The Creation of the Mods and Rockers*. Oxford and New York: Basic Blackwell.

Collin, Matthew (1997), *Altered State: The Story of Ecstasy Culture and Acid House*. London: Serpent's Tail.

Connell, R.W. (1995), *Masculinities*. St. Leonards, NSW: Allen and Unwin.

Considine, David M. (1985), *The Cinema of Adolescence*. Jefferson: McFarland.

Cooper, Anna Julia (1988 [1892]), *A Voice from the South*. New York and Oxford: Oxford University Press.

Corbo, Sally Ann (1997), "The X-er files," *Hospitals and Health Networks* vol. 71(7), April 5, 58–60.

Corliss, Richard (1986a), "Growing pains: *Pretty in Pink*," *Time* vol. 127(9), March 3, 83.

—— (1986b), "Well, hello Molly! Meet Hollywood's new teen princess," *Time* vol. 127(21), May 26, 66–71.

—— (1987), "Killer! *Fatal Attraction* strikes gold as a parable of sexual guilt," *Time* vol. 130(20), November 16, 72–79.

Corneau, Guy (1991), *Absent Fathers, Lost Sons: The Search for Masculine Identity*. Boston: Shambhala.

Coupland, Douglas (1991), *Generation X: Tales for an Accelerated Culture*. London: Abacus.

—— (1995), "Generation X papers: Douglas Coupland commits gen-x-cide," *Details*, June, 72.

Cranny-Francis, Anne (1992), *Engendered Fiction: Analysing Gender in the Production and Reception of Texts*. Kensington, NSW: University of New South Wales Press.

Creed, Barbara (1993), *The Monstrous-Feminine: Film, Feminism, Psychoanalysis*. London and New York: Routledge.

Cresswell, Tim (1996), *In Place/Out of Place: Geography, Ideology, and Transgression*. Minneapolis: University of Minnesota Press.

Critcher, Chas (2000), "'Still raving': social reaction to ecstasy," *Leisure Studies* vol. 19(3), 145–62.

Cubitt, Sean (1991), *Timeshift: On Video Culture*. London and New York: Routledge.

Curtis, Deborah (1995), *Touching from a Distance: Ian Curtis and Joy Division*. London: Faber & Faber.

D'acci, Julie (1997), "Nobody's woman? *Honey West* and the new sexuality," in *The Revolution Wasn't Televised: Sixties Television and Social Conflict*, Lynn Spigel and Michael Curtin (eds). New York and London: Routledge, 72–93.

Daley, David (1999), "How could we forget?" *The Fargo Forum*, April 8. <http://www.mollyringwald.co.uk/article2.html>

D'Arcens, Louise (1998), "Mothers, daughters, sisters," in *Talking Up: Young Women's Take on Feminism*, Rosamund Else-Mitchell and Naomi Flutter (eds). North Melbourne: Spinifex Press, 103–16.

Daugherty, Rebecca (2002), "The spirit of '77: punk and the girl revolution," *Women and Music* vol. 6, December 31, 27–35.

Davis, Mark (1997), *Gangland: Cultural Elites and the New Generationalism*, 2nd edn. St. Leonards, NSW: Allen and Unwin.

Dee, Sandra (1991), "Learning to live again," *People Weekly* vol. 35(10), March 18, 87–94.

Dillard, Brian J. (1998), "*Celebrity Skin*: review." <http://www.armchair-dj.com/reviews/c/celebrity_skin.asp>

Doane, Mary Ann (1984), "The 'woman's film': possession and address," in *Re-Vision: Essays in Feminist Film Criticism*, Mary Ann Doane, Patricia

Mellencamp, and Linda Williams (eds). Los Angeles: The American Film Institute, 67–82.

—— (1991), *Femmes Fatales: Feminism, Film Theory, Psychoanalysis*. New York and London: Routledge.

Doherty, Thomas (2002), *Teenagers and Teenpics: The Juvenilization of American Movies. Revised and Expanded Edition*. Philadelphia: Temple University Press.

Dorr, Aimee and Dale Kunkel (1990), "Children and the media environment: change and constancy amid change," *Communication Research* vol. 17(1), February, 5–25.

Driscoll, Catherine (1999), "Girl culture, revenge and global capitalism: cybergirls, riot grrrls, Spice Girls," *Australian Feminist Studies* vol. 14(29), 173–93.

Dyer, Richard (1998 [1979]), *Stars*. London: British Film Institute.

Eliot, T.S. (1969 [1941]), "Four Quartets," in *The Complete Poems and Plays of T.S. Eliot*. London and Boston: Faber & Faber.

Farley, Christopher John (2000), "Rave new world: it's more than just ecstasy," *Time* vol. 155(23), June 5. <http://www.time.com/time/magazine/article/0,9171,997084,00.html>

Felperin, Leslie (2002), "Darkness visible," *Sight and Sound* vol. 12(10), October, 34–5.

Fiske, John (1989), *Reading the Popular*. Boston: Unwin Hyman.

Foucault, Michel (1978), *The History of Sexuality. Volume 1: An Introduction*, Robert Hurley (Trans.). New York: Pantheon Books.

Frith, Simon and Jon Savage (1997), "Pearls and swine: intellectuals and the mass media," in *The Clubcultures Reader: Readings in Popular Cultural Studies*, Steve Redhead, Derek Wynne, and Justin O'Connor (eds). Oxford and Malden: Blackwell Publishers, 7–17.

Frow, John (1997), *Time and Commodity Culture: Essays in Cultural Theory and Postmodernity*. Oxford: Clarendon Press.

Fuchs, Cynthia (2001), "*Waking Life*: review," *Pop Matters*, November 2. <http://www.popmatters.com/film/reviews/w/waking-life2.shtml>

Fukuyama, Francis (1989), "The end of history?" *The National Interest* issue 16, 3–18.

—— (1992), *The End of History and the Last Man*. New York: Avon Books.

Fyvel, T.R. (1961), *The Insecure Offenders: Rebellious Youth in the Welfare State*. London: Chatto and Windus.

Gallagher, Hugh (1994), "Seven days and seven nights alone with MTV," in *The GenX Reader*, Douglas Rushkoff (ed.). New York: Ballantine Books, 183–203.

Gare, Shelley (1999), "Too much truffle oil: baby boomers and the generation war," in *Future Tense: Australia Beyond Election 1998*, Murray Waldren (ed.). St. Leonards, NSW: Allen and Unwin, 217–30.

Garner, Helen (1995), *The First Stone: Some Questions about Sex and Power*. Sydney: Picador.

Garratt, Sheryl (1998), *Adventures in Wonderland: A Decade of Club Culture*. London: Headline.

Garrison, Ednie Kaeh (2000), "U.S. feminism—grrrl style! Youth (sub)cultures and the technologics of the third wave," *Feminist Studies* vol. 26(1), 141–70.

Gelder, Ken (1997), "Chapter 10: introduction to part 2," in *The Subcultures Reader*, Ken Gelder and Sarah Thornton (eds). London and New York: Routledge, 83–9.

Gerard, Morgan (2004), "Selecting ritual: DJs, dancers and liminality in underground dance music," in *Rave and Religion*, Graham St. John (ed.). London and New York: Routledge, 167–84.

Geyh, Paula E. (2003), "Assembling postmodernism: experience, meaning, and the space in-between," *College Literature* vol. 30(2), 1–29.

Giles, Judy (2002), "National countermemories: narratives of gender, class, and modernity in women's memories of mid-twentieth century Britain," *Signs: Journal of Women in Culture and Society* vol. 28(11), 21–41.

Giroux, Henry (2002), *Breaking in to the Movies: Film and the Culture of Politics*. Malden and Oxford: Blackwell.

—— (2003), *The Abandoned Generation: Democracy Beyond the Culture of Fear*. New York and Houndmills: Palgrave Macmillan.

Goodwin, Andrew (1987), "Music video in the (post) modern world," *Screen* vol. 28(3), 36–55.

—— (1992), *Dancing in the Distraction Factory: Music Television and Popular Culture*. Minneapolis: University of Minnesota Press.

Grant, Eleanor (1988), "VCR'S: no family affair," *Psychology Today* vol. 22(1), January, 14.

Greven, David (2002), "Dude, where's my gender? Contemporary teen comedies and new forms of American masculinity," *Cineaste* vol. 27(3), 14–37.

Grigoriadis, Vanessa (2004), "In his own hothouse," *New York Magazine*, June 28. <http://newyorkmetro.com/nymetro/arts/features/9373/>

Grossberg, Lawrence (1989), "MTV: swinging on the (postmodern) star," in *Cultural Politics in Contemporary America*, Ian Angus and Sut Jhally (eds). London: Routledge, 254–68.

—— (1992), "Is there a fan in the house?: the affective sensibility of fandom," in *The Adoring Audience: Fan Culture and Popular Media*, Lisa A. Lewis (ed.). London: Routledge, 50–61.

—— (1994), "The political status of youth and youth culture," in *Adolescents and their Music: If It's Too Loud, You're Too Old*, Jonathon S. Epstein (ed.). New York and London: Garland, 25–46.

Haaken, Janice (2002), "Bitch and femme psychology: women, aggression, and psychoanalytic social theory," *Journal for the Psychoanalysis of Culture and Society* vol. 7(2), 202–15.

Hall, G. Stanley (1904), *Adolescence: Its Psychology and Its Relations to Physiology, Anthropology, Sociology, Sex, Crime, Religion and Education*. New York: D. Appleton and Co.

Hall, Stuart (1993), "For Allon White: metaphors of transformation," in *Carnival, Hysteria, and Writing: Collected Essays and Autobiography*, Allon White (author). Oxford: Clarendon Press, 1–25.

Hall, Stuart, Chas Critcher, Tony Jefferson, John Clarke, and Brian Roberts (1978), *Policing the Crisis: Mugging, the State, and Law and Order*. London and Basingstoke: Macmillan Press.

Hanson, Peter (2002), *The Cinema of Generation X: A Critical Study*. Jefferson and London: McFarland.

Harris, Anita (2004), *Future Girl: Young Women in the Twenty-First Century*. New York and London: Routledge.

Hartley, John (1992), *The Politics of Pictures: The Creation of the Public in the Age of Popular Media*. London and New York: Routledge.

Haslam, Dave (2001), *Adventures on the Wheels of Steel: The Rise of the Superstar DJs*. London: Fourth Estate.

Hawking, Stephen (1988), *A Brief History of Time: From the Big Bang to Black Holes*. London: Bantam.

Hearn, Jeff (1996), "Is masculinity dead? A critique of the concept of masculinity/ masculinities," in *Understanding Masculinities*, Máirtín Mac an Ghaill (ed.). Buckingham: Open University Press, 202–17.

Hebdige, Dick (1979), *Subculture: The Meaning of Style*. London and New York: Methuen.

—— (1988), *Hiding in the Light: On Images and Things*. London and New York: Comedia.

Heimann, Jim (ed.) (2003), *All-American Ads 50s*. Köln: Taschen.

Heimel, Cynthia (1993), *Get Your Tongue Out of My Mouth, I'm Kissing You Good-bye!* Sydney: Macmillan Press.

Hentges, Sarah (2006), *Pictures of Girlhood: Modern Female Adolescence on Film*. Jefferson and London: McFarland.

Hicks, Carolyn (1996), "The only things that aren't fake are you, me and Sprite: ironies and realities in generation X advertising," *Metro Magazine* issue 106, 71–81.

Hill, Andrew (2003), "Acid house and Thatcherism: contesting spaces in late 1980s Britain," *Space and Polity* vol. 7(3), December, 219–32.

Hirshey, Gerri (2001), *We Gotta Get Out of This Place: The True, Tough Story of Women in Rock*. New York: Atlantic Monthly Press.

Holmlund, Chris (1991), "Reading character with a vengeance: the *Fatal Attraction* phenomenon," *The Velvet Light Trap* issue 27, 25–36.

hooks, bell (1984), *Feminist Theory: From Margin to Center*. Boston: South End Press.

—— (1994), *Outlaw Culture: Resisting Representations*. New York and London: Routledge.

Hopkins, Susan (1995), "Generation pulp," *Youth Studies Australia* vol. 14(3), 14–18.

—— (1999), "Hole lotta attitude: Courtney Love and guitar feminism," *Social Alternatives* vol. 18(2), April, 11–14.

—— (2002), *Girl Heroes: The New Force in Popular Culture*. Annandale, NSW: Pluto Press Australia.

Hornblower, Margot (1997), "Great Xpectations," *Time* vol. 149(23), June 9, 58–68.

Horrocks, Roger (1994), *Masculinity in Crisis: Myths, Fantasies, and Realities*. Houndmills: Macmillan Press.

Howry, Allison Lea and Julia T. Wood (2001), "Something old, something new, something borrowed: themes in the voices of a new generation of feminists," *Southern Communication Journal* vol. 66(4), 323–36.

Hultkrans, Andrew (1994), "The slacker factor," in *The GenX Reader*, Douglas Rushkoff (ed.). New York: Ballantine Books, 297–303.

Hunter, Latham (2003), "The celluloid cubicle: regressive constructions of masculinity in 1990s office movies," *The Journal of American Culture* vol. 26(1), March, 71–86.

Hutchings, David (1986), "Molly Ringwald goes to the head of the teen class with *Pretty in Pink*, but she'd rather play grown-up," *People Weekly* vol. 25(12), March 24, 87, 89.

Hutson, Scott R. (1999), "Technoshamanism: spiritual healing in the rave subculture," *Popular Music and Society* vol. 23(3), 53–77.

Hutton, Fiona (2006), *Risky Pleasures? Club Cultures and Feminine Identities*. Aldershot: Ashgate.

Huyssen, Andreas (1995), *Twilight Memories: Marking Time in a Culture of Amnesia*. New York and London: Routledge.

Inness, Sherrie A. (1999), *Tough Girls: Women Warriors and Wonder Women in Popular Culture*. Philadelphia: University of Pennsylvania Press.

Jefferson, Tony (1976), "Cultural responses of the teds," in *Resistance Through Rituals: Youth Subcultures in Post-War Britain*, Stuart Hall and Tony Jefferson (eds). London: Routledge, 81–6.

Jenkins, Henry (1992), *Textual Poachers: Television Fans and Participatory Culture*. New York and London: Routledge.

Jenkins, Keith (1991), *Re-thinking History*. London and New York: Routledge.

Jones, Kent (2001), "Dream whirl," *Artforum International* vol. 40(1), September, 39.

—— (2002), "To live or clarify the moment: Rick Linklater's *Waking Life*," *Senses of Cinema*, March. <http://www.sensesofcinema.com/contents/01/19/waking.html>

Kaplan, E. Ann (1988), *Rocking Around the Clock: Music Television, Postmodernism, and Consumer Culture*. New York and London: Routledge.

—— (1998), "Introduction to new edition," in *Women in Film Noir*, E. Ann Kaplan (ed.). London: British Film Institute, 1–14.

Kaveney, Roz (2006), *Teen Dreams: Reading Teen Film and Television from Heathers to Veronica Mars*. New York: I.B. Taurus.

Kearney, Mary Celeste (1998), "'Don't need you': rethinking identity politics and separatism from a grrrl perspective," in *Youth Culture: Identity in a Postmodern World*, Jonathon S. Epstein (ed.). Massachusetts and Oxford: Blackwell, 148–88.

Keen, Sam (1991), *Fire in the Belly: On Being A Man*. New York: Bantam Books.

Keesey, Douglas (2001), "They kill for love: defining the erotic thriller as a film genre," *CineAction*, June 22, 44–53.

Kelly, Richard (2003), *The Donnie Darko Book*. London: Faber & Faber.

Keough, Peter (2002), "Dream weaver," *The Phoenix*. <http://www.bostonphoenix.com/boston/movies/documents/01978298.htm>

Kermode, Mark (2004), "Brief encounters," *New Statesman* vol. 133(4698), July 26, 45.

Kerr, Philip (2002), "The curious case of the six-foot rabbit," *New Statesman* vol. 131(4611), October 28, 45.

King, Noel (1992), "Teen movies debate: 'not to be an intellectual'—Adrian Martin on teen movies," *Cinema Papers* issue 89, August, 44, 46–7.

Klein, Hugh (1990), "Adolescence, youth, and young childhood: rethinking current conceptualizations of life stages," *Youth and Society* vol. 21(4), June, 446–71.

Kristeva, Julia (1982), *Powers of Horror: An Essay on Abjection*, Leon S. Roudiez (Trans.). New York: Columbia University Press.

Lee, Christina (2005), "Lock and load(up): the action body in *The Matrix*," *Continuum: Journal of Media and Cultural Studies* vol. 19(4), December, 559–69.

—— (2008), "Introduction," in *Violating Time: History, Memory, and Nostalgia in Cinema*, Christina Lee (ed.). New York: Continuum Books, 1–11.

Leitch, Thomas M. (1992), "The world according to teenpix," *Literature/Film Quarterly* vol. 20(1), 43–7.

Lentz, Kirsten Marthe (1993), "The popular pleasures of female revenge (or rage bursting in a blaze of gunfire)," *Cultural Studies* vol. 7(3), 374–405.

Lewis, Jon (1992), *The Road to Romance and Ruin: Teen Films and Youth Culture*. New York and London: Routledge.

Lightman, Alan (1993), *Einstein's Dreams*. New York: Warner Books.

Linklater, Richard (2004a), "*Before Sunset*—official website (production notes)." <http://wip.warnerbros.com/beforesunset/>

—— (2004b), "From the notebooks" in *Slacker* booklet. Detour Filmproduction, 31–3.

Lowenthal, David (1985), *The Past is a Foreign Country*. Cambridge: Cambridge University Press.

Lumby, Catharine (1997), *Bad Girls: The Media, Sex and Feminism in the 90s*. St. Leonards, NSW: Allen and Unwin.

Lynskey, Dorian (2002), "The old skool reunion," *The Guardian*, January 11. <http://www.guardian.co.uk/friday_review/story/0,3605,630391,00.html>

MacCannell, Dean (1992), *Empty Meeting Grounds*. London: Routledge.

Mantoux, Paul (1961 [1928]), *The Industrial Revolution in the Eighteenth Century: An Outline of the Beginnings of the Modern Factory System in England.* London: Jonathan Cape.

Marcus, Greil (1989), *Lipstick Traces: A Secret History of the Twentieth Century.* Cambridge: Harvard University Press.

—— (1995), *The Dustbin of History.* Cambridge: Harvard University Press.

Marr, Andrew (2007), *History of Modern Britain*, BBC, June 12. <http://news.bbc.co.uk/2/hi/uk_news/magazine/6741127.stm>

Martin, Adrian (1989), "The teen movie: why bother?" *Cinema Papers* vol. 75, September, 10–15.

—— (1992a), "In the name of popular culture," *Metro*, issue 89, 34–46.

—— (1992b), "Teen movies debate: mon cas," *Cinema Papers*, issue 89, August, 45, 48.

—— (1994), *Phantasms: The Dreams and Desires of the Heart of Our Popular Culture.* Ringwood, VIC: McPhee Gribble Publishers.

Martin, Daniel (1999), "Power play and party politics: the significance of raving," *Journal of Popular Culture* vol. 32(4), 77–99.

Marx, Karl (1887), *Capital: A Critical Analysis of Capitalist Production*, Frederick Engels (ed.). London: Swan Sonnenschein, Lowrey.

Mayshark, Jesse Fox (2007), *Post-Pop Cinema: The Search for Meaning in New American Film.* Westport and London: Praeger.

McLeer, Anne (2002), "Practical perfection? The nanny negotiates gender, class, and family contradictions in 1960s popular culture," *NWSA Journal* vol. 14(2), 80–101.

McRobbie, Angela (1994), *Postmodernism and Popular Culture.* London and New York: Routledge.

Measham, Fiona (2002), "'Doing gender'—'doing drugs': conceptualizing the gendering of drugs culture," *Contemporary Drug Problems* vol. 29(2), 335–73.

Melechi, Antonio (1993), "The ecstasy of disappearance" in *Rave Off: Politics and Deviance in Contemporary Youth Culture*, Steve Redhead (ed.). Aldershot: Ashgate, 29–40.

Mencimer, Stephanie (2001), "Violent femmes," *The Washington Monthly* vol. 33(9), September, 15–18.

Merchant, Jacqueline and Robert MacDonald (1994), "Youth and the rave culture, ecstasy and health," *Youth and Policy* vol. 45, 16–38.

Metaphilm (2002–2003), "On the brink of falling skyward," *Metaphilm.* <http://www.metaphilm.com/philms/wakinglife.html>

Mink, Nicolaas (2008), "A (Napoleon) Dynamite identity: rural Idaho, the politics of place, and the creation of a new western film," *Western Historical Quarterly* vol. 39(2), 153–75.

Mulvey, Laura (1992 [1975]), "Visual pleasure and narrative cinema," in *Film Theory and Criticism*, Gerald Mast, Marshall Cohen, and Leo Braudy (eds). New York: Oxford University Press, 746–57.

—— (1989), *Visual Culture and Other Pleasures*. Houndmills: Macmillan Press.

Murphy, Kylie (2001), "'I'm sorry—I'm not really sorry': Courtney Love and notions of authenticity," *Hecate* vol. 27(1), May, 139–62.

—— (2002), *Bitch: The Politics of Angry Women*. PhD Dissertation. Murdoch, WA: Murdoch University.

Myles, James (1850), *Chapters in the Life of a Dundee Factory Boy: An Autobiography*. Dundee: James Myles.

Naglazas, Mark (1999), "Get ready, go for some pulp action," *The West Australian*, August 21, 97.

Nashawaty, Chris (1997), "Teen steam," *Entertainment Weekly*, issue 45, November 14, 24–34.

Nead, Lynda (1992), *The Female Nude: Art, Obscenity and Sexuality*. London: Routledge.

Nelson, Hilde Lindemann (1995), "Resistance and insubordination," *Hypatia* vol. 10(2), 23–40.

Nice, James (2002), "Ludus: genius and damage." <http://home.planet.nl/~frankbri/ludushis.html>

O'Brien, Lucy (1999), "The woman punk made me," in *Punk Rock: So What? The Cultural Legacy of Punk*, Roger Sabin (ed.). London and New York: Routledge, 186–98.

Olsen, Mark (1999), "Riding shotgun: *Go* review," *Film Comment* vol. 35(3), May, 6–7.

—— (2001), "Discovery: Richard Kelly," *Film Comment* vol. 37(5), September–October, 16–17.

O'Neill, Brenda (2002), "What do women think?" *Herizons* vol. 16(2), 20–23.

Osgerby, Bill (2004), *Youth Media*. London and New York: Routledge.

Pateman, Carole (1988), *The Sexual Contract*. Oxford: Polity Press.

Pearce, Sharyn (2001), "'*Secret men's business*': new millennium advice for Australian boys," *Mosaic* vol. 34(2), June, 49–64.

People Weekly (1996), "Molly Ringwald: townies," *People Weekly* vol. 46(10), September 2, 48.

—— (1999), "Ten worst dressed: Molly Ringwald," *People Weekly* vol. 46(12), September 16, 92.

Peraino, Judith A. (2001), "Girls with guitars and other strange stories," *Journal of the American Musicological Society* vol. 54(3), 692–709.

Pierson, John (1995), *Spike, Mike, Slackers and Dykes: A Guided Tour Across a Decade of American Independent Cinema*. New York: Hyperion and Miramax Books.

Pini, Maria (1997a), "Cyborgs, nomads and the raving feminine," in *Dance in the City*, Helen Thomas (ed.). Basingstoke: Palgrave Macmillan, 111–29.

—— (1997b), "Women and the early British rave scene," in *Back to Reality? Social Experience and Cultural Studies*, Angela McRobbie (ed.). Manchester and New York: Manchester University Press, 152–69.

—— (2001), *Club Cultures and Female Subjectivity: The Move from Home to House*. Houndmills and New York: Palgrave.

Place, Janey (1998), "Women in film noir," in *Women in Film Noir*, E. Ann Kaplan (ed.). London: British Film Institute, 47–68.

Polhemus, Ted (1997), "In the supermarket of style," in *The Clubcultures Reader: Readings in Popular Cultural Studies*, Steve Redhead, Derek Wynne, and Justin O'Connor (eds). Oxford and Malden: Blackwell Publishers, 148–51.

Popular Memory Group (1982), "Popular memory: theory, politics, method," in *Making Histories: Studies in History-Writing and Politics*, Richard Johnson, Gregor McLennan, Bill Schwarz, and David Sutton (eds). Minneapolis: University of Minnesota Press, 205–52.

Poster, Mark (1997), *Cultural History and Modernity: Disciplinary Readings and Challenges*. New York: Columbia University Press.

Pulver, Andrew (2000), "Introduction," in *Brat Pack Confidential*, Andrew Pulver and Steven Paul Davies (authors). London: BT Batsford, 5–7.

Rapping, Elayne (1987), "Hollywood's youth cult films," *Cineaste* vol. 16(1–2), 14–19.

Rayner, Jonathan (2003), *The Films of Peter Weir*, 2nd edn. New York and London: Continuum Books.

Redhead, Steve (1997), *Subcultures to Clubcultures: An Introduction to Popular Cultural Studies*. Oxford and Malden: Blackwell.

—— (2000), *Repetitive Beat Generation*. Edinburgh: Rebel.

Reynolds, Simon (1998), "Rave culture: living dream or living death?" in *The Clubcultures Reader: Readings in Popular Cultural Studies*, Steve Redhead, Derek Wynne, and Justin O'Connor (eds). Oxford and Malden: Blackwell Publishers, 84–93.

—— (1999), *Generation Ecstasy: Into the World of Techno and Rave Culture*. New York: Routledge.

Rietveld, Hillegonda C. (2000), "The body and soul of club culture," *The UNESCO Courier*, July–August, 28–30.

Riordan, Ellen (2001), "Commodified agents and empowered girls: consuming and producing feminism," *Journal of Communication Inquiry* vol. 25(3), July, 279–97.

Ritchie, Karen (1995), *Marketing to Generation X*. New York: Lexington Books.

Roberts, Kimberley (2002), "Pleasures and problems of the 'angry girl'," in *Sugar, Spice, and Everything Nice: Cinemas of Girlhood*, Frances Gateward and Murray Pomerance (eds). Detroit: Wayne State University Press, 217–33.

Roberts, Lisa (1997), *From Knowledge to Narrative*. Washington: Smithsonian Institution Press.

Robertson, Barbara (2002), "Life lines," *Computer Graphics World* vol. 25(2), February, 12–17.

Rolling Stone (1997), *Rolling Stone* (United States Edition), July 10–24, 76.

Rose, H.J. (1964 [1928]), *A Handbook of Greek Mythology: Including its Extension to Rome*. London: Methuen.

Rosen, Jody (2000), "90's hipsters dial up with the past with an 80's plaything," *The New York Times*, June 18. <http://www.nytimes.com/2000/06/18/arts/music-90-s-hipsters-dial-up-the-past-with-an-80-s-plaything.html>

Rosenbaum, Ron (1996), "In praise of dangerous women: the beautiful and the damned," *Esquire* vol. 125(3), March, 102–11.

——(2004), "*Slacker*'s oblique strategy," in *Slacker* booklet. Detour Filmproduction, 17–21.

Ross, Andrew (1994), "Andrew Ross' weather report," *Artforum International* vol. 32(9), May 1. <http://www.articlearchives.com/humanities-social-science/visual-performing-arts/927334-1.html>

Rothenbuhler, Eric W. (1988), "The liminal fighter: mass strikes as ritual and interpretation," in *Durkheimian Sociology: Cultural Studies*, Jeffrey C. Alexander (ed.). New York: Cambridge University Press, 66–89.

Ruether, Rosemary Radford (1992), "Patriarchy and the men's movement: part of the problem or part of the solution?" in *Women Respond to the Men's Movement*, Kay Leigh Hagan (ed.). New York: Harper Collins, 13–18.

Rushkoff, Douglas (1994a), "Introduction: us, by us," in *The GenX Reader*, Douglas Rushkoff (ed.). New York: Ballantine Books, 3–8.

—— (1994b), *Media Virus: Hidden Agendas in Popular Culture*. New York: Ballantine Books.

—— (1997), *Children of Chaos: Surviving the End of the World as We Know It*. London: Harper Collins.

Rutsky, R.L. and Justin Wyatt (1990), "Serious pleasures: cinematic pleasure and the notion of fun," *Cinema Journal* vol. 30(1), 3–19.

Samuel, Raphael (1994), *Past and Present in Contemporary Culture. Volume 1 of Theatres of Memory*. London and New York: Verso.

Savage, Jon (1997), *Time Travel*. London: Vintage.

—— (2008), *Teenage: The Prehistory of Youth Culture 1875–1945*. London: Penguin Books.

Schaffer, Michael (2001), "No more fast times at Ridgemont High," *The Washington Monthly*, January, 28–30.

Scheib, Richard (1992), "*Bill and Ted's Excellent Adventure*: review." <http://members.fortunecity.com/roogulator/sf/bill&ted.htm>

Scheiner, Georganne (2001), "Look at me, I'm Sandra Dee: beyond a white teen icon," *Frontiers* vol. 22(2), 87–106.

Shary, Timothy (2002), *Generation Multiplex: The Image of Youth in Contemporary American Cinema*. Austin: University of Texas Press.

—— (2005), *Teen Movies: American Youth On Screen*. London: Wallflower Press.

Shepard, Lucius (2002), "Dark, darker, Darko," *Fantasy and Science Fiction* vol. 102(4), April, 111–16.

Simmons, Jerold (1995), "The censoring of *Rebel Without a Cause*," *Journal of Popular Film and Television* vol. 23(2), 56–63.

—— (2008), "Violent youth: the censoring and public reception of *The Wild One* and *The Blackboard Jungle*," *Film History: An International Journal* vol. 20(3), 381–91.

Smith, Gavin (1996), "Girlpower: Sundance '96," *Film Comment* vol. 32(2), March–April, 51–3.

Speed, Lesley (1998), "Pastel romances: the teen films of John Hughes," *Metro*, issue 113/14, 103–10.

—— (2000), "Together in electric dreams: films revisiting 1980s youth," *Journal of Popular Film and Television* vol. 28(1), 22–9.

Spice Girls (1997), *Real Life—Real Spice: The Official Story*. London: Zone/ Chameleon Books.

Stables, Kate (1998), "The postmodern always rings twice: constructing the *femme fatale* in 90s cinema," in *Women in Film Noir*, E. Ann Kaplan (ed.). London: British Film Institute, 164–82.

Stallybrass, Peter and Allon White (1986), *The Politics and Poetics of Transgression*. Ithaca: Cornell University Press.

Stratton, Jon (1985), "Youth subcultures and their cultural contexts," *Australian and New Zealand Journal of Sociology* vol. 21(2), July, 194–218.

Straw, Will (2001), "Consumption," in *The Cambridge Companion to Pop and Rock*, Simon Frith, Will Straw, and John Streets (eds). Cambridge: Cambridge University Press, 53–73.

Summers, Anne (1995), "Shockwaves at the revolution," *Good Weekend: The Australian*, March 18, 30.

Susman, Gary (1998), "Irresistible force: it's a *Spice World* after all—and we just live in it," *The Boston Phoenix*, January 26. <http://weeklywire.com/ww/01-26-98/boston_movies_1.html>

Syson, Damon (1997), "1997: a spice odyssey," *Sky*, February. <http://www.dreamwater.org/music/sgmagazines/SKYspicegirls.html>

Tagg, Philip (1994), "From refrain to rave: the decline of figure and the rise of ground," *Popular Music* vol. 13(2), 209–22.

Temple, Johnny (1999), "Noise from underground: punk rock's anarchic rhythms spur a new generation to political activism," *The Nation*, October 18, 17–28.

Thompson, E.P. (1967), "Time, work-discipline, and industrial capitalism," *Past and Present*, issue 38, December, 56–97.

Tomlinson, Lori (1998), "'This ain't no disco' … or is it? Youth culture and the rave phenomenon," in *Youth Culture: Identity in a Postmodern World*, Jonathon S. Epstein (ed.). Malden and Oxford: Blackwell, 195–211.

Tropiano, Stephen (2006), *Rebels and Chicks: A History of the Hollywood Teen Movie*. New York: Back Stage Books.

Tulloch, John (1990), *Television Drama: Agency, Audience and Myth*. London and New York: Routledge.

—— (1995), "'But why is *Doctor Who* so attractive?' Negotiating ideology and pleasure," in *Science Fiction Audiences: Watching Doctor Who and Star Trek*,

John Tulloch and Henry Jenkins (authors). London and New York: Routledge, 108–24.

Turner, Bryan S. (1987), "A note on nostalgia," *Theory, Culture and Society* vol. 4(1), 147–56.

Turner, Graeme (2004), *Understanding Celebrity*. London, Thousand Oaks, and New Delhi: Sage.

Turner, Victor (1967), *The Forest of Symbols: Aspects of Ndembu Ritual*. Ithaca: Cornell University Press.

Ulrich, John M. (2003), "Introduction. Generation X: a (sub)cultural geneology," in *GenXegesis: Essays on "Alternative" Youth Sub(Culture)*, John M. Ulrich and Andrea L. Harris (eds). Madison: The University of Wisconsin Press, 3–37.

Urschel, Joanne K. (2000), "Men's studies and women's studies: commonality, dependence, and independence," *The Journal of Men's Studies* vol. 8(3), 407–10.

Variety (1985), "Review of *The Breakfast Club*," *Variety*, February 13, 19.

Walters, Chris (2004), "Freedom's just another word for nothing to do," in *Slacker* booklet. Detour Filmproduction, 22–5.

Walters, James (2008), "When people run in circles: structures of time and memory in *Donnie Darko*," in *Violating Time: History, Memory, and Nostalgia in Cinema*, Christina Lee (ed.). New York: Continuum Books, 191–207.

Walzer, Andrew (2002), "Narratives of contemporary male crisis: the (re)production of a national discourse," *The Journal of Men's Studies* vol. 10(2), 209–23.

Washington, Mary Helen (1988 [1892]), "Introduction," in *A Voice from the South*, Anna Julia Cooper (author). New York and Oxford: Oxford University Press, xxvii–liv.

White, Allon (1993), *Carnival, Hysteria, and Writing: Collected Essays and Autobiography*. Oxford: Clarendon Press.

White, Armond (1985), "Kidpix," *Film Comment* vol. 21(4), 9–15.

Whitney, Allison (2002), "Gidget goes hysterical," in *Sugar, Spice, and Everything Nice: Cinemas of Girlhood*, Frances Gateward and Murray Pomerance (eds). Detroit: Wayne State University Press, 55–71.

Widdicombe, Sue and Robin Wooffitt (1995), *The Language of Youth Subcultures: Social Identity in Action*. Hertfordshire: Harvester Wheatsheaf.

Willis, Paul E. (1979), "Shop-floor culture, masculinity and the wage form," in *Working-Class Culture: Studies in History and Theory*. John Clarke, Chas Critcher and Richard Johnson (eds). London: Hutchinson, 185–98.

—— (1990), *Common Culture: Symbolic Work at Play in the Everyday Cultures of the Young*. Buckingham: Open University Press.

Wójcik, Daniel (1997), *The End of the World As We Know It: Faith, Fatalism, and Apocalypse in America*. New York: New York University Press.

Wolcott, James (2003), "Teen engines: riding with the kid culture," *Vanity Fair*, issue 515, July, 70–87, 132–3.

—— (2008), "Who's up? Hollywood's next wave," *Vanity Fair*, issue 576, August, 92–105.

Wood, Robin (2002), "Party time or can't hardly wait for that American pie: Hollywood high school movies of the 90s," *CineAction*, 2–10.

Woods, Paul A. (1998), *King Pulp: The Wild World of Quentin Tarantino*. London: Plexus.

Woodward, Steven (2002), "She's murder: pretty poisons and bad seeds," in *Sugar, Spice, and Everything Nice: Cinemas of Girlhood*, Frances Gateward and Murray Pomerance (eds). Detroit: Wayne State University Press, 303–21.

Wright, Patrick (1992), *A Journey Through Ruins*. London: Flamingo.

Wyatt, Justin (1994), *High Concept: Movies and Marketing in Hollywood*. Austin: University of Texas Press.

Wyllyams, Beth, Mandy Norman, and Linda Males (1997), *All About the Spice Girls and Me*. New York: Aladdin Paperbacks.

Yeap, Sue (1999), "Tale of a sour teacher fails acid test (review of *Teaching Mrs Tingle*)," *The West Australian: Arts and Entertainment*, October 23, 112.

Zimmerman, Patricia (1993), "The female bodywars: rethinking feminist media politics," *Socialist Review* vol. 23(2), 35–56.

Zuel, Bernard (2004), "A French delicacy," *The Sydney Morning Herald*, August 14. <http://www.smh.com.au/articles/2004/08/13/1092340453918.html?from =storylhs&oneclick=true>

Filmography

American Beauty (1999), dir. Sam Mendes. Universal Studios.
American Graffiti (1973), dir. George Lucas. Universal Studios.
American Pie (1999), dir. Paul Weiz. Universal Studios.
American Pie 2 (2001), dir. J.B. Rogers. Universal Studios.
American Wedding (2003), dir. Jesse Dylan. Universal Studios.
A Scanner Darkly (2006), dir. Richard Linklater. Warner Bros.
Back to the Future (1985), dir. Robert Zemeckis. Twentieth Century Fox.
Basic Instinct (1992), dir. Paul Verhoeven. Lionsgate/Fox Studios.
Before Sunrise (1995), dir. Richard Linklater. Warner Bros.
Before Sunset (2004), dir. Richard Linklater. Warner Bros.
Bend It Like Beckham (2002), dir. Gurinder Chadha. Twentieth Century Fox.
Betsy's Wedding (1990), dir. Alan Alda. Touchstone Pictures.
Better Living Through Circuity (1999), dir. Jon Reiss. MVD Visual.
Beverly Hills, 90210 (1990–2000), created by Darren Star. Spelling Productions.
Bill and Ted's Excellent Adventure (1989), dir. Stephen Herek. MGM/United Artists.
Blackboard Jungle (1955), dir. Richard Brooks. MGM.
Body of Evidence (1993), dir. Uli Edel. MGM.
Boys Don't Cry (1999), dir. Kimberly Peirce. Fox Searchlight Pictures.
Boyz N the Hood (1991), dir. John Singleton. Sony Pictures.
Brady Bunch, The (1969–1974), created by Sherwood Schwartz. ABC.
Breakfast Club, The (1985), dir. John Hughes. Universal Studios.
Bring It On (2000), dir. Peyton Reed. Universal Studios.
Buffy the Vampire Slayer (1997–2003), created by Joss Whedon. Twentieth Century Fox.
Carrie (1976), dir. Brian De Palma. MGM/United Artists.
Clueless (1995), dir. Amy Heckerling. Paramount Pictures.
Commando (1985), dir. Mark L. Lester. Twentieth Century Fox.
Craft, The (1996), dir. Andrew Fleming. Columbia Pictures.
Cruel Intentions (1999), dir. Roger Kumble. Columbia Tristar Pictures.
Cut (2000), dir. Kimble Rendall. MBP, Mushroom Pictures, and Beyond Films.
Cry Baby (1990), dir. John Waters. Universal Studios.
Dawson's Creek (1998–2003), created by Kevin Williamson. Warner Bros.
Dazed and Confused (1993), dir. Richard Linklater. Universal Studios.
Dead Poets Society (1989), dir. Peter Weir. Touchstone Pictures.
Dogfight (1991), dir. Nancy Savoca. Warner Bros.
Donnie Darko (2001), dir. Richard Kelly. Pandora.

Dude, Where's My Car? (2000), dir. Danny Leiner. Twentieth Century Fox.
Electric Dreams (1984), dir. Steve Barron. Virgin/Twentieth Century Fox.
Encino Man (1992), dir. Les Mayfield. Walt Disney.
Faculty, The (1998), dir. Robert Rodriguez. Miramax.
Falling Down (1993), dir. Joel Schumacher. Warner Bros.
Fast Food Nation (2006), dir. Richard Linklater. Twentieth Century Fox.
Fatal Attraction (1987), dir. Adrian Lyne. Paramount Pictures.
Ferris Bueller's Day Off (1986), dir. John Hughes. Paramount Pictures.
Finding Forrester (2000), dir. Gus Van Sant. Columbia Pictures.
Footloose (1984), dir. Herbert Ross. Paramount Pictures.
For Keeps (1988), dir. John G. Avildsen. Columbia Tristar Pictures.
40 Days and 40 Nights (2002), dir. Michael Lehmann. Universal Studios.
Freaks and Geeks (1999–2000), created by Paul Feig. NBC.
Freeway (1996), dir. Matthew Bright. Republic Pictures.
Fresh Horses (1988), dir. David Anspaugh. Columbia Tristar Pictures.
Get Real (1999), dir. Simon Shore. Paramount Pictures.
Ghost World (2001), dir. Terry Zwigoff. MGM.
Gidget (1959), dir. Paul Wendkos. Columbia Pictures.
Gidget Goes Hawaiian (1961), dir. Paul Wendkos. Columbia Pictures.
Ginger Snaps (2000), dir. John Fawcett. Artisan Studio.
Girlfight (2000), dir. Karyn Kusama. Columbia Tristar Pictures.
Girls Town (1996), dir. Jim McKay. Evergreen Entertainment.
Go (1999), dir. Doug Liman. Columbia Pictures.
Gossip Girl (2007–), created by Josh Schwartz and Stephanie Savage. Warner
    Bros.
Grease (1978), dir. Randal Kleiser. Paramount Pictures.
Groove (2000), dir. Greg Harrison. Columbia Tristar Pictures.
Grosse Pointe Blank (1997), dir. George Armitage. Hollywood Pictures.
Hard Candy (2005), dir. David Slade. Lions Gate.
Harry Potter and the Prisoner of Azkaban (2004), dir. Alfonso Cuarón. Warner
    Bros.
Heathers (1989), dir. Michael Lehmann. Anchor Bay Entertainment.
Heavenly Creatures (1994), dir. Peter Jackson. Miramax.
History of Modern Britain (2007), dir. Francis Whately. BBC.
Human Traffic (1999), dir. Justin Kerrigan. Renaissance Films.
It's Impossible to Learn to Plow by Reading Books (1988), dir. Richard Linklater.
    Detour Filmproduction.
Jade (1995), dir. William Friedkin. Paramount Pictures.
Jawbreaker (1999), dir. Darren Stein. Sony Pictures.
Jay and Silent Bob Strike Back (2001), dir. Kevin Smith. Dimension Films.
Juno (2007), dir. Jason Reitman. Twentieth Century Fox.
Karate Kid, The (1984), dir. John G. Avildsen. Columbia Tristar Pictures.
Kids (1995), dir. Larry Clark. Excalibur Films.
King Lear (1987), dir. Jean-Luc Godard. Cinematheque.

Leave It To Beaver (1957–1963), created by Joe Connelly and Bob Mosher. CBS/ABC.

Less Than Zero (1987), dir. Marek Kanievska. Twentieth Century Fox.

Long Kiss Goodnight, The (1996), dir. Renny Harlin. New Line Cinema.

Lost Boys, The (1987), dir. Joel Schumacher. Warner Bros.

Mamma Mia! (2008), dir. Phyllida Lloyd. Universal Studios.

Mean Girls (2004), dir. Mark S. Waters. Paramount Pictures.

My Own Private Idaho (1991), dir. Gus Van Sant. New Line Cinema.

My So-Called Life (1994–1995), created by Winnie Holzman. ABC.

Mystery Date (1991), dir. Jonathan Wacks. MGM.

Nancy Drew (2007), dir. Andrew Fleming. Warner Bros.

Napoleon Dynamite (2004), dir. Jared Hess. Twentieth Century Fox.

National Lampoon's Animal House (1978), dir. John Landis. Universal Studios.

Not Another Teen Movie (2001), dir. Joel Gallen. Columbia Tristar Pictures.

O.C., The (2003–2007), created by Josh Schwartz. Warner Bros.

Out of the Past (1947), dir. Jacques Tourneur. RKO.

Outsiders, The (1983), dir. Francis Ford Coppola. Warner Bros.

Partridge Family, The (1970–1974), created by Bernard Slade. ABC.

Peggy Sue Got Married (1986), dir. Francis Ford Coppola. Columbia Tristar Pictures.

Pick Up Artist, The (1987), dir. James Toback. Twentieth Century Fox.

Pleasantville (1998), dir. Gary Ross. New Line Cinema.

Porky's (1982), dir. Bob Clark. Twentieth Century Fox.

Predator (1987), dir. John McTiernan. Twentieth Century Fox.

Pretty in Pink (1986), dir. Howard Deutch. Paramount Pictures.

Pulp Fiction (1994), dir. Quentin Tarantino. Miramax.

Pump Up the Volume (1990), dir. Allan Moyle. New Line Cinema.

Quadrophenia (1979), dir. Franc Roddam. Rhino/WEA.

Real Genius (1985), dir. Martha Coolidge. Sony Pictures.

Reality Bites (1994), dir. Ben Stiller. Universal Studios.

Rebel Without a Cause (1955), dir. Nicholas Ray. Warner Bros.

Reservoir Dogs (1992), dir. Quentin Tarantino. Miramax.

Risky Business (1983), dir. Paul Brickman. Warner Bros.

River's Edge (1987), dir. Tim Hunter. Island Pictures.

Rock Around The Clock (1956), dir. Fred F. Sears. Columbia Studios.

Romy and Michele's High School Reunion (1997), dir. David Mirkin. Touchstone Pictures.

Roswell (1999–2002), created by Jason Katims. Warner Bros.

Say Anything... (1989), dir. Cameron Crowe. Twentieth Century Fox.

Scream (1996), dir. Wes Craven. Miramax.

Secret Life of the American Teenager, The (2008–), created by Brenda Hampton. ABC.

sex, lies, and videotape (1989), dir. Steven Soderbergh. Miramax.

Sixteen Candles (1984), dir. John Hughes. Universal Studios.

Slacker (1991), dir. Richard Linklater. Detour Filmproduction.
Some Kind of Wonderful (1987), dir. Howard Deutch. Paramount Pictures.
Spice World: The Spice Girls Movie (1997), dir. Bob Spiers. Polygram Filmed
   Entertainment.
Stand, The (1994), dir. Mick Garris. Republic Pictures.
Stand By Me (1986), dir. Rob Reiner. Columbia Pictures.
Superman (1978), dir. Richard Donner. Warner Bros.
Tammy and the Doctor (1963), dir. Harry Keller. Universal Studios.
Tammy Tell Me True (1961), dir. Harry Keller. Universal Studios.
Teaching Mrs Tingle (1999), dir. Kevin Williamson. Miramax and Dimension
   Films.
Teen Wolf (1985), dir. Rob Daniel. MGM.
Terminator, The (1984), dir. James Cameron. MGM/United Artists.
Terminator 2: Judgment Day (1991), dir. James Cameron. Artisan Entertainment.
Time Bandits, The (1980), dir. Terry Gilliam. HandMade Films.
Time Machine, The (1960), dir. George Pal. Warner Bros.
Towelhead (2007), dir. Alan Ball. Warner Bros.
24 Hour Party People (2002), dir. Michael Winterbottom. MGM.
21 Jump Street (1987–1991), created by Patrick Hasburgh and Stephen J. Cannell.
   Fox Studios.
Twilight (2008), dir. Catherine Hardwicke. Summit Entertainment.
View, The (1997–), "Interview with Mollywald Ringwald and Shailene Woodley,"
   episode date: February 6, 2009. ABC.
Waking Life (2001), dir. Richard Linklater. Twentieth Century Fox.
Wall Street (1987), dir. Oliver Stone. Twentieth Century Fox.
Wedding Singer, The (1998), dir. Frank Coraci. New Line Cinema.
Weird Science (1985), dir. John Hughes. Universal Studios.
What's Eating Gilbert Grape? (1993), dir. Lasse Hallström. Paramount Pictures.
Wild One, The (1953), dir. Laslo Benedek. Sony Pictures.

Discography

Baerwald, David (1994), "I'm Nuthin'," *Reality Bites* album. Universal City
   Studios.
Hole (1998), "Celebrity Skin," *Celebrity Skin* album. DGC Records.
Jules, Gary (2001), "Mad World," *Donnie Darko* album. Sanctuary and
   Adventure.
Simple Minds (1985), "Don't You (Forget About Me)," *The Breakfast Club* album.
   Virgin Records.
Spice Girls (1996), "Wannabe," *Spice* album. Virgin Records.
Spice Girls (1997), "Viva Forever," *Spiceworld* album. Virgin Records.

Index

References to illustrations are in **bold**

7 Year Bitch 66
21 Jump Street 34, 51–2
24 Hour Party People 96
40 Days and 40 Nights 115
1950s
    cinema 31, 123
    optimism, *Back to the Future* 122,
        123–4
1980s
    dystopia, *Donnie Darko* 125
    icon, Ringwald as 43, 50, 56
    imagery in films 5
acid house music 99
action films 117–18
adolescence, construction of 27
affect
    and cinema 45
    Grossberg on 29
Agamben, Giorgio 51
AIDS
    epidemic 45, 144
    paranoia 31, 51
Alden, Norman 123
All About the Spice Girls and Me 69
Allen, Virginia, *The Femme Fatale: Erotic
    Icon* 80
American Dream 21, 104, 117, 125, 128,
    137
American Beauty 119, 120–1
American Graffiti 6, 28
American Pie 115
American Pie 2 115
American Wedding 115
Anderson, Paul Thomas 152
anti-advertising 21fn3
Ariès, Philippe 12
Aronofsky, Darren 151
Askew, Desmond 103

Baby Boomers 16, 17, 18, 32, 48, 122,
    123, 125
Back to the Future 10, 111, 121–4, **122**
    1950s optimism 122, 123–4
    Donnie Darko, comparison 125
Bacon, Kevin 153
Baerwald, David, "I'm Nuthin'" 20–1
Bakan, David 12
Bakhtin, Mikhail, on carnival 38
Ball, Lucille 123
Barron, Robert V. 114
Barrymore, Drew 131
Barthes, Roland, on myth 50
Basic Instinct 78
Bauman, Zygmunt, on identity 44
The Beatles 60
    A Hard Day's Night 71
Beckham, Victoria ("Posh Spice") 72
Beesley, Terence 109
Before Sunrise 133, 143, 145, 146, 147
Before Sunset 133, 143–4, 145, 146, 147,
    148
Bend It Like Beckham 152
Bening, Annette 120
Bernstein, Jonathan, *Pretty in Pink: The
    Golden Age of Teenage Movies*
    27–8
Betsy's Wedding 49
Better Living Through Circuitry 99
Beverly Hills, 90210 3, 34
Bexton, Nathan 105
Biehn, Michael 114
Biggs, Jason 115
Bikini Kill 64, 66
Bill and Ted's Excellent Adventure 114–15
Birch, Thora 120
Birmingham Centre for Contemporary
    Cultural Studies 14, 15
bitch
    femme fatale, difference 87
    in *Freeway* 89, 94

in *Heathers* 84–5
in youth cinema 9, 77–8
see also femme fatale
Blackboard Jungle 33, 34
Bledel, Alexis 4
Bly, Robert 18, 19
Bodison, Wolfgang 90
Body of Evidence 78, 82
Boym, Svetlana 51
on nostalgia 46
Boys Don't Cry 3
Boyz N the Hood 3
The Brady Bunch 20
Brand, Stewart, *The Clock of the Long
    Now* 53
Brando, Marlon 32
Brat Pack 47–8
The Breakfast Club 1, 27, 28, 46, 47, **47**,
    48, 52, 57, 58
bricolage, British Mods 15
Bright, Matthew 78, 90, 94
Bring It On 77, 82–3
Broderick, Matthew **35**, 56
Brooks, Trevor Jack 138
Brown, Melanie ("Scary Spice") 72
Buffy the Vampire Slayer 3
Bunton, Emma ("Baby Spice") 72
Buzzcocks 96
Bynes, Amanda 4

Cabaret musical 57
cable subscriptions 19
Caffeine, Jean 134
Capa, Robert 17
carnival
    Bakhtin on 38
    as catalyst 39
    and the grotesque 38
    and transgression 40
Carr, E.H. 113, 124
Carrie 78
Castell, Dominik 143
celebrity
    as genre of representation 73
    status 9, 49, 59, 72
Chambers, Ian 23
Chang, Chris 141
Charles, Josh 116

childhood, changing concept of 12
Chisholm, Melanie ("Sporty Spice") 69
cinema
    1950s 31, 123
    and affect 45
    and Baby Boomers 32
    as interpretive truth 53
    juvenile delinquent in 33, 34
    and memory 45, 54
    see also youth cinema
Clark, Larry 7, 133
Clarke, John 15
Clinton, Bill, impeachment 126
Close, Glenn 79
Clueless 3
Cobain, Kurt 43
Cockrell, Eddie 143–4
Cohen, Phil 14
Cohen, Stanley 18
Collin, Matthew 98, 106
Columbine shooting 54
coming-of-age films 7, 115–16, 127fn3
Commando 117
commodification, Spice Girls 67, 73
commodity fetishism, Girl Power as 67
Considine, David, *The Cinema of
    Adolescence* 8
Coogan, Steve 96
Cooper, Anna Julia, *A Voice from the South*
    62
Cooper, Chris 121
Coppola, Sofia 152
Corliss, Richard 80
Costello, Elvis 71
Coupland, Douglas, *Generation X* 17–18,
    148
The Craft 77
Cranny-Francis, Anne 90
creativity, symbolic 107
    Willis on 102
    Cruel Intentions 77
    Cry Baby 34
Cryer, Jon 48
Cubitt, Sean 21
culture
    malleability of 99
    Willis on 29
    see also popular culture; subcultures

Cumming, Alan 73
Curtis, Ian 96
Cusack, John 151
Cut 56–7

Daugherty, Rebecca 63
Dawson's Creek 3, 13
Dazed and Confused 133
Dead Poets Society 116–17
Dean, James 22, 32, 34, 43, 92, 103
Dee, Sandra
    constructed image 51
    Ringwald, comparison 50, 57
Delpy, Julie 134, **140**, 143, **146**
Depp, Johnny 34
Deverson, Jane *see* Hamblett, Charles
Devoto, Howard 96
Die Hard 91
Diesel, Vin 91
Dietert, Samuel 135
Diggs, Taye 108
Dillard, Brian 68
disc jockeys 95
discography 174
Doane, Mary Ann 86
Dogfight 6fn1
Doherty, Shannen 83, **83**
Doherty, Thomas 32
Donnie Darko 10, 111, 124–32
    1980s dystopia 125
    Back to the Future, comparison 125
    masculinity 126–7
    mental illness in 129–30
Douglas, Michael 119
Downey, Robert Jr 47
Driver, Minnie 151
Dude, Where's My Car? 115–16
Duff, Hilary 4
Duran Duran, "Notorious" 130
Duval, James 108, 124, **128**
Dyer, Danny 109
Dyer, Richard 152
Ecstasy drug 97, 101, 103, 105, 106, 107,
    109
Eisenhower, Dwight 31
Electric Dreams 19
Eliot, T.S., "Four Quartets" 137
Encino Man 3

Estevez, Emilio 47, **47**

The Faculty 31
Falk, Lisanne 83, **83**
Falling Down 119, 121, 130
fandom 56, 59, 73
Fast Food Nation 133
Fatal Attraction 78, 79, 80
feminism
    backlash against 118
    development phases 61–3
    do-it-yourself 63–6
    media manifestations 63
    and punk subculture 63–4
    Spice Girls 70, 75
    third-wave 54, 64
    see also Girl Power; Riot Grrrl
        Movement
femme fatale
    bitch, difference 87
    construction 81
    in *film noir* 80–1
    films 78–82
    iconography 80
    post-modern version 82
    as vampire 80
    violence 79
    see also bitch
Ferris Bueller's Day Off 34–6, **35**, 49, 55
Fichtner, William 106
film noir, femme fatale in 80–1
film types *see* action films; coming-of-age
    films; office films; teen films
filmography 171–4
Finding Forrester 152
Firgens, Mackenzie 109
Fiske, John 8
Footloose 1
For Keeps 49
Foucault, Michel 15
Fox, Kitty 89
Fox, Michael J. 121, **122**
Freaks and Geeks 3
Freeman, J.E. 108
Freeway 78, 88–93, **91**
    bitch in 89, 94
    female violence 89, 91–2, 93
    Red Riding Hood motif 88, 90

Fresh Horses 49
Frith, Simon 30
Frow, John 146–7
Fukuyama, Francis, *End of History* 125–6
    critique 126
Fullilove, Donald 123

Gallagher, Hugh 24
Garner, Helen, *The First Stone* 61
Garratt, Sheryl 97
Garrison, Ednie Kaeh 65, 68
Geldof, Bob 72
Generation X
    and the American Dream 21
    cultural studies approach 1
    film-makers 151–2
    Linklater's films 133–49
    meanings 11, 153–4
    media saturation 18–22
    and media technology 19
    multidimensionality 152
    origins 17
    purchasing power 19
    Reality Bites 144–5
    Slacker 18, 133, 134–8
    tv, experience of 20
    Waking Life 138–42
"Generation X" band 17
Generation Y 151
Genesis P-Orridge 99
Gerard, Morgan 100
Get Real 3
Geyh, Paula 137, 138
Ghost World 3
Gidget 50
Gidget Goes Hawaiian 50
Ginger Snaps 126, 127fn3
Girl Power 59, 60, 68, 69
    as commodity fetishism 67
    as new age feminism 69
    see also Spice Girls
Girlfight 87, 152
Girls Town 152
Giroux, Henry 2, 93, 148
Glover, Crispin 121
Go 97, 103–9, **104**
    female drug dealing 105–6, 107–8
    female transgression 107

'fun' as commodity 105
    identity issues 108
    masculinity 109
    rave backdrop 106, 108, 110
Goodwin, Andrew 67
Gossip Girl 4, 14
Grant, Richard E. 73
Grease 77
Greer, Jane 82
Greven, David 115, 116
Gries, John 5
Groove 109–10
Grossberg, Lawrence 8, 21–2
    on affect 29
Grosse Pointe Blank 5, 151
Gyllenhaal, Jake 124, **128**
Gyllenhaal, Maggie 128

Haaken, Janice 79
Hacienda club 63, 96, 97
Hall, Anthony Michael **47**
Hall, G. Stanley, *Adolescence* 13fn2
Hall, Stuart, on transgression 40
Halliwell, Geri ("Ginger Spice") 69, 75
Hamblett, Charles, and Jane Deverson,
    Generation X 17
Hancock, Martin 96
Hanna, Kathleen 64
Hannigan, Alyson 115
Hansen, Gale 116
Hanson, Peter 145
    The Cinema of Generation X 8
Hard Candy 94
Harris, Anita 61
Harris, Barbara 151
Harrison, Carol 109
Harry, Debbie 63
Harry Potter and the Prisoner of Azkaban
    111
Hartley, John 3
Hartnett, Josh 115
Haslam, Dave, *Adventures on the Wheels
    of Steel* 95
Hawke, Ethan 116, 134, **140**, 143, **146**
    novels
        Ash Wednesday 143fn5
        The Hottest State 143fn5
Hawking, Stephen 111, 113

A Brief History of Time 129
Heathers 78, 83–8, **83**
    bitch in 84–5
    cinematic gaze 86
Heavenly Creatures 152
Hebdige, Dick 15, 16
Hedaya, Dan 90
Heder, Jon 5
Heimann, Jim 16–17
Heimel, Cynthia 118
Henderson, Shirley 96
Hershey, Barbara 119
high school
    as microcosm of society 55
    prom 55–6
hippie 10, 15, 99, 105
history
    dominant view 45
    and identity 44–5
    as ideological construct 113–14
    Jenkins on 113
    Marcus on 153
    as time travel 114
Hole 65, 66
    Celebrity Skin 68
Holmes, Katie **104**, 105
hooks, bell 152
Hopkins, Susan 67, 75
Hornblower, Margot 20
Hoskins, Bob 71, 74
Howry, Allison 62
Huggy Bear 66
Hughes, John 9, 10, 43, 56
    high school films 54–5
    Ringwald films 47–8
Hultkrans, Andrew 23
Human Traffic 95, 107
    masculinity 109
Hunter, Latham 120, 121
Hutton, Fiona 107
Huyssen, Andreas 45

icons
    1980s, Ringwald 43, 50, 56
    female 4
identity
    and history 44–5
    Zygmunt on 44

Idol, Billy 17
Inness, Sherrie 90
It's A Wonderful Life 124
It's Impossible to Learn to Plow by
    Reading Books 141

Jackson, Michael 10
Jackson, Samuel L. **23**
Jade 78
James, Mark 134
Jawbreaker 3
Jay and Silent Bob Strike Back 8
Jenkins, Henry 69
Jenkins, Keith, on history 113
Jewell, David 141
John, Elton 72
Jones, Kent 139
Jonze, Spike 152
Joy Division 96
Juno 152
juvenile, US classification 12
juvenile delinquent, in cinema 33, 34

Kael, Pauline 49
The Karate Kid 1
Kaufman, Michael 92
Kaveney, Roz 2
Kelly, Gene 123
Kelly, Richard 10, 111, 124, 127, 128,
    130, 131, 132
    nostalgia 125
Kerr, Philip 129
Kids 7
King, Noel 28
Kirkwood, Denny 109
Klein, Hugh 13
Kristeva, Julia 37
Krizan, Kim 139
Krull, Suzanne 107
Kutcher, Ashton 115

Leach, Jim 52
Leave It To Beaver 20
Lehmann, Michael 78
Leighton, Claire 97
Leitch, Thomas 32
Leonard, Sean Robert 116
Less Than Zero 51

Lewis, Jon, *The Road to Romance and Ruin* 8
Lightman, Alan 132
Liman, Doug 10, 97, 103
liminality, youth cinema 36–7
Linklater, Lorelei 138
Linklater, Richard 10, 133, 151
    Generation X films 133–49
Lively, Blake 4
Lloyd, Christopher 121, **122**
Loggins, Kenny, "Footloose" 153
Lohan, Lindsay 4
The Long Kiss Goodnight 87
Loomis, Rod 114
The Lost Boys 30–1
Love, Courtney 65, 66, 75
    selling out, accusation 68
Lowe, Rob 47
Lowenthal, David 6
Lucas, George 151
Ludus 63
Lumby, Catharine 66

McCarthy, Andrew 48, 49
McClure, Marc 122
McCormack, Keith 135
McDonnell, Mary 129
McKinney, Mark 74
McLeer, Anne 117
McRobbie, Angela 2, 99
Madonna 79
Majorino, Tina 5
Malone, Jena **128**, 131
Mamma Mia! 4
Mangold, Erni 143
Marcus, Greil 44
    on history 153
Marr, Andrew, *History of Modern Britain* 119fn2
Martin, Adrian 7, 28–9, 36
Martin, Daniel 107
Marx, Karl 67
masculinity
    crisis
        books 118
        films 117–18, 119–21
    Donnie Darko 126–7
    Go 109

Human Traffic 109
Mayshark, Jesse Fox 137
Mean Girls 4, 77
meaning, construction of 73
Measham, Fiona 105
media, subversiveness of 23–5
Melechi, Antonio 108
memory
    and cinema 45, 54
    popular 1, 31, 45–6, 53, 54, 57, 63, 75, 118, 153
    and time 53
Mencimer, Stephanie 91–2
Meyer, Breckin 108
Mods, British, bricolage 15
Mohr, Jay 103
Monroe, Marilyn 22, 72, 123
Moore, Demi 47
Moore, Mandy 4
Moore, Roger 74
Moreland, David 129
Morris, Meaghan 55
Mortensen, Viggo 49
MTV, influence 24–5
Mulvey, Laura 84, 86
Murphy, Kylie 67
My Own Private Idaho 152
My So-Called Life 3
Mystery Date 3
myth, Barthes on 50

Naglazas, Mark 103
Nancy Drew 4
Napoleon Dynamite 5
Nashawaty, Chris 3–4
National Lampoon's Animal House 48
Nead, Lynda 65
Nelson, Judd **47**
Newton-John, Olivia 77
Nixon, Richard 31
Northern Soul music 96
nostalgia 10, 21, 38, 45, 124, 138, 147
    as cultural discourse 5–6
    definition 6
    reflective 6, 46, 151
    restorative 46
Not Another Teen Movie 5, 57

Oakenfold, Paul 101
The O.C. 14
office films 118–20
Olsen, Ashley 4
Olsen, Mark 125, 126
Olsen, Mary-Kate 4
Olyphant, Timothy 105
Osborne, Holmes 128
Out of the Past 82
The Outsiders 34

Page, Ellen 94
Parkes, Shaun 109
The Partridge Family 20
Pateman, Carole 125
Peggy Sue Got Married 14
Peraino, Judith 62, 66
Perkins, Emily 127fn3
Perry, Luke 34
Phoenix, River 6fn1
The Pick Up Artist 49
Pilkington, Lorraine 109
Pini, Maria 97, 101, 108
Place, Janey 81
Pleasantville 3
Plummer, Amanda 88
PLUR mantra, rave subculture 99
Polhemus, Ted 108
Polley, Sarah 103, **104**
popular culture
    accessibility 30
    uses 30
Porky's 48
Poster, Mark 126
Predator 117
Presley, Elvis 15, 32
Pretty in Pink 46, 48, 49, 52, 55, 57
Pulp Fiction 22, **23**
Pulver, Andrew 47–8
Pump Up the Volume 9, 37–41, **39**
punk music, gender discrimination 66fn3
punk subculture 16
    as commodified lifestyle 67–8
    and feminism 63–4

Quadrophenia 6

Rae, Brian 95–6

Rapping, Elayne 28
rave subculture
    dancefloor dynamics 101
    egalitarianism 101
    Ibiza origins 97, 98
    legal sanctions against 100
    liminality 100
    mainstream appropriation 104fn3
    male centeredness 101
    manifestations 100
    moral panic reaction 99–100
    paradoxes 110
    PLUR mantra 99
    smiley face logo 99
    USA 104
    women, invisibility 10, 96–7, 101–2
    see also Go
Raven 4
Rayner, Jonathan 117
Reagan, Ronald 31
Real Genius 34
Reality Bites 144–5
Rebel Without a Cause 32–3
Reckless 28
Redhead, Steve 100
Reeve, Christopher 114
Reeves, Keanu 7, 91, 114
Reservoir Dogs 8
revivalist texts, Speed on 5
Reynolds, Nicola 109
Reynolds, Simon 101
Rietveld, Hillegonda 101–2
Ringwald, Molly 9, 46–52, **47**, 154
    as 1980s icon 43, 50, 56
    Dee, comparison 50, 57
    Hughes films 47–8
    post-Hughes films 49, 56–8
Riordan, Ellen 67
Riot Grrrl Movement 9, 63, 64–6, 70, 89
    and the body 65
    media dissemination 68
Risky Business 34
Ritchie, Karen 20
rites of passage 7, 10, 111
    films 117, 121
    phases 36
River's Edge 7
Roberts, Emma 4

Roberts, Kimberley 90, 92–3
Rock Around The Clock 33–4
Romy and Michele's High School Reunion 5
Ross, Andrew 104–5
Ross, Katherine 129, 131
Roswell 13, 30
Ruck, Alan **35**
Ruell, Aaron 5
Rushbrook, Claire 73
Rushkoff, Douglas 11, 24
    Children of Chaos 25fn5
    Media Virus 23
Rutsky, R.L. 36
Ryder, Winona 83, **83**

Sara, Mia **35**
Saunders, Jennifer 72
Savage, Jon 13fn2, 30, 54
Savoca, Nancy 6fn1
Say Anything... 6, 7
A Scanner Darkly 133
Schaeffer, Michael 54
Schaudies, Jennifer 135
Schwarzenegger, Arnold 114, 117, 118
Scott, Seann William 115–16
Scream 3
The Secret Life of the American Teenager
    58
sex, lies, and videotape 8
Sex Pistols 66fn3, 96
Seyfried, Amanda 4
Shary, Timothy 31
    Generation Multiplex 8
Sheedy, Ally 47, **47**
Shephard, Lucius 125
Sherman, Barry Del 120
Shubert, Jimmy 108
Simm, John 95
Simmons, Jerrold 32
Simple Minds, "Don't You (Forget About
    Me)" 43, 57
Simpson, O.J., trial 126
Singer, Bryan 152
Singer, Joey Hope 119
Sixteen Candles 46–7, 48, 52, 58
Slacker
    episodic structure 135–6
    and Generation X 18, 133, 134–8

    reception 135–6
    slacker generation 10, 137–8
Slater, Christian **39**, 84
Slits 63
smiley face logo, rave subculture 99
Smith, Gavin 89
Smith, Kevin 1, 133, 151
Smith, Patti 63
Soderbergh, Steven 133, 151
Some Kind of Wonderful 52–3, 55
Spacek, Sissy 78
Spacey, Kevin 120
Speed, Lesley, on revivalist texts 5
Spelletich, Kalman 136
Sperber, Wendie Jo 122
Spice Girls 9, 59–60
    commodification 67, 73
    feminist agenda 70, 75
    Real Life - Real Spice book 69
    reunion (2007) 60
    songs
        'Viva Forever' 75
        'Wannabe' 60, 68–9
    Spice album 59, 60
    "Spice Squad" fans 69
    Spice World: The Spice Girls Movie
        59, 70–4, **71**
Spielberg, Steven 151
Stables, Kate 81–2
Stallone, Sylvester 117
Stallybrass, Peter 38
The Stand 57
Stand By Me 6, 29–30
Steedman, Tony 114
Sterling, Linda 64
Stewart, Kristen 4
Stiller, Ben 144
Stoltz, Eric 52
Stone, Sharon 79
Straw, Will 60
subcultural theory 2, 8, 14, 16
subcultures
    mainstreaming 15–16
    Teddy Boy 14–15
    see also punk subculture; rave
        subculture
Summers, Anne 61
Superman 114

Susman, Gary 70
Sutherland, Kiefer 89
Swayze, Patrick 10, 127

Tagg, Philip 100
Tammy and the Doctor 50
Tammy Tell Me True 50
Tarantino, Quentin 22, 133, 151
Taylor, Lili 6fn1
Taylor, Rod 114
Taylor, Teresa 136
Teaching Mrs Tingle 56
Tears For Fears, "Mad World" 126, 131
technologics 65
teen films, disparagement of 27, 28
Teen Vogue 3
Teen Wolf 30
teenagers, cultural construction of 13fn2
Teret, Ray 96
The Terminator 11, 114
Terminator 2: Judgment Day 87
terrorism 148
Thatcherism, and unemployment 97–8
Thomas, Giles 109
Thompson, E.P. 111–12
Thompson, Lea 121
Thurman, Uma 22, 143fn5
time
    gendered 112–13
    industrial 112
    manipulation 112
    and memory 53
    nature of 132
The Time Bandits 114
The Time Machine 114
time travel, history as 114
time travel films 10, 111, 121–32
    male dominance 114
timeshifting, with the VCR 21
Tolkan, James 122
Towelhead 152
transgression
    and carnival 40
    Hall on 40
    youth cinema 38–41
Travolta, John 22, **23**
Tropiano, Stephen 48
Tulloch, John 73

Turner, Bryan 5
Turner, Graeme 73
Turner, Kathleen 114
Turner, Victor 36
Twilight 4
Twisted Wheel Club (Manchester) 95–6

Ubach, Alanna 92
unemployment, and Thatcherism 97–8
USA, rave subculture 104

Valens, Ritchie 43
vampire, femme fatale as 80
Van Damme, Jean-Claude 117
Vanity Fair 4
VCR 20
    ownership 19
    timeshifting with 21
Vicious, Sid 43
Vietnam War 6fn1, 20, 50, 117
The View 58
Virginia Tech shooting 54

Waking Life **140**, 147
    animation component 139
    critique 139
    dreams 142
    episodic structure 138
    and Generation X 133, 138–42
    'journey' motif 141–2
    as process 139–40
    transcendent moments 141
    visuals 140
Walker, Kim 83, **83**
Wall Street 51
Walters, Chris 137
Walters, James 125
Watergate scandal 50, 126
Wayne, John 123
The Wedding Singer 5
Weird Science 49, 55
Weiss, Michael T. 89
Wendt, George 74
West, Honey, tv sleuth 63fn1
What's Eating Gilbert Grape? 152
White, Allon 38
White, Armond 28
Whitney, Allison 12

Wiedlin, Jane 114
Wiggins, Wiley 138, 139, 140, 141, 142
The Wild One 34
Williams, Robin 116
Willis, Paul
    on culture 29
    on symbolic creativity 102
Wilson, Patrick 94
Wilson, Thomas F. 122
Wilson, Tony 96
Winter, Alex 114
Winterbottom, Michael 96
Wise, Bill 141
Witherspoon, Reese 89, **91**
Wolf, Naomi 62
Wolf, Scott 103
Wood, Evan Rachel 4
Wood, Julia 62
Wood, Robin 2
Woodbine, Bokeen 90
Wright, Patrick 45

Wyatt, Justin 36
Wyle, Noah 130

youth
    definitions 12
    as historical construct 8, 12–13
    media images 13
    as Other 30
    as rebel 27
youth cinema 1, 2, 3, 153
    bitch in 9, 77–8
    examples 6–7
    liminality 36–7
    transgression 38–41
    writings on 8
    see also teen films
youth culture, merchandising 14

Zahedi, Caveh 140, 141
Zemeckis, Robert 111
Zimmerman, Patricia 70